New Mexico, Past and Present

New Mexico Past and Present

A HISTORICAL READER

Edited by RICHARD N. ELLIS

Albuquerque
UNIVERSITY OF NEW MEXICO PRESS

Dedicated to France V. Scholes

We owe a great debt to such historians, who have searched for records. Professor Scholes' contributions to the history of seventeenth century New Mexico are unparalleled, and his knowledge of the archival sources is unequaled. In 1971 at the age of seventy-four he is still an active scholar.

Manufactured in the United States of America
Library of Congress Catalog Card No. 71-153941
International Standard Book No. 0-8263-0210-6 (clothbound), 0-8263-0215-7 (paperbound)
Fourth paperbound printing 1983

Contents

Introduction

The large column of soldiers, Indians and animals that departed from Compostela in February 1540 gave the appearance of a vast army on the march. Almost seventy years before the founding of the English colony at Jamestown in Virginia, Francisco Coronado led his command of over 300 Spaniards, accompanied by some 800 Indians and a thousand horses and mules, northward in an effort to emulate Cortes and Pizarro by discovering great wealth and conquering new kingdoms for the Spanish crown. Instead he found the adobe pueblos at Zuni, Tiguex and other locations in New Mexico.

Although Coronado may be used to symbolize the dramatic beginning of recorded history in New Mexico, others had preceded him. The native Americans had been in the area for thousands of years, and archeologists are still at work piecing together the story of how they lived. It was not until the sixteenth century that Europeans arrived on the scene. In 1535 Cabeza de Vaca and other survivors from an ill-fated Spanish expedition along the Gulf of Mexico undoubtedly crossed the southern portion of the state, and in 1539 Fray Marcos de Niza and the slave, Estéban the Black, who had been with Cabeza de Vaca, searched for the Seven Cities of Cíbola. Although there is disagreement regarding the veracity of the friar's claim that he viewed the "city" of Háwikuh, a pueblo of the Zuñi Indians where Estéban was killed, it was in response to de Niza's reports that Mendoza dispatched Coronado to the north.

The romantic image of Coronado and other Spanish explorers has captured the imagination of the American public, and the Spanish conquest of New Mexico is indeed dramatic and colorful. The difficult years of early colonization, the struggle for survival in a hostile environment, and the continuing contribution of Spanish-Americans to the political, economic, social, and cultural history of the state are enduring memorials to the strength of the Spanish imperial thrust. Spain, like other colonial powers in the Americas, was unable to maintain her New World empire, but the long years of Spanish control had a lasting impact on the development of the New World.

The highlights of the Spanish period in New Mexico with few exceptions have been known to early historians. They described the role of Coronado, Oñate, Vargas and others. We are fortunate that Spanish friars and officials maintained records of their accomplishments, but many of the records of the Spanish and Mexican periods were not discovered until recently. Some had been lost or destroyed; others were buried in archives in Spain and Mexico, and research for these periods of New Mexico history must often be conducted in foreign countries.

New Mexico is fortunate in having such a strong Spanish-American heritage, and the proportionate size of the Spanish-speaking population and the influence of its culture is greater than in any other state in the United States. New Mexico benefits also from a strong Indian heritage, and this tri-cultural condition has enriched the state's history. Although the Negro population has never been large, Blacks were numbered among the Spanish soldiers and settlers. The contributions of the Black soldiers of the Ninth Cavalry, the only army regiment in the state during much of the 1870s, have recently been recognized, and Fray Angélico Chávez's controversial article on Pohé-Yemo in Chapter 4 also suggests that a Negro played a critical role in the Pueblo Revolt although his suggestion has not been accepted by all historians.

New Mexico history abounds with controversy, and there are numerous questions for which adequate answers do not exist. Many aspects of the history of New Mexico Indian tribes are unknown because of the absence of a written record and because the general hostility toward Indians by white settlers precluded the development of a more thorough record of Indian history by observant whites. Because the Indian side of the story often does not exist, a balanced picture of Indian-white relations is impossible. In addition, we also lack a comprehensive history of the Mexican period. Historians have not effectively explained New Mexico's reaction to the approach of the American army in 1846. Despite resentment by some individuals and despite the rebellion in Taos in 1847, opposition to American control does not appear to have been deep or widespread. Was American control accepted because of the instability of the Mexican governmental system in the difficult years following independence from Spain, or was it as some have suggested, because the United States promised effective protection from hostile Indians, something which the financially pressed Mexican government had been unable to provide? Although Ralph E. Twitchell describes the conquest and the Taos Rebellion in Chapter 11, he does not provide adequate answers to these questions. Other questions also beg for answers. For example, how important was the Confederate invasion of New Mexico in the overall picture of the Civil War, and what did the Confederates hope to gain? Did they seriously believe that they could hold an area that was so distant from their base of supply, or was it simply a foolish and misdirected expenditure of men and equipment?

New Mexico, Past and Present is designed to provide significant and readable selections, which provide an in-depth treatment of the important events in New Mexico history. It can be used to supplement a general text, and a rough balance exists between the Spanish and Mexican periods and the Anglo period. Some of the selections stand alone while others are extracted from books and monographs which therefore should be consulted for a better understanding of the subject. For example, in Chapter 4 Jack Forbes, author of Section I of The Pueblo Revolt, discusses this event in relation to the widespread Indian uprisings on the northern frontiers of New Spain in his *Apache, Navaho, and Spaniard.* Several of the selections place New Mexico history in the broader context of the history of the Spanish Borderlands and of the United States. In Chapter 8 Professor Max Moorhead of the University of Oklahoma describes the Indian policy on the northern frontier of New Spain, while in Chapter 10 he demonstrates the importance of the Santa Fe trade in Chihuahua as well as to New Mexico and Missouri. In Chapter 18 Professor Robert Larson evaluates the statehood struggle in terms of national politics. Some of the subjects such as the land grant question and the Alianza are of continuing interest as New Mexico enters the decade of the 1970s, and the successful test of the atomic bomb at Trinity Site near White Sands signaled the beginning of the atomic age and was one of the most important events in human history.

I
Coronado in Perspective

In early June 1540 a dusty column of weary, hungry men finally approached Háwikuh, one of the Zuni pueblos. Drawn by tales of gold, silver, and other riches, the Spanish found mud walls, dusty streets, and determined resistance. Francisco Coronado was himself wounded in the fighting which followed, but the well-armed Spanish overwhelmed the defenders and eventually moved on to conquer other pueblos in the Rio Grande Valley and adjacent regions and to claim the area for the King of Spain.

The Coronado expedition of 1540 was but one example of the continuing Spanish expansion following Cortés' conquest of the Aztec empire in 1521. Hernando Cortés' lieutenants led expeditions north and south from Mexico City, the former Aztec capital of Tenochtitlán, as they searched for new riches and new empires to conquer. The Coronado expedition, however, was also bound up in politics, for the young nobleman was sent northward by Antonio de Mendoza, successor and rival of Cortés and first Viceroy of New Spain. It was, in addition, sparked by reports of considerable riches at the fabled Seven Cities of Cíbola.

Undoubtedly the first Spanish visitors to New Mexico were the four survivors of the ill-fated expedition of Pánfilo de Narvaéz which had been shipwrecked on the Texas coast in 1528. Led by Cabeza de Vaca, the four men, including the Moorish slave Estéban probably crossed the southern portion of New Mexico and Arizona on their epic journey to Mexico City. De Vaca's tales of the Seven Cities caused Viceroy Mendoza to dispatch a small expedition under Friar Marcos de Niza which resulted in the death of the guide Estéban, at Háwikuh. The priest reported that there were indeed riches at these "cities" so Coronado led the first large expedition into the region and initiated contact with the numerous pueblos of New Mexico and with other tribes on the Great Plains.

The dramatic story of the Coronado expedition has been told many times but probably never as effectively as by Herbert Eugene Bolton, the leading historian of the Spanish Borderlands. As a writer and a teacher, Bolton stimulated interest in this aspect of the history of the New World, and his study of Coronado is a valuable, readable narrative and interpretation of an important incident in the history of the Southwest. Coronado found no riches despite a persistent search that led him to the plains of Kansas, and as a result Spanish interest in New Mexico declined. Coronado did, however, make major contributions to the geographical knowledge of North America, and he did make contact with numerous Indian tribes in the north. Coronado, writes Bolton, "made one of the significant expeditions of that remarkable era of the opening of the Western Hemisphere by Europeans."

Because Coronado found no precious metals in the regions he explored it has been the fashion to regard his expedition as a pointless jaunt. Nothing could be farther from the truth. Exploration was a necessary antecedent to the colonization, exploitation and social development of any part of the New World. Before the Wright brothers invented an airplane that would work, more than one Darius Green made a flying machine that failed to function. Before Cortés and Alvarado entered the interior of Mexico and Central America, numerous apparently profitless voyages had been made around the shores of the Gulf and the Caribbean. Before the English pioneers crossed the mountains and established homes in the Ohio Valley, it was visited by a whole galaxy of Daniel Boones and by them made known to the people on the eastern seaboard as a Promised Land. In the long perspective of history no exploring expedition was entirely profitless, even if it netted no contemporary a dollar. Negatively or positively, each reconnoissance of any region helped to prepare the way for the next step in the historical process by which the New World became what it is today.

Coronado made one of the significant expeditions of that remarkable era of the opening of the Western Hemisphere by Europeans. He performed in North America a service analogous to what was done in South America by Pizarro, Almagro, Belalcázar, or Quesada; or in Middle America by Balboa, Alvarado, or Cortés. He converted the old trail up the West Coast Corridor into a well-known road that is still in use, and in its time and place just as significant as the Wilderness Road over the mountains to Kentucky. To the map of the interior of North America he added Cíbola, Tusayán, Tiguex, and Llanos del Cíbola, and Quivira, regions which were later combined by Anglo-Americans under the name of the Southwest, or the Spanish Borderlands. Historical tradition in this vast area, all the way from California to Nebraska, runs back to the reconnoissance made by the gallant conquistador.

A notable contribution of Coronado to the larger features of North American geography was the discovery of the Continental Divide—the watershed between the Pacific and the Atlantic Oceans from which two river systems run in opposite directions. Jaramillo observed and correctly stated that in the latitude where they crossed it the Divide was just east of Zuñi. He says that "all the springs, rivers, and arroyos we have found as far as Cíbola, and perhaps also those one or two days beyond, flow to the South Sea, and those farther on to the North Sea." As a matter of general interest it would be appropriate to erect a marker of the Continental Divide on the road leading east from Zuñi where Jaramillo noted the watershed, and on it record his important discovery.

It was Coronado who first acquired a relatively accurate knowledge of the width of the continent in the latitude of his travels. Contemporary maps made in Europe showed North America as very narrow in this area. Cabeza de Vaca's long journey westward from Florida to Arizona had not dispelled the notion that north of Mexico the oceans were close together. Then a new idea dawned. Coronado while he was still at Cíbola was visited by native ambassadors from the Pecos River some two hundred miles farther east, who told of the great Buffalo Plains still beyond. Don Francisco now formed a generally sound opinion regarding Cíbola's relation to both oceans. He wrote from there: "I have gained no information about the North Sea [Atlantic Ocean] nor about the one in the west, nor am I able to tell your Lordship which one we are nearest, but I should judge we are closer to the Western Sea. It appears to me that it cannot be less than 150 leagues from here to there, and that the North Sea must be much farther away." This is a definitely more accurate estimate than the one revealed by Mendoza's instructions to Fray Marcos. The man who furnished the initial data for this important geographical news was no other than our young friend Bigotes, chief of Pecos. He deserves a place in the history of cartography alongside of Jaramillo.

After going east to far-distant Quivira, Coronado concluded that the Tiguex pueblos were "four hundred leagues from the North Sea, and more than two hundred from the South Sea, thus prohibiting all intercourse." This would put Tiguex, on the upper Rio Grande, about one-third of the distance from the Pacific to the Atlantic, which is fairly accurate, and his estimate of six hundred leagues for the total width of the continent, though still too small, was a vast improvement over some of the contemporary maps. Nor was Coronado's opinion a guess; it was based on his long journey from Arizona to Kansas, during which he and his horses had measured every mile of the way in terms of sweat, sore muscles, and bodily fatigue.

If by the North Sea Coronado meant the Gulf of Mexico, as apparently is the case, his calculation of distance was not far from correct.

This idea of the immense span of the continent acquired by Coronado on the basis of his own travels was substantiated and made more exact by the contemporary expedition of De Soto from the eastern seaboard to and across the Mississippi into the regions now called Arkansas, Louisiana, and eastern Texas. Thus the approximate width of the continent was now established on the basis of actual exploration by the two armies which almost met. To the same result Zaldívar's Indian woman contributed her bit. Having fled from the Barrancas of the Panhandle, later on she reached Moscoso's men in eastern Texas, as was learned by Coronado's men after they returned to Mexico. "Thus," Castañeda remarks, "we are led to believe that we were not far from the region they discovered. . . . So it is estimated that the land in that latitude must be more than six hundred leagues wide from sea to sea"—a very fair estimate of the distance from the Gulf of California to the Gulf of Mexico. In the short space of three years these two rival explorers had made known to the world in broad outline nearly a third of the area now contained in the United States, and in several important respects had changed current ideas regarding the entire land mass of North America and its geographical relation to the rest of the globe.

By a strange misunderstanding, recorded by Ramusio and adopted by Gómara, European map makers absurdly reversed the direction of Coronado's long eastward march from Cíbola and the order of the pueblos seen by him, transformed the River of Quivira into a lake, and then shifted the province of Quivira to the shores of the Pacific Ocean, where for several decades it roamed up and down the map. As a corollary to this blunder, Coronado's River of La Señora [the Rio Grande] was shown as flowing west into the Pacific Ocean in northern California—categorical statements by Coronado, Jaramillo, and Castañeda to the contrary notwithstanding. It is safe to say that Coronado never told Mendoza what Ramusio attributed to him. Both Ramusio and Gómara deserve a prominent place in a Southwestern joke book.

Relatively unimportant though these curious mistakes of the map makers may have been, they make it clear that Coronado and his contemporaries had contributed more to North American geography than Europeans could quickly digest. The government of Spain was partly at fault by reason of its secretive policy with respect to the work of its explorers, for after Gómara's history, little was published regarding the Coronado expedition for several decades. French, Portuguese, English, and Russian explorers in America also suffered from the ignorance of their officials in Europe.

It must not be concluded from the strange errors made by map makers that the explorers themselves did not know where they had been, or that they did not understand the relative position of their discoveries with respect to Mexico and adjacent areas. On the contrary, the chroniclers of the Coronado expedition, contemporary Mexican officials, and contemporary frontier promoters had a generally clear idea of what both Coronado and his *vis à vis*, DeSoto, had done; and they made use of the new information in the discussion of problems which immediately arose. More important than the difficulty of educating Europeans was the widening of the horizon of the colonists in New Spain, who made practical use of the new data acquired.

Coronado on his march from the Barranca Grande to the Arkansas River made an interesting contribution to knowledge of the declination of the compass needle in that region and at that date. Writers hitherto have generally approached the problem of the identity of the Barranca Grande backward. Not knowing the topography of the region, in order to locate the great canyon, and noting that Coronado said he traveled by the needle, they consulted scientists regarding the declination of the compass needle in 1541. On confessedly inadequate data the scientists conjectured that the declination along Coronado's route from the Barranca Grande was some two degrees west of true north. In accordance with that guess historians placed the Barranca Grande far east and south of its true location. But the Barranca Grande was unmistakably Palo Duro Canyon. From here Coronado traveled on the high plain, near the escarpment of the Llano Estacado, which runs about eleven degrees east of true north. This happens to be about the average declination of the needle along Coronado's route for the last century, for which we have accurate data based on astronomical observations. The obvious conclusion is that it was about the same in Coronado's day. Hence his record has enabled us to answer a question for which scientists have had no reliable data.

There is a widespread impression, often expressed in print, that the horses in use by the Plains Indians in the seventeenth and eighteenth centuries were descended from the animals left behind when the Coronado expedition withdrew to Mexico. But this opinion, as Aiton states, does not appear to be well founded. In the first place, as has already been noted, among the horses taken to New Mexico by Coronado and his men there were very few mares. In the muster roll of the army drawn up at Compostela when the expedition started north, out of some five hundred mounts listed, only two mares were mentioned. There probably were others but the number apparently was small. Since mounts were at a premium they no doubt were carefully guarded in the course of the long march and at the winter camps in Pueblo Land. In the available records of the expedition there is mention of the disappearance of two or three horses besides those killed by the Pueblo Indians in the Tiguex War. Had there been others, it is reasonable to suppose they also would have been noted.

Moreover, in the accounts of the Spanish expeditions to the Southwest and Kansas in the later sixteenth and early seventeenth centuries no mention is made of horses or mounted Indians, which, if encountered, would have been sure to attract attention. It would seem, therefore, that the horses ridden by the Plains Indians in the eighteenth century as far north as the prairies of Canada were descended from stock which strayed or was obtained from the Spanish settlements after the permanent colonization of New Mexico and Texas in the seventeenth century.

The notion of vast wealth in Tierra Nueva would not down. In spite of Coronado's reports, and of the emphatic testimony of his followers as to the lack of ready-to-hand riches—namely, gold, silver, and precious stones—Don Francisco was criticized for withdrawing to Mexico, and within five years of his return there was official talk of sending a new expedition to colonize Quivira. Contributory motives were the desire to relieve Mexico City of idle adventurers, including some of Coronado's own men, and fear of another intrusion from the east such as that of De Soto. The route to Quivira now proposed was the direct one by which Do Campo had fled to Pánuco and which was paralleled by Moscoso. "Of all this wealth they give great news," wrote a high official of Mexico in 1547, "and it is very proper that your Majesty should order all that country peopled. . . . Now the route is certain and the land so healthful and fertile and abounding . . . with so many provisions and so many millions of cattle which God has scattered there that it appears to me . . . another Promised Land." Do Campo's trail from Quivira to Mexico City was not more than half as long as the one followed by Coronado, hence the route proposed for a return to Kansas.

But the defense of Florida at the moment was more urgent, and to this task attention was now given. Mendoza requested Moscoso's men to return thither overland, "offering them whatever was necessary to establish themselves in that distant land," but many of them went instead to Peru. A colony for Florida was raised in Mexico in 1559, and the man chosen to lead the adventurers was no other than Don Tristán de Luna y Arellano, who had made a good record with Coronado and had high family connections. Six of his captains had been with De Soto, acquired Alabama wives, and with them now accompanied Arellano. Thus Don Tristán was a personal link between Coronado and Florida. The Do Campo-De Soto route was at first contemplated, but the expedition was finally sent by water, which under existing circumstances was more practicable. The wide gap overland was not bridged till long afterward, but the idea persisted and it was initially based on the exploits of Do Campo, De Soto, and Moscoso.

If Coronado may appear less efficient than some of his contemporary conquistadores, it is partly due to his finer sense of the rights and dignity of human beings. He was not a swashbuckler. Don Francisco had many unquestionable qualifications for leadership. When he set forth on his great expedition he was only thirty years old. With five years of American experience behind him, he was still in the bloom of early manhood, and had those precious attributes that make youth so competent, so engaging, and so enviable. He was attractive, optimistic, and unsoured by the hard knocks and disappointments that come with sordid worldly contacts. There is abundant evidence that Coronado organized his army well, and led it in an orderly manner all the way to Cíbola, Tiguex, the Buffalo Plains, and Quivira. His treatment of the Indian allies whom he took in his train was notably more humane than that practiced by some of the conquerors of the period. Mendoza's orders regarding this matter were strict, and Coronado was zealous in carrying them out. He was so successful in this particular that on the long march of more than four thousand miles, from Mexico City to eastern Kansas and back, and embracing a period of more than two years, including two cold and hungry winters in Tiguex, few Spaniards were lost and not more than thirty Indian allies were sacrificed. No other contemporary record could match this one.

Coronado was reputed by his followers to be a strict disciplinarian, even something of a martinet, and it is well known that he sometimes punished his soldiers for misconduct, especially for offenses against the Indians. But on only one occasion, so far as the available record goes, was he charged with being harsh and arbitrary with his men. This was when some of the soldiers opposed his decision to abandon conquest and return with the whole army to Mexico. When, as we have seen, some sixty men on that occasion proposed to remain in Tiguex, or to return to Quivira with Father Padilla, Coronado threatened to punish—even to hang—anyone who remained or so much as talked about remaining. He had decided to return to Mexico for what he regarded as good reasons, and now it was his duty to enforce his orders.

If Don Francisco had been an incompetent leader some of his followers might well have clamored to turn back after the shocking disappointment experienced at Cíbola, when they saw the much advertised city was nothing but a "huddle of mud huts"; and they might have done the same after new disappointments at Tiguex, or after the hardships of the first winter there. But not many faltered, and apparently nobody deserted except some of the men left with brutal Alcaráz in Sonora Valley. Without a commander who inspired confidence and enthusiasm for the gamble this could not have been true.

There is no doubt of Coronado's dash and nerve, qualities which endeared him to his soldiers, and made them willing to follow him through thick and thin. At Cíbola he led his men into battle, receiving blows and wounds which caused his comrades to despair of his life, and to admire him all the more in consequence. His conduct in the Tiguex War was brave and soldierly. It took real stamina to march with only thirty men through unknown country from the Barrancas of the Texas Panhandle five or six hundred miles to Quivira, whose ruler had been represented as a powerful monarch who commanded an army of giants and inflicted awful punishment upon anyone who opposed his will.

The testimony of Coronado's comrades was put in phrases that leave no doubt of the loyalty and admiration of his followers. Hernando del Valle declared that the general, in the course of the expedition, "suffered great hardships from hunger, cold, heat, and loss of blood from many wounds which the natives of those lands gave him and from which he was at the point of death; and many times his life was put in great peril and danger in the service of his Majesty." Juan Bermejo, royal notary of the expedition, at Cíbola saw Coronado "at the point of death, and beyond the hope of all who went with him on the expedition, because the Indians of that valley wounded him with arrows in many places." Melchior Pérez "saw that the natives of the principal pueblo of Cíbola wounded the governor . . . when he went to enter it, because he was in the vanguard. And such were the wounds and blows they gave him on his head and his body that he lost much blood; and they carried him on their shoulders as dead to the Spanish camp." Pedro de Castro testified that at Cíbola when Coronado was leading the van and encouraging his men, the natives gave him so many wounds that they thought him dead. "They carried him out in their arms and he became very ill from his wounds." Juan Pastor declared that "in all the encounters . . . Coronado, like a good captain, was always in the vanguard, and that . . . he many times came out wounded, and was at the point of death, as is notorious among the men who went in that army." All these and many more testimonials to Coronado's qualities and deeds were given in a secret and not wholly sympathetic inquiry, conducted with a view to obtaining frank expression of opinions.

It is not without human interest to learn how the chief participants in this truly great exploring expedition passed their last days, and what was their reward. Coronado spent the few remaining years of his short life in Mexico City, nursing his broken health and taking part in the government of the capital. He resumed his duties as a member of the council and was elected by that body to serve as procurator mayor for two different years, 1545 and 1551. Don Francisco seems to have made his second term of office noteworthy chiefly by the erection of a pillory in the plaza of the city. A stir was created in the council by the former governor when, in the spring of 1545, he was notified he must carry the city banner in a procession on the feast of San Hipólito. Coronado objected that inasmuch as he had been absent in Jalisco on the King's business when his turn had come up, he was not liable for such service until the duty had made its full rounds. He apparently was not flattered by the honor. The argument continued for more than two months, but at last, on July 3, Don Francisco agreed to function as standard-bearer.

Coronado retained the friendship of Viceroy Mendoza, and in 1547 he was one of the most important witnesses for the defense in the great official's residencia. Two years later, on February 14 and again July 5, presumably because of this friendship, Coronado was designated by the council to visit Mendoza, who was ill at Guastepec, and consult with him on certain matters of city business. In the same year, 1549, in spite of Tejada's condemnation, Coronado received a royal grant of Indians in encomienda "for meritorious services in discovery and conquest." He regarded this as only a partial vindication, and in 1551 he was still pressing his suit to regain the estates of which he had been deprived by Tejada. His health continued to decline, and on June 5, 1553, he obtained permission to leave Mexico City in an effort to improve his condition, for he had never fully recovered from the effects of his accident in Tiguex. By August 1, however, weary though he was, he had again taken up his duties in the cabildo. The records of the council show that Don Francisco was absent for some time during the early months of 1554, and on June 21 the sick man petitioned the King to appoint as regidor in his place Bernaldino de Bocanegra, who was betrothed to Coronado's daughter Doña Isabel, of chain and locket fame. Don Francisco gave ill health as the reason for his resignation but promised to continue to serve the King to the best of his ability until formal appointment of a successor should be made. This was not to be for very long, for although, in accordance with his pledge, he appeared in council meetings on July 3, 6, and 9, "Francisco Vázquez de Coronado died and passed from this present life on the night of a Saturday which was accounted the 22nd day of September of this year of 1554."

The remains of Don Francisco, his celebrated wife, Doña Beatríz, and other members of the explorer's family lie buried in Mexico City in the famous church of Santo Domingo, three blocks north of the Cathedral and across the street from the old Inquisition building. Paul A. Jones and Joaquín Meade y Sáinz Trapaga recently identified the Coronado shrine. With justifiable gratification, Jones writes: "When a Kansas country editor and a Mexico City building contractor had satisfied themselves from the only available records that they knew the spot where all that is mortal of Francisco Vázquez de Coronado now reposes, they went to Santo Domingo church and stood at the gospel or left side of the main altar, confident and proud that they were the first two living persons, representing the two most interested nations, to make the pilgrimage and pay such homage to a brave man across a span of nearly four hundred years. The editor, visibly affected, felt that years of travel and research had been rewarded."

With the death of Francisco Vázquez Coronado, the central figure of one great episode in the pageant of the New World passed from the scene. Many another actor in that vast drama, who had played a part either large or small in the Coronado sequence, already had made his final exit or was soon to spin out his rôle. After his release from the prison into which Pérez de la Torre had ordered him thrown, Nuño de Guzmán, founder of Coronado's province of Nueva Galicia, returned to Spain at the King's command, and spent his remaining years in an attempt to vindicate himself and urge his rights to a share in the northern conquests. There in poverty he died in 1544.

Cortés, the ablest of the conquerors, Guzmán's bitterest enemy, and Coronado's rival in the race for the Seven Cities, likewise passed his last years in Spain, pressing the recognition of his claims in the New World. He left Mexico in 1540 never to return, although just before his final illness he was making plans to set sail for the land he had won for his king. The Marquis of the Valley died, an old man at sixty-two, on December 2, 1547, in the village of Castillejo de la Cuesta, near Seville.

Just a few months later, on June 3, 1548, after twenty illustrious years in Mexico in the service of the Church, the venerable Bishop Zumárraga expired. It was he who had sponsored Fray Marcos and urged Mendoza to put the Coronado expedition into effect. The weight of the Bishop's opinion had been an important factor in the genesis of the great adventure. Highest honors had come to the prelate—but too late. Only nine days before his death, documents arrived naming him first archbishop of Mexico, but he was so feeble that he could not accept the imposing office.

In 1551 Coronado said a last farewell to his good friend, Antonio de Mendoza, with whom he had so carefully and so hopefully planned the expedition north to see the wonders reported by Cabeza de Vaca and Fray Marcos. The parting was far different from that which took place at Tepic in 1540 when the viceroy, having seen Coronado and the army well on their way to the Seven Cities, had turned back to his capital and his official duties. For several years Mendoza had petitioned the King for release from those duties and permission to return to Spain. At last another viceroy was appointed for Mexico, but only death could free Don Antonio from service to his King, for he was now requested to go to Lima to become the viceroy of Peru. Ill and longing for his homeland, the loyal servant of His Majesty set sail from one of the ports on the Pacific Coast of Mexico and arrived at his new capital on September 12, 1551. Less than a year later he died there, on July 21, 1552, and was laid to his final rest in the cathedral beside Pizarro, the conquistador who had found gold at the end of his rainbow.

Soon after Coronado's death—probably in 1556, according to his biographer, Morris Bishop—Cabeza de Vaca ceased his earthly wanderings. He had returned to Spain to get permission to conquer Florida, only to learn that Hernando de Soto, over whom the waters of the mighty Mississippi were soon to roll forever, had already won the post. One would assume that Vaca had seen enough of that land of his misfortune. As an alternative to Florida, he was appointed governor and captain-general to rule at Asunción in Paraguay, South America. His luck there was no better, and after a free-for-all fight with his enemies he returned to Spain defeated and a prisoner. On January 20, 1546, not quite three weeks after he had brought charges against Cárdenas in connection with the Coronado expedition, Villalobos, the King's fiscal and enemy of conquerors, filed suit against Cabeza de Vaca before the Council of the Indies. The case dragged on, and it was not until 1551 that Vaca was finally released from prison, to spend his last years in penniless obscurity.

Meanwhile, in Mexico, Fray Marcos, who with Vaca's black companion, Stephen, had gone to verify the wonders of which the Narváez castaways had told, was nearing the end of a trail which had led him across the wide Atlantic Ocean, west to Guatemala, south to Peru, and north to Cíbola. After his return from the Pueblo country Fray Marcos became crippled, with paralysis, it is said, and repaired to Jalapa to profit by its warm climate. Later he went to live in a monastery at Xochimilco, the suburb of Mexico City, famous for its so-called floating gardens. In 1546, in response to a plea from the friar telling of his illness, Bishop Zumárraga promised to furnish him an arroba of wine each month as long as he, the bishop, should live. Two years later Zumárraga died. Who concerned himself about Marcos's ills during the last decade of the friar's life we do not know. The date of his death is reported by Vetancurt as March 25, 1558.

Cristóbal de Oñate, over whose failure to receive a salary for his services as lieutenant-governor for Coronado in Nueva Galicia there was so much talk during the governor's residencia, with the discovery in 1546 of rich mines at Zacatecas, became one of the wealthiest persons in America—perhaps a millionaire. Ironically, it was the man who had stayed behind when the treasure-seekers trailed north searching for cities of gold, on whom Fate bestowed her munificence. Just how long a time was allotted Don Cristóbal to enjoy his wealth we do not know, having evidence only that he was still living in 1550.

At Culiacán, that outpost so important in Coronado tradition, Don Pedro de Tovar, who had been chief ensign of the expedition and discoverer of the Hopi pueblos, lived for many years. As alcalde mayor, the old post of Melchior Díaz, his former companion in arms who had long lain buried far in the north beside the Camino del Diablo, Tovar won distinction. Described as "the most virtuous and accomplished gentleman in that kingdom," he married Doña Francisca de Guzmán, daughter of a former governor of Cuba and, says one chronicler, "a lady of much Christian fervor, courage, discretion, and beauty, so perfect in every respect that I doubt if there was any one in those regions who could equal her in virtue or quality." When Tovar died is not known, but Tello informs us that the event occurred in Culiacán and that Don Pedro was buried there, as was so fitting.

Like Coronado and Cárdenas, ill and travel-weary, Tristán de Arellano, who had been in command of the main army for many miles in the Cíbola enterprise, made his way back to Mexico City. After recuperating at the home of a friend, Luís de Castilla, Don Tristán went to Oaxaca, where, in 1545, he married a wealthy widow, Doña Isabel de Rojas. Three years later, while Coronado was attending town council meetings in Mexico and Cárdenas was alternately in and out of jail in Spain, Arellano put down a serious Indian uprising in Oaxaca. Ten years later, as we have seen, he was commissioned governor and captain-general of Florida by Viceroy Luís de Velasco, with instructions to lead an expedition to that region and establish a bulwark against foreign intrusions into territory claimed by Spain. As the fortune of Doña Beatríz had been poured into the Cíbola venture, that of Doña Isabel now dissolved in the Florida gamble. The expedition having failed, Don Tristán went to Madrid in 1561 to regain favor, but without success. Poverty-stricken, he returned to Mexico about 1567, and, until his death on September 16, 1573, was again given a home and cared for by his old friend, Luís de Castilla. Arellano's will made provision for the repayment of this debt, but so depleted was the estate of the man who had been cast in leading roles in two great expeditions in the New World that even his funeral expenses had to be met by his benefactor. Not republics alone are ungrateful to their servants.

SUGGESTED READINGS

A. Grove Day, *Coronado's Quest* (Berkeley 1940);
George P. Hammond and Agapito Rey, editors, *Narratives of the Coronado Expedition, 1540–1542* (Albuquerque 1940);
Fray Angelico Chavez, *Coronado's Friars* (Washington 1968);
Arthur S. Aiton, *Antonio de Mendoza, First Viceroy of New Spain* (Durham, N.C. 1927);
Cleve Hallenbeck, *Alvar Núñez Cabeza de Vaca* (Glendale, Calif. 1940).

2
Oñate and the Colonization of New Mexico

Although Coronado failed to find riches in New Mexico or on the Great Plains, it was not long before interest in the northern region revived. In the 1580s a series of expeditions to New Mexico led to eventual colonization. Agustín Rodríguez and Francisco Chamuscado began these expeditions by leading a small party of friars and soldiers probably as far north as Taos. In the following year Antonio de Espejo visited the area and returned with tales of wealth which not only caused several illegal expeditions but also brought royal approval to colonize the region. The contract was awarded to Juan de Oñate.

In the introduction to *Don Juan de Oñate, Colonizer of New Mexico, 1595–1628*, a collection of documents on the founding of New Mexico. George P. Hammond and Agapito Rey describe the Oñate expedition and its antecedents. The long delay between the date of the contract and the march northward provides an example of inefficiency in the Spanish colonial system; in 1598, however, the colonization of New Mexico finally began. Unfortunately the Spaniards failed to find great wealth. Oñate and his lieutenants explored to the east and west and crushed Indian resistance in the bloody battle at Acoma; but the colony was plagued by internal discontent, and Oñate fell into disfavor.

Don Juan de Oñate, colonizer of New Mexico, its first governor and only adelantado, merits a high place among the first pioneers of the United States. It was Oñate, who, after he finally received the coveted privilege of conquering and pacifying the province of New Mexico in 1595, established the first European settlements—San Juan de los Caballeros and San

---

Gabriel—in northern New Mexico, more than a thousand miles from Mexico city. At this great distance from the heart of the Spanish empire in the New World there now arose a new center of expansion, a new focus for exploration of the land and for conversion of the Indians.

Throughout the next three centuries, New Mexico remained a Spanish province, completely isolated by distance from other parts of the empire, but the Spanish language was her mother tongue, and Spanish forms of government, law, and religion were the basis of her institutions. The coming of the Americans in 1846 introduced a new language and a new form of government. These, superimposed on the old, brought changes, but the two peoples lived peacefully together, though their language and customs gradually reflected the blending of the two cultures.

Don Juan de Oñate and his colonists were the agents of the greatest government on earth. They came in response to man's age-old quest to explore the unknown, probe its mysteries, seek adventure and profit, and, as Spaniards, to extend the dominion of the Spanish crown and bring the benefits of their religion to the heathen peoples who dwelt in this unknown land. These men did not flee from a persecuting government, but proudly carried aloft the banners of Spain and defended her colors with their arms. In return for these services, they expected to reap honor and reward, as Hernán Cortés, Francisco Pizarro, and so many others had done before and as Spanish law permitted.

Half a century before Oñate's day, another adventurer had dreamed of fame and fortune in Pueblo land. This was Francisco Vásquez Coronado, friend and confidant of the great viceroy, Antonio de Mendoza. In 1540, urged on by the glowing tales related by Fray Marcos de Niza after his dauntless trip into the unknown north, Coronado led a brilliant and well-organized army up the west coast of Mexico into the heart of the pueblos of the Río Grande country. Though he explored valiantly for two years from his Tiguex headquarters, he found none of the treasures that he sought—precious metals or settled and civilized Indian nations that could be exploited. Coronado returned saddened and empty handed. Men now gave up the search for quick riches in "the beyond," in return for cattle ranching and mining around Zacatecas, Querétaro, and other promising fields of investment closer to the settled areas in Mexico.

Meantime, as the sixteenth century progressed, these old-style military expeditions, so characteristic of the Spanish conquest in its heyday, fell into disfavor. The New Laws of 1542, issued by a benevolent government at the insistence of missionaries and friends of the oppressed Indians, sought to stamp out the heartless encomienda system, by which landlords exploited the Indians like chattels. A little later, in 1573, came another set of laws, designed to benefit the heathen Indians by regulating colonization and settlement. By this code, no military adventurer could hope to duplicate the deeds of men like Cortés. Now only missionaries were to be allowed to venture among new tribes in remote places. These were the new conditions of exploration and settlement that prevailed by the end of the sixteenth century when Oñate asked to be made governor of New Mexico.

The advance into the mining areas of Northern Mexico had by this time reached the Conchos river in modern Chihuahua. Since the natives of the area traded with those of New Mexico, it was not long before stories of the Pueblo Indians of New Mexico and Arizona and tales of their many-storeyed houses became known in the mining settlements and cattle ranches on the Chihuahua frontier. So it was that Father Agustín Rodríguez, a lay brother of the Franciscan order stationed at San Bartolomé in the Conchos valley, obtained the viceroy's permission to investigate the rumors of settled towns farther north. With him went Francisco Sánchez Chamuscado, a small group of soldiers and Indian servants, and two other friars, Francisco López and Juan de Santa María. They set out from the mining settlement of Santa Bárbara south of the Conchos on June 5, 1581, and made one of the most significant expeditions in New Mexico's history. Without fanfare of arms or robbing the Indians of their food and clothing, these men explored as far north as Taos, east to Pecos and the Canadian river, and west to Acoma and Zuñi. They heard of the town-dwelling Hopis on their mesas in northeastern Arizona, but were unable to visit them, owing to a shortage of provisions.

For a whole year, this party reconnoitered New Mexico and visited almost the entire region that had been explored and partially devastated by Coronado. Hernán Gallegos, one of the soldiers, wrote an account of their adventures, which has fortunately been preserved. Nowhere did these men find the Indians hostile. Father Juan de Santa María, eager to bring immediate news of the great success in finding such an advanced society, set out on the return trip before the other members of the party. Unfortunately, he was slain on the way, adding another name to the roll of Franciscan martyrs in New Mexico. His associates, Fathers López and Rodriguez, anxious to begin the conversion of the natives, decided to remain in New Mexico when the soldiers left. They stayed at the pueblo of Puaray, near Bernalillo on the Río Grande, while the soldiers made their way home. Captain Chamuscado, the leader, being old and ill, died on the way.

The return of the expedition with news that they had discovered a large number of pueblos with a high degree of civilization created a sensation in Mexico. The Franciscans, however, became much concerned about the fate of the two friars at Puaray who had remained behind without escort of any kind, for it now became known that Father Santa María must have been killed on his lonesome journey.

At this opportune moment, Antonio de Espejo, a wealthy merchant, offered to lead a relief expedition. This proved satisfactory, and it was organized with only a few months' delay. One friar, Bernardino Beltrán, accompanied the party, which consisted of fourteen soldiers and some Indian servants. The party left San Bartolomé near the Conchos river on November 10, 1582, almost exactly seven months after the return of Chamuscado's soldiers.

During the next few months, Espejo's men explored literally all of New Mexico and much of Arizona. Their specific mission was soon ended, for among the first pueblos on the Río Grande they learned that the two friars were dead. The men chose to go on, nevertheless, to see for themselves what kind of country they were in. They visited all the major pueblos,—Pecos, Taos, Jémez, Acoma, and Zuñi. Even more; they went on to the Hopi towns, and a long distance beyond, in search of mines. The return journey was down the Pecos instead of over the now-familiar Río Grande route. The party got back home in September, 1583, after an absence of ten eventful months.

While Espejo and his party were thus looking for mines all over the Pueblo country, the king, on April 19, 1583, in response to the viceroy's report of the discoveries of Rodríguez and Chamuscado, issued a cedula authorizing the conquest of New Mexico. Naturally, this must be without cost to the crown, and the arrangements must satisfy the Council of the Indies. The contract must also be in conformity with the laws of 1573, which were now to receive a major test, for the conquest of New Mexico was the first great venture of this nature attempted under this code.

In view of the sensational nature of the news of the Pueblo country, there were many applicants ready and eager to enter into a contract with the crown for pacification of the region. Some of these were prominent men; others we know little about, but all demanded numerous concessions and favors. There was Cristóbal Martín of Mexico, who offered to explore a thousand leagues beyond New Mexico and to establish posts on the North and South seas (i.e., the Atlantic and Pacific oceans), in return for many royal favors. Espejo, too, sought the honor, but his reputation had been besmirched by a charge of complicity in the murder of two men, and he was passed by; Hernán Gallegos of the Rodríguez expedition was a candidate claiming special knowledge of the land; and Francisco Díaz de Vargas of Puebla proposed to explore from Quivira to the strait of Anián; Juan Bautista de Lomas y Colmenares of New Galicia, in order to obtain exclusive rights to the country beyond the Conchos in Chihuahua, put on pressure to get the honor, but failed, as did Francisco de Urdiñola, governor of Nueva Vizcaya, who had been charged with the murder of his wife. Both of these men actually had contracts drawn up, but in the end they were deemed inadequate for the high post.

The long delays attendant upon the choice of a governor inspired the two illegal expeditions that now invaded New Mexico. The first was led by

Gaspar Castaño de Sosa, lieutenant governor of Nuevo León, who set out for New Mexico in 1590 from his mining camp of Nuevo Almadén (Monclova), with his entire colony of about a hundred and seventy persons. He went up the Pecos and crossed over to the Río Grande from Pecos pueblo, but soon the law caught up with him. Since he had no license to make the journey, a Captain Juan Morlete was sent to arrest him and bring back his people, who returned without serious remonstrance.

This unhappy venture was followed by one even more pathetic, under the leadership of Francisco de Leyva Bonilla and Antonio Gutiérrez de Humaña, or Umaña, as the name is usually written in the Oñate documents. These men started from Nueva Vizcaya in 1593, but few details are known of their journey except for the report of an Indian servant who escaped and told the story of how they went to the pueblo of Bove, modern San Ildefonso, New Mexico, and then set out for the buffalo plains to the east. On the way, Humaña had some disagreement with Leyva and stabbed him to death, but later he and almost his entire party were killed by the Indians. When Oñate set out for New Mexico, the fate of these men was not known in Mexico, and he therefore had instructions to bring them to justice.

At this time, perhaps as early as 1592, Don Juan de Oñate had become a contestant for the governorship of New Mexico. In view of the time needed to draw up an agreement and to get the required consideration and approval, it would seem logical that he must have begun negotiations with the viceroy long before 1595. In any case, the viceroy approved a contract with him for the pacification and conquest of New Mexico on September 21 of that year.

Oñate came from a distinguished and wealthy family. His father, Don Cristóbal, had come to the New World with the first conquerors under Cortés. For the adventurous, it was a time of opportunity, and Don Cristóbal played his part well. In 1538, he became for a brief period governor of Nueva Galicia, and then, under Francisco Vásquez Coronado's administration, lieutenant governor. When the Mixtón war broke out in 1540, Don Cristóbal distinguished himself by his military courage and skill against the Indians entrenched on their craggy heights. Shortly afterward, with three partners, one of whom was the renowned Juanes de Tolosa, he became the discoverer of the mines of Zacatecas. These mines, among the most famous in New Spain, brought wealth to the crown and honor and distinction to Don Cristóbal de Oñate and his associates. When the king gave the city of Zacatecas a coat of arms, Don Cristóbal was one of the four founders of the city whose pictures were placed on its escutcheon. Clearly, the elder Oñate was one of the notable men of the Nueva Galicia frontier.

Of Don Juan de Oñate's earlier years we know very little, except that he married well and served the king faithfully. His wife was Doña Isabel de Tolosa, daughter of Juanes de Tolosa and Doña Leonor Cortés, a natural daughter of Hernán Cortés, and a granddaughter of the Aztec ruler. Evidently Don Juan took part also in the subjugation of the Indians of the frontier and opened mines, for he says, that "from the time he was old enough to bear arms," he fought the "Chichimecos and Gua[chi]chiles Indians in company with Viceroy Don Luis de Velasco," and that he discovered and conquered the mines of San Luis, Chicu, and Charcas at his own cost. These mines, he asserted, had yielded millions in royal fifths to the crown; they must have been very rich.

In addition to his own wealth, Don Juan had influential friends. There were his nephews, the four Zaldívar brothers, two of whom served as his chief officers. He had the friendship and support of numerous officials, cattle ranchers, and miners, and his family was looked upon with favor by the viceroy, Don Luis de Velasco II, who had resided in the country for many years.

With these facts in mind, one can surmise that Oñate heard with much interest the stories that came from the New Mexico frontier on the return of the Rodríguez-Chamuscado and Espejo expeditions. What more natural than that he, whose family had served the crown so faithfully in discovering new lands, subduing Indians, and exploiting mines in Nueva Galicia should have an ear cocked to these new rumors and have offered to serve the king as governor of New Mexico?

As soon as Oñate received the contract on September 21, 1595, he chose his chief lieutenants and began to recruit men. As his highest officer, he appointed his nephew, Don Juan de Zaldívar, as maese de campo; another nephew, Vicente de Zaldívar, became sargento mayor and recruiting officer. Among the many other distinguished captains was the celebrated Gaspar de Villagrá, whose epic poem, published in Spain a decade before the Pilgrims landed in New England, extols the deeds of the Spanish conquerors of New Mexico. His historical poem is a gem among the early records of American history.

Recruitment of colonists and soldiers now began in earnest. The lists were opened with pomp and ceremony at the viceroy's palace in Mexico city, and with drums and banners in Puebla, Zacatecas, and other towns near the frontier. This was the area where Oñate and his family had lived and conquered, and most of his followers came from the towns of this region.

Oñate's contract is an interesting document. It gives in detail not only the general terms and conditions of the conquest, but also his specific obligations. Don Juan proposed, for example, to recruit at least two hundred men, fully equipped, to provide quantities of flour, maize, and jerked beef for food, wheat for sowing, and one thousand cattle, three thousand sheep, one thousand rams, one thousand goats, one hundred black cattle, one hundred and fifty colts, one hundred and fifty mares, and a profusion of other things, such as footgear, medicine, iron tools, paper, sackcloth, and blacksmiths' bellows, all at his own cost. For his personal use, he offered to provide twenty-five horses, twenty-five mules, several carts, and weapons and clothing in abundance, all of which were duly listed.

By his contract, Oñate got the title of governor and captain general for two generations. He was to receive the title of adelantado on taking possession of the land, and it was to be valid for two generations also. In each case, he asked that these honors be extended for two more generations, in view of the great cost and hardship of the expedition.

The king provided Oñate with three fieldpieces, thirty quintals of powder, one hundred of lead, and a dozen coats of mail (though Oñate was to pay for these). He had asked for harquebuses, but got none, as they were not available. He asked for a loan of ten quintals of mercury, which was granted, and the right to commandeer carts, if necessary, paying a just price for them. He received, too, a loan of six thousand pesos from the royal treasury.

Oñate sought also the right to allot lands and Indians in encomienda, to appoint the officials of the expedition, and to have his colonists recognized as hidalgos, with the same privileges as hidalgos of Castile. He asked, too, for thirty square leagues of land, including the subjects on it, for the title of marquis (which was not granted), and for a salary of eight thousand ducats of Castile (he was given six thousand). In addition, he asked for the office of alguacil mayor, for the right to establish an office of the royal treasury in New Mexico, for the privilege of taking up mining claims subject to a tax of a tenth instead of the usual fifth, for authority to appoint alcaldes mayores and corregidores, and for the privilege of using local revenues in putting down any rebellion that might occur.

Very important was Oñate's request to be placed under the immediate jurisdiction of the Council of the Indies, which would have made him virtually independent of the viceroy of Mexico. He sought permission also to recruit additional soldiers as needed, exemption from payment of the alcabala (sales tax) and import duties for a period of twenty years, power to appoint a successor and to levy tribute on the Indians according to the fruits of the land, and, finally, assurance that all the ordinances for new colonies would be kept insofar as they did not violate the royal ordinances of 1573 for new discoveries and settlements.

These were Oñate's major requests. In every instance, the viceroy replied by granting him what was allowed by the ordinances of 1573, nothing more. The fact that Oñate had asked for greater favors than he received would of course leave the door open to requests for additional honors in case of great success or extraordinary hardships.

Oñate's petition to become governor and captain general of New Mexico was made at an unfortunate moment in history. His family friend, Don Luis de Velasco, who had been viceroy of Mexico from 1589 to 1595 and had made a fine record as a benevolent ruler, was promoted to the viceroyalty of Peru and was therefore unable to aid his protege in launching the New Mexico expedition. To take Velasco's place, the king had named the Count of Monterrey as viceroy of Mexico, and it was Oñate's bad luck that he should arrive just at the moment when the contract was being signed.

The Count of Monterrey, with the grandeur of Spain's barren mesas and mountains ingrained in his nature, took up his duties in Mexico with considerable caution, obviously impressed with the riches of the country and of the opportunity that this wealth presented. Of Mexico's problems, its people, and its government he knew but little, and it was to his credit that he was in no haste to make decisions. At Vera Cruz, where he arrived with his retinue in September, 1595, he listened to those who sought his ear—the ambitious and the disgruntled. At Acolman, on the way to the capital, he conferred formally with the outgoing viceroy. In both places, Oñate's friends and enemies sought to influence the Count, but since he had so much to learn about his new government, he listened and waited without taking positive action.

In their conferences, Viceroy Velasco impressed upon him the importance of the New Mexico project and Oñate's fitness for the position of its governor and captain general. The Count, biding his own time, permitted Velasco to go on with the plans he had under way and to issue Oñate's appointment as governor and captain general of New Mexico and to give him a specific set of instructions. Both were issued on October 21, a fortnight after the new viceroy had reached Mexico city and taken up his duties. At the same time, Velasco gave the king an account of what he had done and sent him a copy of Oñate's contract, which had been made in conformity with the royal ordinances, he assured the monarch. When the king read this letter a few months later, he wrote in the margin: "Write to the Count of Monterrey and urge him, in view of the arrangements made by Don Luis de Velasco for this pacification, to favor it . . . for it is an important matter and has been sought for a long time."

As Viceroy Monterrey gathered information about Oñate and his project, he must have been impressed by the grandiose nature of the new governor's plans. Oñate's desire to be independent of the viceroy of Mexico, his demand for the right to raise troops freely, and his request to found ports on the Atlantic and Pacific oceans, pointed toward independence from Mexico, though the new province must inevitably be dependent on New Spain for food and other supplies and reinforcements. Added to the viceroy's doubts about the wisdom of Oñate's schemes were the rumors of Oñate's unfitness for the office of governor, rumors which finally reached Spain some months later and added fuel to the fire of his opponents. Some critics said that though he was the son of a rich miner of Zacatecas, he had wasted his property and gone heavily into debt.

Pondering these doubts, the Count of Monterrey resolved them by asking the king to take no action in Spain even if Oñate or his friends should demand ratification of the contract, and by curtailing Oñate's contract rigorously. He made seven significant modifications, each of which was vital. He limited Oñate's right to recruit soldiers and colonists to "this occasion only"; deprived the governor of the power to appoint the first royal officials of New Mexico and to determine their salaries; denied his claim to be under the immediate jurisdiction of the Council of the Indies; rejected the privilege of bringing two ships each year to his province (it was believed that New Mexico faced the Atlantic ocean); took away his authority to determine the amount of tribute which the Indians were to pay; required him to account for and obtain confirmation, within three years, of the encomiendas that might have been granted; and limited the right of the colonists of becoming "hidalgos" to those who persevered in the conquest for five years.

These modifications of Oñate's contract were bitterly opposed by his family and friends, but in view of the viceroy's power, there was nothing to do but to accept the situation. This they did, doubtless with tongue in cheek, hoping that their luck in the new venture or their influence with the crown would bring the changes they desired. Oñate's faith in his project remained unimpaired, and he and his officers vigorously recruited soldiers and colonists for the expedition and gathered supplies and foodstuffs of all kinds.

The city of Zacatecas, where Oñate's family and friends were most numerous, was the center of activity. Fortunately, it was also situated on the frontier where men were ready and eager to believe the stories of greater Indian kingdoms in the distant unexplored regions.

Throughout the autumn of 1595 and the spring and summer of the next year, Oñate and his captains eagerly pursued their business, waiting at the same time for the final word from King Philip or the Council of the Indies that would send them on their way to fame and fortune in New Mexico. Instead of receiving a go-ahead signal, however, there came a decree from the king in September, 1596, when the army was stationed at the Río de las Nazas in the southern part of modern Chihuahua which deprived Oñate of the right to make the expedition to New Mexico until he should receive further orders.

For Don Juan de Oñate and his people, this was a terrible blow, but they had to face still greater disappointments, for when the Council of the Indies read Viceroy Monterrey's letters about New Mexico, it concluded that the viceroy was not very enthusiastic about Don Juan or his ability to carry out the proposed conquest. The Council had learned, too, so it was charged, that he was not an effective leader, that he had mismanaged other affairs, and that he had exhausted his financial resources.

At that very moment, moreover, it had found another candidate for the new post. This was a venerable gentleman from Bailén, Spain, Don Pedro Ponce de León, who had visited Mexico with the Count of Coruña nearly twenty years earlier and was said to have made many friends there. His standing in Spain was so good, said the Council, that men would flock to his standard, and it recommended, therefore, that the king give the charter to Ponce de León. If Oñate had incurred any expenses in his preparations that merited recompense, the Council continued, he might be reimbursed by this new applicant for the position of governor of New Mexico.

While Ponce's star was still in the ascendancy, he reached an agreement with the Council for a contract to conquer New Mexico, and the king, as though doubtful of this deal, reaffirmed the decision that no one else should make the conquest. That winter, however, the new conqueror fell ill, his bank account ran low, and he asked the king for a loan. This was a horse of a different color, and the penny-pinching Philip II now asked to see all the papers relating to the New Mexico affair. The Council, nevertheless, when it reviewed the claims of the two applicants, again strongly urged that Don Pedro Ponce be awarded the honor of conquering New Mexico and be sent to New Spain at once, though it admitted that the Count of Monterrey was now more favorably disposed toward Oñate. In this situation, King Philip showed the kind of ruler he was by ordering the Council to keep Don Pedro waiting "with good hopes" and requested that the viceroy be advised secretly to allow Oñate to proceed if he still had everything in readiness, and, if he did not, to report further.

Thus Don Pedro Ponce's hopes of empire crashed about his ears, and by a quirk of fortune, Oñate's star rose again. Key factor in the situation was Viceroy Monterrey, who now looked with greater favor on Oñate. The reasons for this change are obscure, but Don Juan's friends had not been idle. Captain Villagrá suggests that their intervention in his behalf had helped the viceroy to change his mind. By this time, too, the latter had probably come to realize that an old conqueror from Mexico would do much better at this sort of business than a newcomer from Spain, unfamiliar with the country and unknown among the men of the frontier.

While these events unfolded in Spain, Oñate's forces were being inspected by the viceroy's agent, Don Lope de Ulloa y Lemos. Oñate had repeatedly asked for an inspection, insisting that he had fulfilled the terms of his contract and that failure to send an inspector would justify his holding it himself, in order to vindicate his rights. These urgings finally led the Count of Monterrey to send Don Lope de Ulloa, who carried out a complete inspection of the New Mexico expedition in December, 1596, and January, 1597. At the conclusion of the review, it was found that Oñate had a total of two hundred and five men, or five more than he was obliged to provide. Of supplies and provisions he had a surplus of more than four thousand pesos. In all respects, Oñate had met the requirements of his contract, but it was an empty victory. The royal ban of suspension was still in effect. Neither Oñate nor any of his staff could guess what would happen. Would the king finally permit them to conquer New Mexico or would he give the honor to someone else? How long would he force these soldier-colonists, who had set out with so much spirit to serve their God and king in distant lands, to vegetate and rot on that northern frontier? In spite of adversity, Oñate had courage and skill and above all a firm belief in the righteousness of his cause that enabled him to keep most of his followers together. This faith carried the expedition through months of trials and hardships.

This period of tribulation came to an end when the king finally authorized the viceroy to permit Oñate to continue the conquest of New Mexico, if he still wanted to go. This good news reached Mexico during the summer of 1597. When Viceroy Monterrey informed Oñate of the royal order, it must have caused an outburst of enthusiasm among the drooping colonists and revived their determination to carry on. Now no one thought of turning back, and Oñate made strenuous efforts to prepare for the great adventure.

Viceroy Monterrey, who was responsible for deciding whether Oñate had fulfilled his agreements, made immediate preparations for holding another inspection of the expedition in order to make sure that everything was in order. As royal inspector he appointed Juan de Frías Salazar, an elderly mine operator from the famous mining community of Pachuca, and since he feared that there might be disorders among Oñate's people, he gave this agent full authority to cope with any situation that might arise.

Salazar was on his way immediately and within a month reached Santa Bárbara, where he notified Oñate to hold himself and his people in readiness for the inspection. Now followed the usual wrangling over procedure. Much of the goods was stored in warehouses, and therefore the expedition could not be put in marching order as promptly as Salazar demanded. Obviously, Oñate had trouble getting his men and supplies together, to say nothing of rounding up his livestock from distant pastures, and he was stalling for time. The troops were indeed in the three separate localities of Casco, La Puana, and Santa Bárbara, a good many leagues apart. In addition, the inspector was evidently a hardboiled old fellow, who had his instructions from the viceroy. Perhaps the Count would not be sorry if Oñate still should fail.

As the inspection began, a welter of official orders came from Salazar regarding arrangements for holding the review. The army was finally set in motion on December 18, 1597, after repeated orders of the royal agent, but when it got to San Bartolomé, a couple of leagues away, it was ordered to halt, as this was the site chosen by Salazar for the inspection. Villagrá described the spot as destitute and barren. Cattle, horses, sheep, goats, supplies, everything had to be assembled for the inventory. From December 22, 1597, to January 8, 1598, the ordeal dragged on, ending, finally, with the review of the soldier-colonists on the last day. This ceremony took place within the church at the mines of Todos Santos. As each man appeared, his name was recorded, together with his birthplace, his father's name, a personal description, and a statement of his weapons and armor. There were one hundred and twenty-nine men who proudly stepped forward and answered the roll call that January morning and enlisted for the conquest of New Mexico.

These men did not go alone. Many took their women and children, although no specific list of those who went at this time seems to have been compiled. In New Mexico, some of these women appear on the pages of history. Villagrá speaks eloquently of the courage of Doña Eufemia, the wife of Peñalosa, the royal ensign, in times of trouble. When the reinforcements came in 1600, there were many women, children, and servants on the expedition. Of these we have a detailed report.

In some categories, Oñate had fallen short of his contract. He needed seventy-one men to make up the required two hundred, and he was short of cattle and supplies. But the viceroy's orders permitted him to make good such deficiencies by giving bond, and so Don Juan called on a cousin, Juan Guerra de Resa, and his wife, Doña Ana de Zaldívar y Mendoza, for support. They had already backed Don Juan with funds, and they loyally stood by him now and gave bond to pay the costs of eighty soldiers and the necessary equipment and supplies. When this document was signed at Aviño on January 21, 1598, the formalities of the inspection were over and Oñate and his army of soldier-colonists were ready to undertake the conquest and pacification of New Mexico, their new home.

Frías de Salazar accompanied the expedition until it crossed the Conchos river, and there he gruffly took leave of the colonists without any intimate words of encouragement or good will. In fact, Oñate was later convicted of enjoying an insulting caricature of Salazar that some mulattoes had made to mock him. From this incident we may be sure that there was much bad feeling between the inspector and the members of the expedition.

Now came the serious business of organizing the great caravan for the march. Previous explorers had descended the Conchos to its junction with the Río Grande and had then followed its course upstream to New Mexico, thus being assured of water. But Oñate sought a shortcut and sent Vicente de Zaldívar and a small party to reconnoiter. They came back on March 10, after nearly a month's absence, and reported that they had found a direct road with adequate water through the sand dunes. The main army, in the meantime, had remained in camp, awaiting the Franciscan friars who were to accompany it. These arrived a week before Zaldívar's return, escorted by Captain Marcos Farfán, who had accompanied Inspector Salazar homeward but now returned to join the march to the north.

The Franciscans had been active in their support of the New Mexico conversion for several years, the first friars for this venture having been appointed in 1596. Fray Rodrigo Durán, who had the title of commissary, headed this group, and he was accompanied by five other friars. These included Fray Diego Márquez, the representative of the Inquisition, Fray Cristóbal de Salazar, Oñate's cousin, and Fray Francisco de San Miguel. A dispute soon arose between the Franciscans and the Holy Office of the Inquisition, however, and the commissary asked for the recall of Fray Márquez, charging that he was a native of Mexico and an intimate friend of Oñate. The main point of the argument was that the Franciscans challenged the right of the Inquisition to send an agent to New Mexico. In the end, Fray Márquez was recalled and no one was named in his stead.

SUGGESTED READINGS

George P. Hammond, "Don Juan de Oñate and the Founding of New Mexico," *New Mexico Historical Review,* vol. I (January, April, July, and October 1926), vol. II (January and April 1927);

George P. Hammond and Agapito Rey, *The Rediscovery of New Mexico, 1580–1594: The Explorations of Chamuscado, Espejo, Castaño de Sosa, Morlete, and Leyva de Bonilla and Humaña* (Albuquerque 1966);

Philip W. Powell, *Soldiers, Indians and Silver: The Northward Advance of New Spain, 1550–1600* (Berkeley 1952);

Herbert E. Bolton, *Spanish Exploration in the Southwest, 1542–1706* (New York 1916);

Gaspar Perez de Villagra, *A History of New Mexico* (Los Angeles 1933);

Florence C. and Robert H. Lister, *Chihuahua: Storehouse of Storms* (Albuquerque 1966).

3
Church and State in New Mexico

Seventeenth-century New Mexico was characterized by a long, bitter struggle between Church and State. Similar strife occurred throughout the empire but rarely did it reach the intensity of the controversy in New Mexico. Basic disagreements included the treatment and use of the Indians and the position of the Church as a privileged institution.

New Mexico was primarily a mission area, and the Church was therefore abnormally influential. The friars believed that the most important duty of laymen was to aid and protect the missions, and they were also overly zealous in the defense of their privileges. Governors resented many actions of the Church as unwarranted interference in political affairs. Difficulties were compounded by the fact that the missionaries were all Franciscans and thus presented a degree of unity which was absent in other areas of the empire. Ecclesiastical authority was concentrated to a remarkable degree, and no bishop had jurisdiction over New Mexico before 1680. The clergy's attitude toward the treatment of Indians also caused difficulties. They were quick to denounce any infringement on Indian rights, but colonists were angered by such criticism when they saw the Church exploiting Indians and when at times the combined resources of the Franciscans were greater than that of the colonists.

The office of governor was inherently difficult, for civil officials were entrusted with the often contradictory tasks of aiding and protecting the missions while promoting the economic development of the province. When exploitation of Indians provided the only source of wealth, as it did in New Mexico, discord was inevitable, and some governors contributed to the problem using their position to enrich

Reprinted by permission. By France V. Scholes; first published in the *New Mexico Historical Review,* vol. XI, No. 4 (October 1936), pp. 297–325.

themselves. Governors violated laws forbidding them to trade, conducted slave raids against the nomadic tribes, and some were intemperate and immoral.

It is not surprising then that a struggle between Church and State developed in New Mexico. From 1610 to 1650 the intensity of the conflict increased until it almost resulted in civil war. This account of the administration of Luís de Rosas (1637–41) by Dr. France V. Scholes, the outstanding authority on seventeenth-century New Mexico, describes the various elements of the conflict. In time New Mexico divided into two armed camps; individuals were beaten and killed; and eventually Rosas was murdered because of a trumped-up charge of adultery. The impact of these events on the underdeveloped and sparsely populated province was unquestionably great.

With the possible exception of Diego de Peñalosa, who was governor from 1661 to 1664, Luís de Rosas was the most interesting of all the men who ruled New Mexico prior to the Pueblo Revolt. He was an outspoken, hard-hitting soldier, fearless in action. He made his decisions quickly and executed them ruthlessly. He had the qualities useful in a leader of a faction, but unsuited to the civil administration of a province where passions had already been deeply aroused. Men admired him or hated him, for his character was of that direct and positive sort that leaves no room for neutral ground.

Rosas was appointed governor of New Mexico by the viceroy, Marqués de Cadereita, and the clergy of New Mexico later charged that he was merely Cadereita's servant. The first glimpse of Rosas, in the spring of 1636 probably soon after his appointment, shows him anxious to set out for his province, for he had petitioned the viceregal authorities for permission to leave for New Mexico in advance of the regular supply caravan. He was obliged to curb his restlessness, however, and wait for the caravan that left later in the year. He arrived in New Mexico in the spring of 1637, and on April 19 took over the province from his predecessor, Francisco Martínez de Baeza.

During Rosas' term of office (1637–1641) the spirit of faction and bitterness between the two jurisdictions that had been developing ever since the days of Peralta came to a climax in a series of tragic events which left the province a house divided. Father Manso's optimism was not justified; Rosas, instead of giving the Church "pleasure and peace," soon came to be regarded as the mortal enemy of the clergy.

Curiously enough the Inquisition played only a very minor role during the Rosas period. An explanation is not difficult to find. Friar Estéban de Perea continued to exercise the authority of local representative of the Holy

Office during the decade of the 1630's. To the end of his life Perea retained his old zeal, and instead of taking his ease at the pueblo of Sandía he assumed the responsibilities of a new mission post in the pueblo of Cuarac. His quarter-century of experience in all phases of missionary business, his terms as prelate, and the vindication he had received in Mexico City in 1627–1629 gave him great personal influence, and as a member of the committee of definitors he kept in touch with details of local administration. But active leadership had passed into other hands. Friar Cristóbal de Quiros and Friar Juan de Salas who bore the brunt of the conflict with Baeza and Rosas were old associates of Perea, and they probably relied on him for counsel. But they made the final decisions, not Perea.

Age was demanding its inevitable price: the Perea of the 1630's was not the Perea of the old quarrel with Eulate. During the last four or five years of his life, he exercised his functions as agent of the Holy Office sparingly. He did not seek to initiate investigations and summoned only a few witnesses when a situation had been presented to him in a voluntary declaration. His death, which probably occurred in the winter of 1638–1639, came just at the moment when Custodian Salas and Governor Rosas were "clearing the decks" for a finish fight. By the time the Holy Office could appoint a new agent for New Mexico the situation had passed the investigation stage and demanded more stringent action than could be taken under the cumbersome methods involved in an inquisitorial process.

Thus in the great crisis of 1639–1642 the weapons which Perea had eagerly sought as an aid to the Church lay unused. In the preliminary skirmishes of 1638 a few sworn declarations of evidence were made and duly transmitted to the Holy Office, but they are important now only as a source of information concerning certain events of that period. Faltering hands wielded the weapons of the Inquisition—and those hands were Friar Estéban de Perea's!

Rosas' first important duty as governor was to take the residencia of his predecessor. The clergy confidently expected that he would submit Baeza to severe rebuke and punishment, but to their amazement he refused to permit himself to be made their instrument of vengeance. It was charged several years later (1641) by the anti-Rosas faction that he accepted a bribe from Baeza in return for which he made no strict investigation of the latter's official conduct. This was not unlikely, as bribery was not an uncommon means of escaping a strict residencia. It is evident in any case that Rosas refused to take the side of the Church with regard to the recent difficulties with Baeza, and his independent action, whether it involved the acceptance of a bribe or not, brought him adverse criticism.

This was merely the first cause of friction between the two jurisdictions. More important was the old problem of Indian administration, for Rosas appears to have adopted the system of exploitation that had been employed by his predecessors. The most explicit, as well as the most detailed, indictment on this charge is contained in a general accusation presented in 1641 by Capt. Francisco de Salazar, one of the governor's enemies and a leader in the clerical, anti-Rosas faction. Additional information is found in depositions made before Friars Perea and Salas and transmitted to the Holy Office. The accusations contained in these documents may be divided into two groups: (1) those dealing with the exploitation of the converted Pueblos, and (2) those which relate to Rosas' policy toward the nomadic tribes.

With regard to the Pueblos Rosas followed Baeza's example and required the Indians of the several villages to weave mantas and other textiles. He also established a workshop in Santa Fé where the Indians, both Christian and unconverted, including Apache and "Utaca" captives, were forced to labor for long hours under conditions of virtual servitude, and it was said that Rosas himself was often to be found there, surrounded by Indians and so covered with dirt that only by his clothes could he be distinguished from the Indians. Indian labor was employed also in planting great quantities of food. Likewise, the frontier pueblos were used for barter and trade with nomadic Apaches. The pueblo of Pecos was one of the most important of these frontier trading posts, and from time immemorial the Indians had bartered for the buffalo hides and meat brought in by the Apaches. To Pecos Rosas took a large quantity of knives to be used in trade, but apparently he had little success in this venture. The governor blamed the friars in charge of the mission, and had one of them arrested and placed under guard. It was also charged that, in order to induce the Indians of Pecos to greater activity, he promised them permission to revert to some of their old pagan and idolatrous customs if they could furnish more mantas and hides.

The denunciations of Rosas' policy toward the nomadic, unconverted tribes were equally severe. Against the "Utacas," a bellicose people living beyond the Pueblo area, but from whom the Spaniards and Pueblos had received no harm, Rosas was said to have made unjust war. Several of the Indian warriors were killed during the encounter, and a group of eighty were captured, some of whom were sent to labor in Rosas' Santa Fé workshop.

More serious were the complaints made concerning Rosas' Apache policy. The Apaches were already becoming a serious problem, for although some of the tribes traded now and then at Pecos or with the pueblos in the Tompiro area, the general trend of Apache-Pueblo relations was becoming more and more hostile. During Baeza's term of office the raids had become fairly frequent, but he made no serious attempt to deal with the problem. Consequently the Apaches were emboldened, and continued their marauding adventures. Captain Salazar complained that Rosas not only neglected to prepare an adequate defense, but even failed to organize any counter attacks after raids had been successfully executed. On the other hand, it was charged that he was directly responsible for a definite sharpening of Apache hostility, for during an expedition to the plains of Quivira he permitted treacherous attacks to be made on a friendly Apache tribe during which several of the Indians were killed and others were made prisoners. Some of the prisoners were impressed as laborers in the Santa Fé workshop and others were sent to New Spain as slaves. In short, Rosas aroused the Apaches by acts of treachery, and then failed to protect the frontier pueblos when counter-raids were made.

Another group of Indians whom Rosas antagonized were the Ipotlapiguas who lived in northern Sonora. For several years the friars had been interested in the possibility of evangelizing these tribes and their neighbors, the Zipias, and in the spring of 1638 a group of five friars and an escort of forty soldiers commanded by Rosas himself set out for the Ipotlapigua country. The friars regarded the expedition as essentially a missionary enterprise, and they expected to remain with the Ipotlapiguas and the Zipias as resident missionaries in case their labors were successful. But according to available evidence—all of it is hostile—the governor turned the expedition into a venture for his own profit. As soon as the party arrived in the Ipotlapigua area he forgot his duty toward the friars and their mission and made all sorts of unjust demands on the Indians. He forced them to bring in feathers and hides, robbed them of their clothing, even the garments that covered their nakedness, and threatened to burn their villages if they did not comply with his demands. The protests of the friars against these abuses were without avail. Rosas continued to follow his policy of extortion, and the Indians, who had seemed willing enough to listen to the teachings of the friars, fled to the mountains when they realized the nature of Rosas' motives. The mission to the Ipotlapiguas was thus a failure, and the friars who had expected to remain with them as ministers and teachers returned to New Mexico with the military escort.

Such were the most important complaints made against Rosas on the score of exploiting and maltreating the Indians. The charges were made by his personal enemies and by the clergy, and should be viewed with a certain amount of caution, although there is no doubt that Rosas laid a heavy burden of labor on the Indians and exploited them to the limit. It should be noted, however, that some of the evidence is not so hostile. The charge that Rosas mismanaged the Apache problem was contradicted by Sargento Mayor Francisco Gómez, one of the founders of the province and its most important military figure during the first half of the seventeenth century. In a letter to the viceroy, Gómez praised Rosas' conduct and especially his successful expedition to Quivira and the resolute action by which he had forced the Apaches to accept peace.

According to the clerical party it was the purpose of Rosas to destroy all ecclesiastical privilege and authority. As an example of his lack of respect for the immunities of ecclesiastical persons, the arrest of one of the friars stationed at Pecos was cited. Investigation of the conduct of the guardian of Taos whom the Indians accused of grave immorality was doubtless another case in point. It was also reported that during the journey to the Ipotlapigua country in 1636 Rosas questioned the authority of Friar Antonio de Arteaga, commissary of the clergy who had been appointed to the Ipotlapigua mission, on the ground that the custodian had no authority to grant Arteaga the powers of a legitimate prelate. Likewise, it was said that he made certain general statements implying doubt concerning the just authority of the Church as a whole. Friar Arteaga decided that it was necessary to correct these errors as well as to denounce the governor's exploitation of the Ipotlapiguas. In the course of a sermon which he preached on St. Mark's day, he explained that all Catholic princes were subject to the laws of the Church and were in duty bound to defend them. He cited the king of Spain as an example of such a Catholic prince, and in order to press the point home he also stated that although it was possible for a man to be relieved of obedience to the civil law of one state by moving to another state, it was impossible for any man ever to become exempt from obedience to the laws of the Church. In fact, any man who refused such obedience would be a heretic. Angered by these remarks Rosas rose from his place and shouted, "Shut up, Father, what you say is a lie." And with these words he left the services and most of the soldiers followed him. When he reported this incident to Friar Perea several weeks later, Arteaga said:

> Seeing that they left without wishing to hear the sermon and mass, and having had experience with the depreciations with which they regard excommunications, I did not wish to deal so severely with them. Instead, I merely told them that in the name of God, whose minister I was, I ordered them to listen; and that if they did not do so, the curse of God and of St. Peter and St. Paul would fall upon them.

The Indians who were present, especially the Christian Pueblo Indians who had accompanied the expedition, were scandalized by Rosas' action. They remarked that if the governor could call a priest a liar, how, then, could they henceforth believe what the friars taught?

The question that finally forced the issue between Rosas and the clergy was the status of the representatives of the Santa Cruzada in New Mexico.

The Bull was first preached in New Mexico in 1633. Friar Juan de Góngora, the custodian, was appointed commissary subdelegate, and he continued to serve in that capacity when his term as custodian came to an end in 1635. The first treasurer was Capt. Roque de Casaus, who was later succeeded by Alférez Juan Márquez.

From the beginning there had been difficulty. In the first place, Father Góngora failed to present his patent as commissary subdelegate to the cabildo of Santa Fé for formal acceptance. This touched the pride of the local officials and also raised some doubt concerning the validity of Góngora's exercise of authority. Second, many persons could see no justice in preaching the Bull in New Mexico where the citizens were engaged in a real crusade against pagan enemies, such as the unconverted Apaches and Navahos who threatened the existence of the missions. And it was reported that certain friars shared this view.

In the course of time complaints were made concerning the arbitrary manner in which the commissary subdelegate and the treasurer exercised their authority. The procurator general of the province informed the tribunal of the Crusade in Mexico City that the treasurer was using his authority to obtain special advantages in the settlement of private business operations. The tribunal denounced such action and ordered the treasurer to use his official position only for collections of sums due for purchase of bulls. Father Góngora added to the discontent by publishing an edict on August 6, 1638, imposing the censure of excommunication on all persons who were in arrears on sums owed for bulls.

But there is another aspect of the general situation which deserves notice. The clericals testified in 1644 that a certain Juan de Trespalacios, who had returned to Mexico after a brief service in New Mexico as a familiar of the Crusade, forwarded to Father Góngora a viceregal order guaranteeing to the citizens of the province complete liberty in their private business operations, especially in carrying on trade, and the right of free movement to and from the province. Góngora turned this order over to Capt. Nicolás de la Mar y Vargas, notary of the cabildo, for formal presentation. According to the notary's own testimony, and substantiated by the testimony of others, Rosas considered this act a great affront, and would have sent the notary to the garrote if friends had not intervened. The governor blamed Góngora for the entire incident, and from that moment displayed open hostility toward the friar and the business of the Crusade.

Finally in January, 1639, the treasurer Márquez was arrested and charged with "certain grave offenses," and Father Góngora sought to defend him by an assertion of ecclesiastical privilege. The alcalde ordinario, Capt. Roque de Casaus, brought the matter to the attention of the cabildo in a formal petition on January 28. He questioned Góngora's authority on the ground that the friar had never formally presented his appointment as commissary subdelegate of the Crusade before the cabildo. He complained that Góngora had constantly acted in a high-handed manner, disturbing and scandalizing the province with excommunications and interdicts, protecting guilty parties and doing injustice to the citizens, opposing governmental officers and interfering with civil jurisdiction. He also accused both Góngora and Márquez of using their offices and privileges to seize property unlawfully. The last item was a grave charge. In justice to the accused, it must be pointed out that the clerical faction later stated that Márquez had attempted to force Captain Casaus to give an accounting of funds received when the latter had served as treasurer of the Crusade, and that Casaus took advantage of his position as alcalde ordinario of Santa Fé to prevent such an accounting.

Whatever the cause, the arrest of Márquez forced the issue of ecclesiastical jurisdiction. During the early weeks of 1639 the civil authorities entered into an open controversy with Father Góngora and demanded that he give proof of his appointment as commissary subdelegate to the cabildo. Góngora refused to comply, stating that in accordance with his original instruction he had presented his papers to Governor Mora Ceballos when the Crusade had first been preached and that he was under no obligation to present them to the cabildo. Moreover, when the cabildo notified him of the decree of the central tribunal of the Crusade forbidding the treasurer to use his official position for private ends, Góngora countered by declaring that the tribunal's action had been based on false information supplied by the procurator general, and that the tribunal had later restated the right of agent of the Crusade to exercise jurisdiction in the collection of private debts. The cabildo called upon Góngora to present the text of this new provision, but he replied that he had sent all the papers to Mexico by a special emissary. He also reiterated his refusal to present his patents of appointment as commissary subdelegate.

The immediate outcome of this affair is not known, at least so far as Márquez is concerned. But Captain Salazar and other members of the anti-Rosas group testified that the governor sought to have Custodian Salas order the withdrawal of Góngora from the province, a request which Salas refused on the ground that he had no jurisdiction over a representative of the Crusade. Rosas then banished Góngora on his own authority, and according to our informants the friar died of grief!

Thus the relations between Church and State had once more reached the breaking point. The clergy were thoroughly aroused, and they made free use of the penalty of excommunication. From 1638 until his death on January 25, 1642, Rosas was under ecclesiastical censure continuously. And the governor, in turn, became increasingly hostile to the clergy and their supporters.

Captain Salazar's list of complaints also included many charges of arbitrary and unjust action toward members of the lay community. It was stated, for example, that Rosas always seized the best of the goods or supplies obtained by trading parties sent out to barter with the unconverted nomads; that he controlled all local commerce for his own benefit; that he seized looms owned by private citizens in order to give his own workshop a greater monopoly over local textile production; that he seized and slaughtered approximately one-third of the cattle owned by private citizens in order to provide food for the laborers in his workshop, or in order to pay for the goods that the Indians of the various pueblos made for him. All these acts of injustice resulted from the eager desire of Rosas to accumulate stocks of merchandise for shipment to New Spain. Even the private lives of some of the citizens did not escape the heavy hand of his tyranny, for he was accused of compelling certain persons to marry against their will.

The cabildo of Santa Fé played an important part in the dispute with Father Góngora created by the arrest of Treasurer Márquez, and during the succeeding two years it actively supported Rosas during the open breach of relations with the clergy. It is apparent that Rosas secured this support by manipulation of cabildo elections in order to build up a faction favorable to his interest, but in doing so he alienated the sympathies of a group of the professional soldier-citizens who immediately espoused the cause of the Church. This phase of the general Rosas episode was of prime importance because it led to an open breach in the law community itself, and gave the clergy the support of a military clique which became bitterly resentful of the governor's policy.

It appears that members of the cabildo who were in office during the first year of Rosas' term of office opposed some of his policies. Captain Salazar stated in his general petition of complaint that Rosas wished to destroy the authority of both the Inquisition and the Crusade in New Mexico and sought to have the cabildo join him in a formal denial of the jurisdiction of these tribunals. Three of the regidores, Alférez Cristóbal Enríquez, Capt. Diego de la Serna, and Alférez Diego del Castillo, resisted his demands, and the governor showed his displeasure by maltreating them by both word and deed. Against Enríquez, who was apparently the leader of the dissenting group, Rosas employed physical violence.

Finding that most of the regidores opposed his policies, Rosas undertook to secure the election of a new cabildo that would do his bidding. This was a fairly easy matter, as he had the right to confirm the annual election of regidores and alcaldes ordinarios. The effectiveness of his influence is clearly indicated in the complete support which he received from the cabildo in January and February of 1639 during the controversy with Father Góngora caused by the arrest of Treasurer Márquez. From

1639 to 1641, when Rosas' term came to an end, the cabildo was made up of men who were partisans of the governor.

The resentment caused by Rosas' manipulation of cabildo elections is clearly indicated by the slurs and insults directed against his supporters by members of the clerical party. One of the friars called the new regidores "those four mestizo dogs," and in 1644 the Rosas faction was described as consisting mostly of "a foreigner, a Portuguese, and mestizos and sambohijos, sons of Indian women and negroes and mulattoes."

Care must be exercised, however, in dealing with these characterizations of members of the Rosas faction. One of the governor's loyal defenders was Sargento Mayor Francisco Gómez, a time-tried citizen who had had wide experience in provincial affairs. Capt. Roque de Casaus, who served as alcalde ordinario after the new election, had held the same office six years earlier and, as noted above, had served as first treasurer of the Crusade. The second alcalde ordinario was Francisco de Madrid, member of a family that served the Crown faithfully throughout this early period. One of the regidores was Diego de Guadalajara who was leader of the famous expedition into Texas in 1654. Another was Matías Romero, member of one of the oldest conquistador families, although it must be admitted that the family deteriorated during the seventeenth century. It is perfectly clear that toward the middle of the century mestizos and even negro castes obtained office. It was an inevitable trend, due to the lack of immigration. And on no other occasion were the castes so fiercely denounced. It is difficult to avoid the conclusion that the epithets directed against the Rosas faction by their enemies expressed personal and political passion rather than any deep feeling with regard to the character and race of members of the government party.

But whatever the facts may have been, it is perfectly clear that Rosas antagonized a group of powerful soldier-citizens. Capt. Francisco de Salazar, whose general indictment of Rosas' conduct has been cited so often, was a member of the disaffected party which also included Antonio Baca, Diego Márquez, and Juan de Archuleta.

To sum up, the most important result of the first two years of Rosas' administration was to arouse the opposition of both the Church and a considerable part of the lay community. The clergy saw in Rosas the arch-enemy of the missions and of all ecclesiastical authority. The discontented soldiers were cut to the quick by his arbitrary governmental policy, and probably by acts which affected their pride. A clerical-military coalition was thus formed, and during the succeeding three years it played a very interesting role in provincial politics.

The preceding discussion has been based almost completely on evidence and petitions presented by the anti-Rosas party. It is necessary now to review the situation from the point of view of the governor and his faction.

In 1637 and again in 1638 representations were made to the viceregal court concerning the arbitrary manner in which the clergy exercised jurisdiction, and on one of these occasions substantiating documents were submitted. These documents form the expediente cited as *Diferentes Autos* in preceding chapters of this essay. The first group of papers dealt with an incident of the Oñate period,—the banishment of a soldier from provincial headquarters at the instigation of the Father-Commissary. The second item was the original trial record in the Escarramad case. (See Chapter II). The remaining documents were from the Baeza period, such as the papers on the controversy over the Zuñi mission escort, decrees of excommunication, etc.

To the several groups of documents were appended statements which well illustrate the point of view of the anticlerical faction. The following is the most inclusive:

> [This document] is transmitted in order that it may be seen what an old practice it is for the friars to wield a strong hand in New Mexico . . . and if they are contradicted, they start lawsuits and disturbances, calling [their opponents] enemies of the Order of St. Francis, and denouncing governor and citizens as heretics, as they did with Governor Don Pedro Peralta whom they imprisoned.

In 1638 Governor Rosas dispatched to the Holy Office the testimony and general complaint concerning the misconduct of the guardian of Taos, and took occasion to make certain observations concerning the manner in which the business of the Inquisition was conducted in New Mexico. And at the same time Sargento Mayor Francisco Gómez wrote a strong letter defending the administration of Rosas and calling attention to the tremendous power and influence of the clergy and the unbridled manner in which they interfered in provincial affairs.

The controversy with Father Góngora further aggravated Church and State relations, and about the same time another source of irritation was created. The prelate, Friar Juan de Salas, gave orders to the guardian of Santa Fé not to administer the sacrament of penance to citizens seeking it, and complaints were made to the governor. Rosas issued a formal *auto* summoning the cabildo to a conference for the purpose of discussing the situation. The statement issued by the cabildo as a result of this meeting contained a bitter denunciation of the friars and their alleged abuse of authority. This petition and the papers relating to the Góngora case were transmitted to the viceroy in February, 1639, and were accompanied by a long justificatory dispatch by the cabildo.

The most serious complaint dealt with the wide and varied powers enjoyed by the clergy. The struggling lay community found itself under the thumb of three kinds of ecclesiastical authority and of three tribunals, each with its own chief and lesser officials. The custodian exercised the powers of local prelate with authority to grant or withhold the sacraments, to excommunicate and to absolve, to institute ecclesiastical process, and to sentence the guilty. It was said that for the most minor cause the citizens found themselves cut off from the sacraments and placed under ecclesiastical penalties. The sacrament of penance was often withheld, especially during Lent, unless the penitent signed papers praising the clergy and denouncing civil authority. The case of Governor Baeza was cited as an example. The governor and several other persons refused to sign the prescribed papers and were denied confession. The cabildo made a special trip to Santo Domingo, the ecclesiastical capital, to intervene in the governor's behalf. The custodian received them with open discourtesy and apparently refused to entertain their good offices.

The commissary of the Inquisition possessed authority to investigate cases of heresy, to pry into the lives of citizens, and to summon witnesses great distances, merely stating that it concerned the business of the Holy Office. The Crusade, likewise, had its own chieftain and lesser officers, independent of all authority except that of the tribunal of the Crusade in Mexico City.

Each of these three jurisdictions enjoyed special powers and immunities, and each had its notaries and assistants, all enjoying the privileges of the ecclesiastical *fuero*. To make matters worse, these powers and privileges were all exercised by members of one and the same Order, inspired by a community of interest and purpose. Thus, according to the cabildo's complaint, the Franciscans had become "so powerful that, while enjoying the quiet and ease of their cells and doctrinas, they are able to disturb and afflict the land and to keep it in [a state of] continuous martyrdom." Conflicts or differences with one jurisdiction thus became a conflict with all. Excommunications, interdicts, and denials of the sacraments were lightly ordered and, "what is worse," these were frequently issued against the governors and other civil authorities. Moreover, the censures were sometimes pronounced at most inconvenient times. The Commissary of the Crusade, for example, had posted an edict of excommunication against the civil authorities, just at the time when Rosas was preparing to undertake a campaign against the nomads, and had caused confusion in the midst of the preparations. The slight revenue received from the Crusade was more than offset by the fact that it gave the clergy means for disturbing and scandalizing the province. And the cabildo was especially bitter in denouncing the abuse of authority and privilege by officials of the Crusade in private business operations.

The cabildo did not question the inherent justice of ecclesiastical jurisdiction, but it did believe that the community was too small to warrant the existence of three separate tribunals. The complaint stated that the Church had as many, or more, officials than the civil government, and that some of these officials, being laymen, were sorely needed as soldiers. And the special jurisdictional privileges enjoyed by familiars of the tribunals made the administration of justice exceedingly difficult. Moreover, the heads of the three tribunals seldom lived in the same pueblo and none of them, apparently, made their headquarters in Santa Fé, so that citizens, when summoned on ecclesiastical business, found it necessary to travel great distances back and forth across the province. Representations had been made to the Father-Custodian concerning abuses, but they had served merely to create new sources of conflict and irritation. And whenever the clergy learned that the civil authorities reported cases of violation of civil jurisdiction to the viceroy, they would clamor that the authorities had thereby violated ecclesiastical immunity.

In addition to the long and bitter complaint about the exercise of ecclesiastical authority, the cabildo also discussed the fundamental economic conditions which caused difficulties between Church and State, particularly the rivalry over lands, labor, and the breeding of livestock. It resented the complaints of the clergy that the estancias of private citizens infringed on the communal holdings of the Indians, and took pains to point out that the friars themselves were in possession of thousands of head of stock which grazed on the pueblo ranges. "Each friar possesses one or two thousand sheep, whereas there are few citizens who have as many as five hundred, others do not have even a hundred, and those who live in the villa do not have farms or livestock." The cabildo suggested that inasmuch as the Crown supported the missions, the clergy should not engage in herding. Let their herds be divided among the poor. Such action would aid the struggling soldier-colonists and at the same time decrease the burden of labor on the Indians, for at every mission numerous Indians were constantly employed as cooks, carriers of wood, grinders of corn, and herdsmen. As many as thirty or forty were sometimes thus engaged in a pueblo of fifty or sixty houses. And whereas the friars all had twenty, thirty, or even forty horses, there were many soldiers so poor that they could not even buy horses and arms. Moreover, the clergy had more arms and weapons, shields, swords, arquebuses, and pistols than all the rest of the land. "We beg Your Excellency to order these arms deposited in the Casa Real in the power of the governor in order that he may apportion them out in time of need, since there are none in the Royal Armory." Last of all, the viceroy was asked to investigate certain financial operations of Father Perea that had not been regarded as honest and straightforward.

These complaints went to the root of the difficulties between Church and State and indicated once more the fundamental issues: (1) the Church controlled by a single Order; (2) the exercise of wide and thoroughgoing powers over the citizens in every phase of their spiritual and moral life—with no appeal except to far-away Mexico on the one hand or to the local representative of the Crown in New Mexico on the other; and (3) the economic basis of the conflict. The appeal of the cabildo calls forth sympathy for the struggling community, a population of a few hundred isolated on a distant frontier, which supported the labors of the friars by military service and was burdened by the weight of three ecclesiastical tribunals watching every move for signs of heresy and apostasy and wielding the heaviest of ecclesiastical censures.

What were the remedies which the cabildo proposed? In the first place, it sought to have secular clergy appointed to the parish of Santa Fé in place of the Franciscans. The reasons for this petition are obvious, and we can have considerable sympathy for the cabildo's motives.

Second, the viceroy was requested to retain Rosas in office. The cabildo's characterization of the governor is interesting, even though it was doubtless written at the instigation of Rosas himself.

> We are in duty bound to inform Your Excellency that our Captain General has resisted these hardships with great valor, and that he has also served Your Majesty . . . in journeys, punitive expeditions, and discoveries which he has made, conquering difficulties, not permitting peace or praise to impede him, holding and preserving the citizens and soldiers in peace and justice; therefore, we beg, Your Excellency . . . to preserve him in this office, for it will be a great comfort and relief in the labor and afflictions which we suffer.

Finally, the cabildo urged the concentration of all ecclesiastical authority in the hands of one person who would serve as custodian, commissary of the Inquisition, and agent of the Crusade. This proposal was highly dangerous because it might give the prelate power equal to or greater than that of the governor. But the cabildo thought that the personal aspect of the problem was more important than the question of policy. It stated that in the past the prelacy had been passed around among three or four of the older friars who had long been involved in the quarrel between the two jurisdictions. But all would be well if the viceroy could bring about the election of Friar Juan de Vidania, a newcomer, as prelate.

> He will reform these disorders because he is a friar . . . virtuous and of exemplary life, . . . modest, unassuming, and on very good relations with the authorities and citizens . . . He has preached to us . . . as he should, interested only in declaring the Holy Gospel . . . without display of passion and discourteous words.

Who was this Friar Juan de Vidania in whom the cabildo put so much confidence? Nothing is known concerning his early career except that he had entered the Franciscan Order in the Province of Michoacan after having been expelled from the Society of Jesus. Nor do we have information concerning his service in New Mexico prior to 1638. But from 1638 on, he was openly identified with the Rosas faction. He became the chief aid and closest adviser of the governor, searching the law books and papal decrees for precedents to justify the governor's policies. By the other friars he came to be regarded as a thoroughgoing traitor and scoundrel. His interpretations of ecclesiastical law and custom were said to be so false and inaccurate that one friar declared he should have been refused the privilege of reading Scripture and the canons. His Latin was said to be so crude that he deserved to be deprived of the exercise of divine offices. He brooked no correction from his superiors, and the friars who undertook to challenge his actions became his enemies. Rosas and Vidania, in the eyes of the Church an unholy pair: Rosas, "one of the worst men of these centuries;" Vidania, an evil friar defying the authority of his prelate; the one ruthless and violent, and the other shrewd and clever in defense.

The alliance between the governor and friar dated from 1638. At the meeting of the custodial chapter in that year Vidania was re-assigned to the pueblo of Picurís, and Father Domingo de Espíritu Santo to Santa Fé. But Father Domingo was not *persona grata* to the governor, and the latter called upon Custodian Salas to appoint Vidania to Santa Fé in his place. Rather than cause trouble, Salas consented.

It is difficult to follow the events of the succeeding year and a half in strict chronological sequence. The clergy insisted that Vidania lost no time in espousing the governor's cause, especially in the Crusade affair, and that he began to give advice on legal phases of the Church and State relations with a view to limiting, if not destroying, the jurisdictional authority of the clergy.

The death of Father Perea left the Holy Office powerless for the moment. And as a result of the Góngora controversy, the Crusade was apparently without a legally recognized leader. Thus there remained only the power of the custodian, and so the next move was to question Father Salas' authority. Sometime during the year 1639 the governor and cabildo challenged the validity of Salas' official acts on the ground that he refused to present his patent of appointment for verification and record. Salas had already been serving as prelate for more than a year, and deemed this action insolent and unwarranted.

The general ordinance of 1574 dealing with the royal patronage had specifically stated that prelates of monastic orders before being admitted to office should give notice "to the viceroy, president, audiencia, or governor who may be in charge of the superior government of the province, and present the patent of his appointment and election," etc. Thus there was a clear obligation for the custodian to present his patent to the civil governor on taking office. We have no documents to illustrate actual practice in New Mexico, although Vidania, who acted as adviser to Rosas on all legal matters, stated that Friar Isidro Ordóñez had failed to present his papers and that Governor Peralta had therefore questioned his authority. Friar Bartolomé Romero, an associate and contemporary of Salas, argued that the proper procedure was for the definitors and other friars to receive the custodian, examine his papers, and formally accept him as prelate; and that when this had been done, formal certification of the friar as legal prelate would be made to the civil authorities. Romero stated that this form had been followed in the past without any question. It is obvious that this procedure did not conform to the letter of the law, which provided that the *patent of election* should be presented to the governor. Thus if Salas refused formally to present his appointment to Rosas, his authority could be questioned. But it is not clear whether this was the issue, or whether it had been demanded that he present his patent *before the cabildo*. Romero gave the impression that it was the latter, and if that was true, then the demand was not justified. For although cabildos were sometimes recognized as superior governing authorities of a province during vacancies in the governorship, the cabildo of Santa Fé was not so functioning when the demand for presentation was made.

The important fact is that Rosas and Vidania took the position that Salas' failure to produce his papers deprived him of authority as legal prelate, and that his orders and censures had no validity.

In the meantime Vidania's relations with his Franciscan colleagues were strained to the breaking point. Toward the end of 1639 he had a violent disagreement with Friar Alonso Yanes, one of his subordinates in the Santa Fé convent. The custodian immediately sent another friar, Father Antonio de Aranda, to assume the presidency of the convent and make an investigation. Not long thereafter occurred another incident which brought about a violent breach of relations between the civil and ecclesiastical jurisdictions.

A certain Sebastián de Sandoval incurred excommunication for having posted "infamous libels" against Custodian Salas and other friars. Instead of punishing the offender for such lack of respect for the prelate, Rosas was more cordial to him than before. Emboldened by the governor's favor, he indulged in slander against various leading citizens and their wives, "and dared to do other shameful things, living in a scandalous manner." Early in January, 1640, he was secretly murdered.

According to reports sent to the viceroy by the provincial authorities several persons were involved in the murder, including two friars one of whom had predicted the deed. When Rosas attempted to investigate, the clergy protected the guilty persons and he was obliged to abandon the inquiry. Three years later Governor Pacheco reported that Rosas actually arrested Capt. Juan de Archuleta, as a participant in the crime, but was forced by the pressure of public opinion to release him. Whatever the facts may have been, the investigation was permitted to lapse and officially at least the case remained unsolved.

Friar Antonio de Aranda, who had assumed the presidency of the Santa Fé convent, was absent when the crime was committed. Rosas turned to Vidania, and with the latter's consent had Sandoval buried in the Santa Fé church, despite the fact that he had died excommunicate. Father Aranda hastened back to his post and ordered Vidania confined to his cell pending orders from the custodian.

The governor immediately went to the aid of his ally. Taking a group of soldiers, Rosas entered the convent grounds and talked to Vidania through the window of his cell. It was agreed that the governor would forcibly remove the friar to the Casa Real and appoint him "Royal Chaplain." Vidania, in return for this favor, would absolve the governor and his associates from all the censures that had been pronounced against them during the preceding months. This interview took place on January 12 and was carried out without delay. "By force of arms" Rosas entered the convent and escorted his ally to the Casa Real.

The following day (January 13) all of the other friars who were serving in Santa Fé were ordered to withdraw from the villa, under threat of death, thus leaving Vidania in complete control. On January 14 the Blessed Sacrament was removed from the church to a room in the Casa Real which henceforth served as a chapel for the parish. The convent and the Hermita de San Miguel were closed.

Custodian Salas immediately summoned Vidania to appear and defend his conduct, promising to "receive him with peace and love and let him explain all." When Vidania refused to answer the summons, the prelate declared him excommunicate and apostate, and forbade the citizens under penalty of excommunication to accept the sacraments from his hands. But the friar made light of this action and questioned the legality of the prelate's decrees on the ground that failure to present the patents of his office had invalidated his authority. The custodian then called upon Rosas and the cabildo to hand over the apostate and permit the appointment of another friar as parish priest. This request was denied, and for more than a year Vidania continued to serve as spiritual adviser and leader of the parish of Santa Fé.

The exact chronology of events between January, 1640, and the spring of 1641, when a new prelate and a new governor arrived, cannot be determined with certainty. Consequently the following discussion of the major incidents may be open to some question, although it is based on a careful study and reading of the available documents.

On February 8, 1640, Father Salas summoned the clergy to a conference at Santo Domingo. This action was taken on the advice of several friars. Rosas had made threats, general and specific, against the custodian and other friars, especially the threat of seizing Salas and expelling him from the province. In certain pueblos the governor had ordered the Indians not to obey their ministers. At Taos the Indians had cast off all restraint, and killed the guardian of the convent, Friar Pedro de Miranda, and two other Spaniards. They had then moved on Picurís, but the friar-in-charge fortunately had been absent from the pueblo. Such were the reasons for calling the conference, as given in a formal statement issued by Salas and his associates on March 16.

When the friars assembled at Santo Domingo they canvassed the situation and decided that they would all accompany the prelate if he were expelled. Rosas, in turn, immediately characterized the conference as open rebellion and fulminated a decree condemning the clergy as traitors to the Crown and ordering them to leave the province within three days under penalty of "fire and blood." Although this order was not enforced, the friars deemed it dangerous to return to their respective missions, and remained in Santo Domingo for several weeks longer.

With the clergy there also assembled a number of prominent soldiers. Although some of them may have been inspired by a genuine concern for the safety of the friars, others were motivated either by a desire for personal revenge against the governor or by fear of his displeasure. Five of them subscribed to the manifesto issued by the clergy on March 16 explaining the reasons for the conference. They were Antonio Baca, Juan de Archuleta, Francisco de Salazar, Juan Luján, and Cristóbal Enríquez. The signatures of Archuleta and Enríquez need no explanation. The motives of Baca, Salazar, and Luján are not clear. But, as will be noted in due course, Salazar and Baca became the effective leaders of the anti-Rosas faction.

In April the friars decided to return to their *doctrinas,* and a formal document recording this decision was drawn up on April 8. It was further decided to make another attempt to bring Rosas to reason by sending a special mission of two friars to Santa Fé. For this delicate task was chosen Friar Bartolomé Romero who had been serving for more than ten years as guardian of Oraibi. Because his mission was so far removed from Santa Fé he had had no contacts with the governor, no reason to inspire his displeasure. Friar Francisco Núñez, an aged lay-brother, was to accompany him.

On April 24 Romero and Núñez set out from Santo Domingo, and early the next morning they arrived at the outskirts of Santa Fé. Tired and weary, they entered the Hermita de San Miguel to rest, while soldiers whom they had met outside the villa went to inform the governor of their arrival. Rosas immediately summoned a squad of soldiers and proceeded to San Miguel where the two friars awaited him outside the building. A shameful scene ensued. Rosas began to berate the friars, and finally became so enraged that he beat them with a stick. He attacked Friar Núñez first, breaking a stick over his head, and then, calling for another, rained blow after blow on Father Romero. Soon the two friars were "bathed in blood." And all the while Rosas continued to revile them, calling them liars, pigs, traitors, heretics, schismatics, etc. He finally placed them under arrest and took them to the Casa Real where they were held under guard.

During the remainder of the day there was much coming and going between the governor's quarters and the room in which the friars were being held. Rosas, Roque de Casaus, and others appeared from time to time and engaged in all manner of arguments, legal and theological, with the prisoners, and Father Romero later asserted that he was certain that Vidania was directing and guiding the proceedings. During the day there were threats and rumors of dire punishment—whipping, the garrote, etc.—for the friars. But at the end of the day a formal decree was issued expelling them from the villa. Friar Núñez had been so weakened by the ordeal that he had to be carried part of the way, but about midnight the friars found refuge in a ranch house. The next day Vidania said mass for the governor and his associates and gave them absolution for their deeds.

These events made impossible any reconciliation between the two jurisdictions, and for another twelve months the breach remained unhealed. There is a remarkable lack of documentary material for this period, despite the fact that numerous reports were made by both factions. Moreover, the Rosas residencia of 1641 and the records of the formal charges that were preferred against Vidania in the same year have not been found. The most important available source is a series of letters, opinions, etc., of Father Vidania, but these contain little factual information.

The clergy sent two sets of dispatches, one by Juan de la Serna, the ex-regidor, and one by Friar Diego Franco. And during the long interval while they awaited a reply to their appeals, they maintained as much unity and strength as possible. Many returned to their missions, at least for shorter or longer periods, probably spending a few days or weeks in Santo Domingo from time to time. But the three Tewa pueblos of San Ildefonso, Santa Clara, and Nambé were without friars for a whole year. According to the clerical party, Rosas sent a troop of soldiers to these pueblos to expel the missionaries—Friar Andrés Juárez, Friar Antonio Pérez, and Friar Diego Franco—and to drive off the mission herds. And a presidio was established in San Ildefonso. But Vidania's version of this affair was much different. He stated the clergy had already left the pueblos when the herds were taken, and he defended the establishment of a garrison in San Ildefonso on the ground that the pueblo had been fortified in defiance of the civil government. In any case, the three missions were without clergy until the spring of 1641.

Apparently an increasing number of soldiers abandoned the governor's cause for that of the Church. In addition to the five who subscribed to the manifesto of March 16, we may note the following who apparently took an active part: Diego Pérez Granillo, Juan Ramírez de Salazar, Fernando de Chávez y Durán, and Andrés López de Gracia. And there were many others whose names are not known. Against the soldiers who thus espoused the cause of the Church, Rosas brought formal action, canceled their warrants as officers in the local militia, and declared their encomiendas vacant. In most cases these formal suits were filed, tried, and judgment pronounced in the absence of the accused.

Rosas and Vidania accused the soldiers and clergy of fortifying Santo Domingo and using it as a base whence they raided the countryside, attacked the royal ensign, and interfered with the dispatch of mail to New Spain. Vidania asserted that the *portería* of the convent was made into a guard room, that the friars gave lessons in tactics, the art of fortification, and the machines of war. The soldiers he characterized as "infernal gladiators," and the entire movement was denounced as another Comunero Revolt. Custodian Salas was accused of unfurling the standard of the Faith and proclaiming that the entire province should recognize him as legate of the pope and obey him in place of the governor. But Vidania's excited *pronunciamientos* are so patently prejudiced and so highly colored that it is difficult, if not impossible, to distinguish truth from fiction. It seems fairly clear, however, that the clergy adopted the point of view that the governor forfeited all right to exercise the prerogatives of his office. It was Rosas, they said, who defied law, both human and divine; whereas the friars and their associates were the real defenders of the authority of the Crown. Rosas—another Henry VIII; Vidania—the arch-enemy, leader of the conspiracy, renegade, a sort of local anti-pope!

Rosas' administration of provincial affairs became at once increasingly arbitrary and less effective. One of his first acts subsequent to the Romero incident was to raze the Hermita of San Miguel. Sometime during the year 1640 raids were made on the convents of Sandía and Cuarac, although it is not clear whether they occurred before or after the calling of the Santo Domingo conference. At Cuarac the room that served as headquarters for the business of the Holy Office was desecrated, and this fact doubtless indicates that the raids were directed in part against the memory of Friar Estéban de Perea, who had served as guardian of both Sandía and Cuarac. At Socorro the sacristy was violated, and Capt. Sebastián González put on the habit of a Franciscan and summoned the Indians to kiss his hand.

It is not surprising that the Indians became increasingly restless. The Taos case has already been cited. The guardian of Jémez, Friar Diego de San Lucas, was also killed, although the circumstances are obscure. When informed of these cases, the governor was reported to have remarked: "Would that they might kill all of the friars." He finally made a belated expedition against the Taos, but he took advantage of the occasion to rob the Indians, with the result that many fled from the pueblo.

And during this same tragic year a pest spread among the Indians, taking a toll of three thousand persons, or more than ten per cent of the total Pueblo population. The Apaches also seized the opportunity offered by the bitter factional rivalries to raid the Pueblo area, burning and pillaging. The amount of maize that was burned was estimated at twenty thousand fanegas. It is not surprising, therefore, that the Pueblos began to return to the old ways, to the native religion and ceremonial, for solace and hope.

During the long months of violence, anxiety, and impatient waiting for news from Mexico, Vidania attempted to maintain the confidence of the citizens, and at the same assure the governor—and himself!—that the cause was just. In a long series of sermons, pronouncements, legal formulae, and letters he discussed and reviewed the situation *ad nauseam*. Some of these papers have been preserved. They are a hodge-podge of citations from Scripture, the Fathers, papal decrees, and the canons, interspersed with outbursts of denunciatory rhetoric.

Vidania defended Rosas' authority to intervene in ecclesiastical affairs. Was he not the representative of the Crown, who in turn was legate of the pope by virtue of the Bulls of Donation and Patronage? The Crown and Council possessed wide authority over the Church, and he, as governor, made one body with them. He had every right to investigate the conduct of clergy and report to the viceroy such actions as infringed on secular authority. But even if some of Rosas' acts were not strictly legal, necessity made the illicit licit.

And by what right did the Custodian and his followers deny Rosas' authority as governor? Had not the popes and learned doctors denounced the error of rebellion against constituted authority? The friars and their faction had disobeyed the governor's order to disband and had thereby declared their loyalty. Treason had been encouraged by the slogan, "Death to the governor!" It was the governor's duty to strike down sedition wherever he found it.

In equally strong terms he denied the prelate's legal authority and justified his own conduct in disobeying the prelate's decrees. Right or wrong, he had remained loyal to the king's representative. More—he had given the citizens the solace of the sacraments, even under the most trying conditions; he had performed the office for which he received alms from the royal treasury. Had the custodian done the same?

At long last the anxious days came to an end. In the spring of 1641 Father Salas was succeeded as prelate by Friar Hernando Covarrubias who had been sent from New Spain with wide powers to govern the local Church. The authority of the Inquisition, which had been in abeyance since the death of Perea, was restored by the appointment of Salas as commissary. And on April 13 a new governor, Juan Flores de Sierra y Valdez, relieved Rosas of office. The day of reckoning was at hand.

SUGGESTED READINGS

France V. Scholes, "Church and State in New Mexico, 1610–1650," *New Mexico Historical Review*, vol. XI (January, April, July, and October 1936), vol. XII (January 1937);

Scholes, "Troublous Times in New Mexico, 1659–1670," *New Mexico Historical Review*, vol. XII (April and October 1937), vol. XIII (January 1938), vol. XV (July and October 1940), vol. XVI (January, April, and July 1941);

Scholes, "Civil Government and Society in New Mexico in the Seventeenth Century," *New Mexico Historical Review*, vol. X (April 1935);

Scholes, "The First Decade of the Inquisition in New Mexico," *New Mexico Historical Review*, vol. X (July 1935);

Scholes, "Problems in the Early Ecclesiastical History of New Mexico," *New Mexico Historical Review*, vol. XI (January 1932);

Richard E. Greenleaf, *The Mexican Inquisition of the Sixteenth Century* (Albuquerque 1969).

4
The Pueblo Revolt

In 1680 Spain had occupied New Mexico for more than eighty years, but her hold on the area was tenuous. In August 1680 the Pueblo Indians revolted; they killed an estimated four hundred Spaniards, drove the remainder from the province, and held it for thirteen years. News of the successful revolt sent shock waves throughout the empire and influenced defensive policies on the northern frontier of New Spain. In the same period other tribes in New Spain also took up arms against their conquerers in a general though uncoordinated uprising, which Professor Jack Forbes has described as the Great Southwestern Revolt.

The New Mexico Indians had many causes for discontent, and, while there had been minor outbreaks before, Pueblo unity had been lacking. By 1680, however, the situation had changed. The Pueblos had been exploited by Church, State, and settlers, and the Church-State struggle described by Professor Scholes was a disruptive force that eroded respect for Spanish authority. A severe drought between 1667 and 1672 added to the suffering of the Pueblos while Apache raids, caused largely by Spanish raids for slaves, increased in intensity and forced the Indians to abandon several pueblos east of the Manzano Mountains. Most important, however, the missionaries were determined to stamp out the Indian religion. Native ceremonies were prohibited; kivas were raided, and ceremonial paraphernalia destroyed; and Indian leaders were whipped and imprisoned. Among those punished by the Spanish was a San Juan Indian named Popé.

In the selections that follow, Jack Forbes describes the revolt and its results, and Fray Angelico Chavez offers a provocative interpretation of the leadership of the revolt. Most historians credit Popé with the organizational skill and leadership which brought the separate pueblos together, but Chavez suggests that Popé's role was limited and

---

that the real leader of the revolt was a Negro or mulatto of the Naranjo family of the Santa Cruz-Santa Clara Valley.

I

The year 1680 was a momentous one in the history of the American Southwest. It was the high point in the Pueblo Indians' long struggle for religious and political freedom. It represented a tremendous setback for the Spanish Empire in the area of northern New Spain. It was to mark the beginning of an era worthy of this title: the period of the Great Southwestern Revolt.

For decades the Pueblo Indians had been preserving their ancient religion and beliefs in spite of harsh persecution by fanatically intolerant Spaniards. Secretly, they had passed on ancient lore from generation to generation, and during periods of temporary freedom they practiced their ceremonies in public. Gradually they had learned the method of conforming outwardly to the Roman Catholic religion while keeping faith inwardly with their old beliefs. Apparently, few Spaniards could see that conversion by naked force was a failure in New Mexico until it was too late. In 1681 one European stated rather bitterly that "most of them have never forsaken idolatry, and they appear to be Christians more by force than to be Indians who are reduced to the Holy Faith." If dedicated Christians had come peacefully among the Indians of New Mexico, teaching the doctrine by means of love and high-minded examples, then many Indians might conceivably have been converted in a manner worthy of the founder of the Europeans' faith. This, unfortunately, was not the method of conversion used by the Spaniards, and it is not surprising that both the Pueblo tribes and the Athapascans continually rejected the hypocritical beliefs of their cruel taskmasters.

The revolt which began in the summer of 1680 was both a political and religious phenomenon. Certainly the pueblos desired to be free of Spanish control and to have the ability to restore the old peaceful relationship with neighboring Apaches. Apaches who took part in the first stages of the revolt were likewise motivated by a political desire: the wish to see their Taos, Picuris, and Pecos friends free once again and to eliminate Spanish invasions of their own lands. On the other hand, the Pueblo Indians would possibly never have undertaken such an enterprise without a deeper motive, that is, the desire to restore a spiritual climate which meant the preservation of the people and to destroy the religion of the Europeans which was destroying the tribe and absorbing it into the Hispano-Catholic community. All testimonies agree that the primary motive for rebellion was a desire for religious freedom.

The first stage of the Great Southwestern Revolt was planned very well.

All of the Pueblo tribes except the unnotified Piros were involved, along with at least one Athapascan group. Plans had been in the making for years, and final decisions of the leaders were circulated by means of knotted cords, each knot representing a day of life left for the invaders. On August 9, the Spaniards first learned that trouble was at hand, thanks to some Tano Indians who turned two Tewa messengers over to the Europeans. From these prisoners they discovered that revolt was planned for several days later and that all of the Pueblo tribes and the Apaches were confederated for the undertaking.

Before the governor, Antonio de Otermín, could organize his followers, the natives began to rebel in various pueblos simultaneously, killing all the Franciscans and soldiers that they could and sending squads of warriors onto the highways to halt communications. Taos and Picuris, accompanied by Apaches del Acho, liberated the northernmost regions and killed all of the Spaniards except one soldier, who was just returning from a trip to the Utes. By August 13, it was clear that all of the tribes had joined the movement, and Otermín had to content himself with making preparations to defend Santa Fe. This defense soon developed into quite a problem, for squads of Tanos, Pecos, and Keres warriors began to appear on the outskirts of the *villa*, and they were soon reinforced by Tewas, Taos, Picuris, Jemez, Apaches, and others. On August 15, Otermín arranged to speak with a Tano chief who had previously been friendly and who, with other warriors, had entered the Mexican (that is, the Nahuan) section of the town. The chief informed Otermín that the Indians carried two crosses or banners—one being red and the other white. Red symbolized the war which the Spaniards could choose, and white represented the peace which would prevail if the invaders agreed to abandon New Mexico. In connection with the latter choice, the Indians asked that

> all classes of Indians who were in our power [the Spaniards] be given up to them, both those in the service of the Spaniards and those of the Mexican nation of that suburb of Analco. He demanded also that his wife and children be given up to him, and likewise that all the Apache men and women whom the Spaniards had captured in war be turned over to them, inasmuch as some Apaches who were among them were asking for them.

This request symbolizes the growth of a "Pan-Indian" spirit and also shows that the Europeans were making great use of slaves as late as 1680. As many as 700 Indian servants and captives must have been at Santa Fe when the siege began, but the Spaniards showed no inclination toward leaving New Mexico peacefully or giving up their human property.

Having chosen war, the Spaniards sought to dislodge the Indians from Analco, and many days of bitter fighting followed. Finally, on August 20, the Europeans succeeded in driving the Indians from the *villa*, killing 300 of the enemy, and executing 47 prisoners taken in the battle. Among the native dead were Pueblo Indians of all tribes and also Apaches—these

Apaches contradicting Otermín's earlier belief that there were no Apaches among the attackers. Many Spanish-speaking servants had apostatized and gone over to the rebels, indicating perhaps a success for the Pan-Indian appeal.

The number of Athapascans who took part in the siege has not been established; but on August 17 the rebels had reportedly summoned Apaches, and some Apaches del Acho had probably accompanied the Taos and Picuris to the attack.

On August 21, 1680 Governor Otermín and his followers determined upon retreating downstream and abandoning Santa Fe. This refugee group included approximately 100 fighting men and 1,000 persons in all—the same number which had resided in the *villa* in the 1620's. Their departure led to a sacking of Santa Fe by the victorious Indians, although the *villa* was not destroyed—nor was the governor's palace, which is still standing. The retreating Spaniards found the Tiwa pueblos abandoned and the natives in revolt. They also learned that the Spanish-speaking population of the lower Río Grande area had united at Isleta but had since left for El Paso upon seeing that the Tiwas of Isleta wished to revolt. Subsequently, the Spaniards of Isleta declared that the rebels in that area had many guns taken from 120 dead men, along with large numbers of cattle, horses, and other supplies. These provisions could support the Apaches for four months in a siege, said the commander of the Isleta Spaniards, Alonso García. However, one wonders where 120 armed men had come from.

García led his followers to the Piro region, where the Indians of Sevilleta abandoned their pueblo and went with the Spaniards to Socorro. Socorro proved unsafe, however, as Apaches were in sight and the Piros were restless, having received an emissary from the rebels. García then moved to the place called Fray Cristóbal and waited for news from El Paso. There he learned that Otermín was also retreating downriver, and later the two Spanish-led groups united still farther downstream. Fortunately for the fleeing invaders, Fray Francisco de Ayeta was at El Paso with succor from New Spain, and the refugees were thus able to remain in the El Paso region. However, many of them wished to flee to Parral and other areas, and they had to be kept near El Paso by force. The refugees were reportedly harassed by the Apaches, and this irritation probably added to their desires to bid farewell to New Mexico.

Governor Otermín held muster at a place called La Salineta, a few leagues from El Paso, and reportedly there were almost 2,000 persons, of which 317 were Indians of Isleta, Sevilleta, Alamillo, Socorro, and Senecú pueblos, apparently brought against their will from their homelands. The other 1,700 persons included only 155 fighting men, from which fact one may conclude that the balance—or 1,500 persons—were women, children, and Indian servants and captives. Reportedly, 21 priests and 380 other persons had died in the revolt, but the latter figure must have been only an estimate based upon who was missing, and as it turned out many Spanish-speaking mestizos and servants had gone over to the rebels.

II

The point of highest drama in New Mexico's long history is the Indian Pueblo Revolt of 1680, when the pueblos managed to unite briefly for one concerted effort which put an end to the Spanish colony and the Franciscan missions for a time. Twenty-one friars and several Spanish families were massacred in one day, August 10, and the Spaniards were soon forced to retreat to the distant and southernmost mission center of Guadalupe del Paso, now Ciudad Juárez in Mexico. The causes for the rebellion were several, but ancient pueblo belief was the one adduced by the main leaders as the rallying cry. It was the "ancient ones" of the pueblos versus the God and the saints of the Spaniards. For eighty years the Franciscans had clamored for the complete elimination of the estufas (now called kivas), which in their estimation were hotbeds of idolatry; also, that of the masked dances and related native practices which they considered not only idolatrous, but grossly immoral from the Christian point of view. These they lumped together under the term *cachinas.* Simply to provoke the missionaries, or else bribed by the Indian ritual leaders, certain Spaniards in the succession of governors and their henchmen refused to cooperate, so that the abolition of kivas and cachinas was occasional and sporadic; those eliminated were promptly restored in most pueblos.

Such internal Church-State dissensions, to be sure, did nothing to improve the Indian ritual leaders' regard for the Spaniards. Moreover, and this is something never considered before by historians, some of the principal and most intelligent ones among the leaders were not pure-bred Pueblo Indians. Some were the offspring of an unscrupulous Spanish colonist and a pueblo woman; others were descended from Negroid-Amerindian servants, brought from New Spain by the first colonists, who married into the pueblos; and so during those first eighty years certain mestizos gravitated into pueblo life. A complicated inner resentment against the prevailing caste system had made them identify themselves further with the Pueblo Indian and his beliefs, while their native and acquired capabilities were superior to those of the inbred pueblos who knew little outside their individual restricted cosmos. Otherwise, the ordinary run of Pueblo Indians had been happy with the many material benefits brought them by the padres. Their limited grasp of Spanish Cath-

---

olic doctrine and external worship dovetailed nicely with a native mythology which was their very life. They appreciated the protection which Spanish arms afforded against their perennial enemies, the Apache and other marauding tribes. In a way, for these common people, who in their simplicity had quietly combined interior ancestral belief with the external Catholic forms of worship, any demands made by the friars were less onerous than those made by their own ritual leaders, from whose complete influence they were being wooed. Native pueblo ritual and government required total surrender of the person.

It was the ritual leaders in each pueblo, the "representatives" of superior beings in a native mythology, which we will have to consider briefly, who resented European domination, no matter what the material benefits. The most resentful, and also potentially dangerous, were those hybrid leaders just mentioned. Nor can we eliminate a certain amount of laudable nativistic feeling on the part of the people in general, although it was far from the modern notion of "patriotism" anachronistically attributed to them by current American writers. Power and revenge, in the guise of native belief, were the prime motive. We might compare the situation with that of the fifteenth-century monarchy of Spain, with its closely interlaced feudal nobility and church hierarchy, which set up the Inquisition under the banner of the Faith to consolidate and preserve its position against the divisive forces that it saw in the Moors, the Jews, and the Protestant Reformation. Except that these poor Indian leaders in the past had been altogether incapable of conjuring up any such Inquisition, or even a swift and definite revolution. The pueblo people in general, besides being satisfied with things as they were, were slow to respond to a war cry. Their agelong sedentary life of primitive agriculture and continuous ceremonial had made them a "peaceful people," seldom able to defend themselves against the warlike Apache hunters who from time immemorial had invaded the pueblos at harvest time. To stand up to Spanish firearms and European martial skills was suicidal, as some few found out on different occasions during that eighty-year period. Moreover, different pueblo groups were divided from each other by language and ancient animosities. And there was that internal struggle of long standing among the ritual leaders themselves in each pueblo, a fact noted by modern anthropologists as well as the pioneer missionaries.

But the fact is that the many pueblos did manage to unite most effectively in that year of 1680, to the great surprise of the Spaniards, and to the wonder of serious historians ever since. In all subsequent histories the tactical genius has been thought to be El Popé of San Juan, from many scattered testimonies recorded in the Otermín journals of 1681. Yet, from the very start, Governor Otermín and his captains sensed that El Popé could not have done it all alone, and therefore tried to discover the chief culprit, or culprits, by interrogating their first prisoners. On August 9,

1680, two young men from Tesuque were caught bearing a message of rebellion and a hide thong with two knots signifying the number of days left. All that the frightened youths could reveal under pressure was a "common report among all the Indians that there had come to them from very far away toward the *north* a *letter* from an *Indian lieutenant* [*teniente*] *of Po he yemu* to the effect that all of them in general should rebel, and that any pueblo that would not agree to it they would destroy, killing all the people. It was reported that this *Indian lieutenant of Po he yemu was very tall, black, and had very large yellow eyes*, and that everyone feared him greatly." The Spanish officials simply took this for a fable, concluding that the Indian leaders had deluded these youths and the people in general with this reference to one of their heathen "gods" or "spirits." It is evident that the young pair had divulged all they knew, and that Otermín and his men failed to detect a real human instigator behind their statement. For it certainly looked like the description of some grotesquely masked mythological creature which the Spaniards regarded as the "devil."

Again, a similar interrogation took place on August 20, after the Governor's forces broke a painful siege of Santa Fe by putting more than fifteen hundred warriors to rout, killing three hundred, and taking forty-seven prisoners. On being questioned, these unfortunate captives confessed that they "had a mandate of an *Indian* who lives a very long way from this kingdom, toward the *north*, from which region *Montezuma came*, and who is the *lieutenant of Po he yemu;* and that this *person* ordered all the Indians to take part in the treason and rebellion. . . . *For fear* of this they all joined together, killing the priests and the Spaniards. . . ." Once again it is evident that this was all the poor prisoners knew, else at least one of the forty-seven would have revealed the identity of that "person." And again Otermín took this as an affront to his intelligence; in his anger he had them all shot for mocking him with a mere Indian fable. To him and his men the person of the *teniente* and *Pohé-yemo* himself were one and the same pagan demon. But we shall soon see that he was a very human person—I shall translate *teniente* as "representative" from now on. It expresses more fully the double function of someone "taking the place of" and "assuming the person" of Pohé-yemo. The French-derived "lieutenant" has too many European military and political connotations.

What first led me to suspect a real human person in the Representative of Pohé-yemo, a man who was unusually tall and black in comparison with the average small and not too tawny Pueblo Indian, and one with big yellow eyes, which promptly suggests a mulatto, was the records of a controversy in Santa Fe in 1766. It involves five generations of the Naranjo family of the Santa Cruz-Santa Clara valley whose antecedents were Negroid and who, most significantly, were accused of having fomented Indian insurrections in the past. Then, there is an amply documented legend, originating with the ordinary Spanish colonists of those Revolt times, which told of the Devil appearing as a black giant during the 1680 siege of Santa Fe. All this provided me with enough incentive and material for a thorough investigation of the problem, concerned mainly with a big Negro or black-complexioned mulatto named Naranjo, who at some period before the Revolt of 1680 insinuated himself among the ritual leaders of the pueblos, several of them hybrid individuals like himself. Either to enjoy personal power, or to avenge himself on the Europeans who for so long, and sometimes most cruelly, had lorded it over the primitive colored races, or for both reasons, he most cleverly employed the myth of Pohé-yemo to unite the ever-dissident Pueblo Indians for a successful blow. It is not the first time that an African spoiled the best-laid plans of the Spaniard in American colonial times, but it was the most dramatic. More active and restless by nature than the more passive and stolid Indian, he was more apt to muddle up some serious Hispanic enterprise.

In order to grasp the truth and flavor of the whole episode, we need to have some knowledge and sympathetic understanding of Pueblo Indian mythology and its workings on Indian behavior—in this case particularly concerning a mythical being called Pohé-yemo. This is something the captains and friars neglected to procure, to their sorrow. As they kept repeating in their official acts and letters, it was Satan himself and none other who had inspired the "apostasy and rebellion" against the twin Majesties of God and Catholic King.

The daily life of the Pueblo Indians was closely and intricately bound with year-round rites and ceremonials intended to tap, as it were, the mysterious Power permeating their little world of earth and sky. The Power was impersonal, nothing more than the invisible energy that made nature tick. Each pueblo's cosmos was limited to the visible horizon around it. Upon the earth the Power made trees and plants grow, and the wild animals to reproduce themselves; and from the sky above the Power supplied sunlight and rain, all to insure a food supply for the people in their planting and hunting. Also, through herbs and animals the Power furnished means for curing the people when sick. Naturally, the Power also made human babies grow from their parents to insure the continuity of the community. And, as with other primitives, there was a division of the Power's activities into male and female: sky phenomena were masculine as compared with the passive feminine reproduction in the earth. Hence fertility rites acquired certain open sexual manifestations, pointed out by ethnologists, and by some of the old padres who naturally labeled them obscene.

Because the Power was so erratic in its activities, mainly as regards rainfall and fertility in an arid land, what was needed to insure good crops, good hunting, a healthy people and healthy newborn, was the right effective knowledge, or "know-how," that could make the Power work in their behalf. All that one needed was "to know." This "know-how" rested in their ritual leaders, the Representative Chieftains and Medicinemen, to whom it had been passed down through countless generations from the "ancient ones" since the Pueblo People came out of the earth. The ritual leaders, according to each one's office, prepared themselves by purificatory bathing, fasting, and considerable vomiting, in order to better "represent" the "ancient ones" in putting the "know-how" to work. The better the preparation, the closer a leader came to "becoming" an "ancient one" for that particular function. And the greater the results.

Now, the pueblos had no Creation Myth. Their ancestors came out of a Hole, or vertical Cave, in the already existing earth. It lay somewhere beyond the northern horizon of each pueblo's little world. These first people were as ignorant and helpless as babies emerging from the womb. But just as helpless infants have parents and adult clan relatives to assist them through childhood, so the first people encountered other people, and also animals, who were ready to help and teach them. These were the "ancient ones." These primordial counterparts of the ordinary human and animal world were real corporeal beings. They differed from ordinary folk and animals in this one important respect—they had a perfect "know-how" for using the Power. Through this perfect knowledge they made themselves immortal, and they could perform all sorts of marvelous feats, like making themselves invisible and changing from one place to another in the twinkling of an eye. This instant travel was sometimes done with the aid of primordial birds and animals having the same "know-how." Each one of them specialized in the phenomena of one distinct phase of nature.

These benign "ancient ones" stayed with those first people and taught them how to plant and hunt and fend for themselves. Those who were animals taught them the art of curing with herbs and chants. But there were skeptics even in those days, folks who said the "ancient ones" were nothing but ordinary people disguised in masks and paint and feathers. This unbelief hurt those benefactors, so they decided to go away from the ordinary people forever. But, before departing, they taught the true believers how to use their masks and perform dances with them, and how to employ other paraphernalia such as feather bunches, feathered sticks, and tiny stone fetishes, and how to sing the right songs, to make sure that the people would always have a means of tapping the Power for corn and meat and health, even if in a much more limited degree.

Chief among these kindly beings were the Earth-Mother (*Yaya*) who dwelt by the Hole of Emergence (*Shipapu*), and the Twin-Warriors and Hunters (*Másewi* and *Oyóyewi*), who stayed with her but frequently roamed all over. Most popular were the *Shiwanna* or Rain-Makers who dwelt beyond the western horizon, or some other direction, depending on a particular pueblo's location with regard to prevailing rain clouds. Among these many single individuals controlling some phase of nature was *Pohé-yemo,* who made the sun shine upon the people when they first came out upon the dark and dreary earth's surface. He and the other beings varied in name, concept, and particular functions among the different pueblos, and even in those of the same linguistic group.

Pohé-yemo is called *Pose-yemo* among the Tewa (Santa Clara where Naranjo lived). It means "he who strews morning dew." Another name is *Pose-ueve* (dew from sky), but he is also referred to as *Pose-yemo T'ansendo* (our sun father *Pose-yemo*). The Keres of Santo Domingo know these Tewa terms but also have their own: *Payatyamo* (youth) who is the being in charge of the sun. In Cochiti *Payatyama* (sun-father) is used in contradistinction to *Sanatyaya* (moon-mother), but in action he is identified with *Oshatsh,* the sun. Both in Santo Domingo and San Felipe, *Payatyamo* appears among the fetishes used in preparing for the cachina dances. There are two masks among those of the minor side-dancers which are called *Payatyamo,* resembling the mask of the sun, *Oshatsh.* Dances originally performed for *Payatyamo* now are directed to the Rain-Makers, both at Santo Domingo and Cochiti. From this and other instances, it is clear that the person of the sun-youth was considerably less "performed" than those of the bringers of rain, and this is very natural. In the arid Southwest the sun shines perennially, and therefore needs much less invoking than those beings who control the much needed rain clouds, or those who cause the corn to grow and the wild game to multiply abundantly. Santo Domingo also uses the term *Poshaiyanyi* (our father from east coming with sun), but this is plainly a derivation from the Zuñi *Poshaiyankia.* He is the being who taught the Zuñi, the Taos, and other peoples, the arts of planting and ceremonial curing. Among the Jemez, *Pestya-sode* figures in a legend similar to one among the Zuñi, the prefix *pe* meaning "sun" in their language. But they also use *Peyatyambo* (their version of Keres "youth") for the ritual leader of the Pecos sun clan. The mask of *Pehehmiyoe* (sun on head) has features of the Keres sun-mask, *Oshatsh.*

In short, the original concept of this youth and father having the "know-how" of the sun has not only gotten mixed up in linguistic form but also in the "know-how" pertaining to other mythical persons. He also figures in later tales of the Zuñi, Jemez, Tewa, and Keres, as relayed by investigators like Bandelier and Cushing, but these are more properly current folktales than old ancestral mythology. What we have been arriving at is the fact that, in that fateful year of 1680, all the pueblos knew of Pohé-yemo under one linguistic form or another, when word came from a kiva in Taos that a Chieftain or Medicineman therein had a most extraordinary "know-how" of Pohé-yemo and was *representing* him. In performing the preparatory rites he must have fasted and vomited so effectively that he now represented Pohé-yemo to perfection—he *was* Pohé-yemo at this time. El Popé and the few select leaders let the people know that he was a black giant with big yellow eyes for greater effect. This created more than the usual fear and awe. His human identity was of no consequence, for at the time he fully represented Pohé-yemo.

Why Naranjo chose to represent Pohé-yemo instead of the mighty Twin-Warriors, *Másewi* and *Oyóyewi*, we do not know. But we can guess. It could be the connotation of "sun" with "fire." For Naranjo himself knew of the Aztec god of Fire and War, as we shall see later on. Reared among the Spaniards and cognizant of the real Indian idolatry of New Spain, he imbued his self-assumed mysterious personality with a cruel inner strength unknown to the placid and less sophisticated pueblos. He could communicate with some of the principal leaders in their own tongue, but also in Spanish with those outstanding ones who were mestizos and *coyotes;* and to some of these he could send written letters. His grasp of Spanish psychology showed him how to catch the enemy off guard, and how to hide his identity from them in case the plot should fail, as it almost did. Because the captains as well as the padres looked upon the "ancient ones" of the pueblos as the evil spirits given in the Bible, Pohé-yemo would be regarded as the Devil himself. And so he was.

The blow fell on August 10, 1680, and the success was almost perfect, marred only by the bloody resistance of the Spaniards in Santa Fe. Governor Otermín and his people held on to the villa for a spell, but considered it wise to abandon it and the whole kingdom for the time being. In his questioning of Indian captives, for future reprisals, Otermín got nothing from them, even when they unwittingly described Naranjo physically. For he had made his personal identity known only to a few main leaders, perhaps instructing them not to reveal it to the pueblo people in general. But as soon as the Spaniards left, the pueblos fell away from each other, forgetting all about Pohé-yemo's Representative. For the deed was done. And no ritual leader, after all, could "represent" an "ancient one" indefinitely. At the same time the other ritual leaders of separate pueblos assumed their own little stances of importance, especially El Popé, who went about boasting that he alone had at last defeated the invincible Spaniard and restored the influence of the "ancient ones." Many among the common people did not like this new surge of tyranny, which now had more of a sharp European flavor than the halcyon former rule of the "ancient ones." If Naranjo himself had harbored any ambition of making himself the supreme lord of all the pueblos, it was a rude awakening.

Otermín's return with his forces in the following year was largely one of reconnaissance. Individual Indians of every type were captured from among the southern Rio Grande pueblos, then questioned minutely as to the leaders and causes of the Revolt. The governor's findings were mostly a confirmation of what he had heard the previous year, and these were written down by his clerks in Spanish Christian terms and concepts. One old Indian of Alameda said that Indian resentment had built up from the very beginning of the colony and missions, because the friars and Spaniards took away their *idols* and forbade *sorceries and idolatries.* Another accused El Popé of San Juan, whom all feared because he *talked with the devil;* he killed his own son-in-law, who was the (Spanish-imposed) governor of San Juan, because he was too friendly with the Spaniards and might reveal the plot to them. He went about with El Saca of Taos boasting that he alone had carried out the uprising, and proclaiming that the *devil was very strong and much better than God.* Another told a captain that El Popé had made all the Indians crazy and was like the whirlwind. He had given them to understand that the *father of all the Indians, their great chieftain, who had been such since the Deluge,* had ordered El Popé to make all the pueblos rebel, or else be laid waste. Still others declared that the rebellion had been motivated by the Taos and El Popé, whom all regarded as a *great sorcerer,* and who presented himself as a great chieftain. He went about destroying Christian vestiges and enforcing the ancient customs. Friars and captains wrote that it all was the result of *diabolical* cunning and conspiracy, discord which *the devil had sown,* apostasy caused by *blind fiends of the devil.* After eighty years of baptism, the *most intelligent and favored among them,* with complete secrecy, acted as the moving spirits and guides. They pointed out some of these intelligent leaders: besides El Popé there were Alonso Catiti, *coyote* of Santo Domingo, Luis and Lorenzo Tupatu of Picuris, Nicholás Jonva, and Francisco El Ollita, *coyote* of San Ildefonso. But nobody mentioned a certain Naranjo, the *negro* or *mulato* of Santa Clara operating from a kiva in Taos. His identity had been kept too well hidden except for that dangerously close description of the previous year: a black giant with big yellow eyes. However, certain Naranjo individuals did enter the picture at this time, and these will now be treated more at length as we work out the Naranjo family relationship.

SUGGESTED READINGS

Charles W. Hackett, *Revolt of the Pueblo Indians of New Mexico and Otermin's Attempted Reconquest, 1680–1682* (Albuquerque 1942);

Anne E. Hughes, *The Beginnings of Spanish Settlement in the El Paso District* (Berkeley 1914);

Hackett, "Retreat of the Spaniards from New Mexico in 1680," *Southwestern Historical Quarterly,* vol. XVI (October and December 1912);

France V. Scholes, "Troublous Times in New Mexico, 1659–1670," *New Mexico Historical Review,* vol. XII (April and October 1937), vol. XIII (January 1938), vol. XV (July and October 1940), vol. XVI (January, April and July 1941).

5
Vargas and the Reconquest

The successful expulsion of the Spanish from their country by the Pueblo Indians was a severe setback to the Spanish Empire, but although the Reconquest was not accomplished until 1693, some efforts were quickly made for the restoration of Spanish control. In 1681 Antonio de Otermín returned briefly to the Pueblo country, and seven years later Domingo Jironza Petriz de Cruzate made a similar expedition and sacked the Pueblo of Zia, killing a large number of Indians in the process.

In 1692 the new governor, Don Diego de Vargas, visited the Pueblos with a small command. Vargas proved to be an able diplomat, skillfully exploiting the factionalism that had developed among the Indians and securing their approval for the return of the Spanish. In the following year, therefore, Vargas returned to New Mexico with some eight hundred colonists and settled at Santa Fe which was still occupied by the Indians. Friction was inevitable because of the hard winter and the lack of food, and the Spanish resented the continued presence of the Indians in the old provincial capital. Soon a crisis developed, and in the battle which followed the Spanish drove the Indians from the town, killing some and executing and enslaving others. Despite the victory, hostilities with the Pueblos continued sporadically for several years. Vargas, however, effectively reestablished Spanish control of New Mexico.

While Vargas calmly made plans for the refounding of the missions and for the distribution of the missionaries at Santa Fé and eleven other pueblos, whispers were abroad in the Spanish camp. Rumor had it that the Tewas and Tanos had merely feigned obedience in order to cloak their treachery. Had not the governor of Pecos, Juan de Ye, come to Vargas' tent with reports of secret meetings on the mesa of San Juan between Tewas, Tanos, Picuríes and many Apaches? Juan de Ye had learned of battle plans of these allies from a relative, who in turn had heard it from a Zuñi Indian. The warriors were equipped for war in Spanish fashion, even to leather jackets, leather horse armor and shields. And this Antonio Bolsas, he had heard, was the guiding genius, goading on the people. In Apache style, they were to steal horses, until the Spaniards were forced to foot; then the moment for swooping down upon them would be propitious.

Juan de Ye was very serious about his story. He volunteered to get reinforcements from his pueblo. There was ample evidence to warrant trust in his assertions. None of the natives of Santa Fé bothered to hear Mass or pray at the camp of the Spaniards, the few vegetables they traded were very dear, and they showed other signs of bad faith. When several soldiers were sent into the walled villa for food, everyone stayed out of sight. All that could be obtained was eight sacks of maize brought from Tesuque and Nambé—sufficient to feed only a few of the soldiers.

Due to these circumstances, the custodian presented Vargas with a petition in which he pleaded against the distribution of the missionaries at this time. He regarded such an act as dangerous and injudicious, and urged that the warnings of the ever faithful Juan de Ye of Pecos be heeded. Was it not he, he argued, who in 1680 warned the Spaniards of the impending revolt twenty days before the outbreak by notifying Sergeant Major Francisco Gómez, repeating his warning twelve days later? And after he had seen that no one believed his story, had he not pleaded with his minister, Fray Fernando de Velasco Pacheco, repeating his knowledge of the plot and offering reinforcements? Vargas acknowledged the truth of the custodian's arguments, but failed to take immediate action. Meanwhile, the Spanish women and children were undergoing severe hardships due to the rigors of winter, inadequate shelter, and lack of food. The custodian's complaint was followed by another by the *cabildo*, requesting possession of the *casas reales*, or former government buildings, theirs, they argued, by natural right and legitimate and ancient possession. The Spaniards had come to repopulate Santa Fé, they said, and to place the royal banner upon its walls.

Meanwhile, Vargas went with some of the military leaders to examine the ruined church or hermitage of San Miguel, which had formerly served as the parish church of the Mexican Indians of Santa Fé. It was decided to have the natives throw down the walls, repair the light shaft, and reconstruct the chapel under the direction of Governor José and Antonio Bolsas, in order to provide a decent home for "Our Lady of the Conquest . . . who was enclosed in a wagon; and that if our Lady came they were obliged to provide a house for her." In the cathedral at Santa Fé, on a side altar, there is today a beautiful Virgen del Rosario, a statue about three feet tall, that is the special object of veneration. It is called *La Conquistadora*, Our Lady of the Conquest, and according to legend still current it is the same one that was brought to Santa Fé by the reconqueror Vargas; apparently the one referred to in the above passage. Earlier events already had given this particular statue special importance. It had been saved from the fury of the natives and carried to El Paso in 1680.

Next day, December 19, Miguel Luján returned from San Juan, San Lázaro, San Cristóbal, Nambé, and San Ildefonso, with five loads of flour. He had been given a happy welcome everywhere. Also, Governor Francisco of San Ildefonso arrived at camp to render obedience, and he promised additional grain supplies in return for some hoes, which he was granted. The day following Governor Francisco Pacheco of Taos and Don Luis also came to assure fealty. Luis asked that Father Muñoz de Castro be designated as the pastor at San Juan. Pacheco said that the only reason why his people had not begun to construct a church and convent for the two missionaries destined for their pueblo was that all the roads to Taos were snowbound, which condition rendered difficult the bringing in of the necessary timber; but in return for a roll of cloth he offered to send maize. Luis and Francisco both left very happy.

Meanwhile, Governor José and Antonio Bolsas obstinately informed Vargas that they considered it better to open an *estufa*, or kiva, in the first square of the villa for a chapel, instead of the specified chapel of San Miguel. It was difficult to obtain timber from the mountains on account of the heavy snow, they said, and it was preferable to hear Mass within the walls of the city anyhow. Vargas went to inspect the *estufa*. It was round, low roofed, and entered by an opening in the roof by means of a wooden ladder, just like any pueblo kiva of the present day. He ordered the natives to tear open a door, whitewash the whole interior, make an altar out of adobes, and set aside two rooms of an adjoining house as the living quarters for the missionary. One door should face the altar, and another the adjoining living quarters. But after the structure was completed, the custodian objected to it as a suitable place of worship because it had once been used by the Indians for idolatrous and prohibited religious rites, and this despite Vargas' argument that there were a number of churches and cathedrals in Spain which were formerly Moorish mosques.

During this time all the attempts to obtain grain were disappointing. Five more loads of flour, and three of maize, were brought in from San Ildefonso, San Lázaro, San Cristóbal, and other Tano and Tewa pueblos, and ten loads of flour and maize from Pecos. The rigorous weather continued, with tempestuous snow storms and cold winds. Sickness was rife. Children and infants were dying. Many had already succumbed to the elements. There were repeated complaints. Vargas employed all his talents in his efforts to obtain food. A fortunate incident gave Don Diego an opportunity to use his wits. On December 23, Captain Diego Arias arrived with three of the cowardly deserters captured at Ancón de Fray García two weeks before. The sight of the prisoners, for the moment at least, proved a boon and blessing, for their arrival was witnessed by Governor José and Bolsas. The Spanish leader immediately took Machiavellian advantage of the situation by saying that these were the vanguard of an army of two hundred reinforcements coming to his aid. This stratagem was invaluable, for by it the natives of Santa Fé were frightened into supplying twenty sacks of maize on very short notice. As a trick to obtain still more, Vargas said that the reinforcements were bringing a large supply of powder and bullets to use against the Apaches, but that they lacked provisions, and had sent for two hundred sacks of maize. This series of unforeseen circumstances gave the colonists renewed confidence, and fired them into complaining more loudly of their suffering due to exposure, which they believed could and should be remedied. Twenty-two had already died of exposure, and were buried beneath the snow. Their designs, obviously, were upon the dwellings of the natives of Santa Fé.

It was high time for Vargas to call a general council of war. Composed of all of the leading citizens, the missionaries, and the military officers, the gathering was held in his tent, and there petitions and complaints were registered and opinions expressed. On motion of the *cabildo* this gathering took officially the form of a *cabildo abierto*, or open town meeting. Of fourteen of the most conspicuous leaders consulted, there was unanimity in agreement with the petition of the *cabildo*: namely, that the Tanos be obliged to return to their former pueblo of Galisteo, and the buildings of the city be reoccupied by the Spaniards. Six of these favored the expulsion of the natives by fire and sword if necessary. The missionaries, whose only interest was safety, deemed the time not yet auspicious to distribute the missionaries as the governor had planned. For these reasons it was decided to ask the Indians of Santa Fé to return to Galisteo.

These meetings could be clearly observed by the Indians, who watched at the ramparts with growing anger and suspicion. They knew full well what the settlers were demanding, and were ready for resistance. They were already harboring some of the Spaniards beneath their roofs, against the will of the majority; an attempt was being made to fleece them of their grain; now the Spaniards wanted to drive them from their homes. The atmosphere of the whole city was charged as if with electricity. For the Spaniards it was a matter of life or death, without compromise, among a people who had committed treason against their God and their king, and the spirit of the reconquest of Spain from the Moslem infidel still ran in their veins. For the Pueblo Indians, who were not warlike by nature, it was a noble and just defense of life, property, and religion at any cost. Under such circumstances war was inevitable.

The rebels countermured their houses, and kept their guns, darts, and arrows in readiness, under the pretext of preparing for a deer hunt. Crafty sentinels on the ramparts continuously watched every move of the Spaniards. Among those members of the expedition of mixed blood who were living in the villa, were Jerónima Márquez, living with a native aunt named Ángela. According to her reports, for the past two days Tanos and Tewas had been entering and leaving the city all night long, taking their food and belongings to the mountains, she believed. The natives had seen through the hoax regarding the alleged reinforcements. They were very angry, and on the night of the 26th the leaders harangued in the *estufa* until dawn. Their disgruntlement simmered down to this query: if the Spaniards wished to destroy them, let them commence; but why attempt to fleece them of food and house and home? The creoles and mestizos of Vargas' colony who were living in the villa were warned by native friends to join their own camp, for the majority of the natives were defiant, and as a consequence several families abandoned the shelter of the villa for safety.

The tightening of nerves continued on through the hours of the following day and night, and in the false dawn of the 28th there came a break. All night long the restless natives had been gathered in the patio around their fires, listening to the harangues of their leaders. At four in the morning Vargas was suddenly aroused from sleep by a youth, a messenger from Miguel Luján, a Spanish soldier quartered in the *estufa* of the pueblo which had been partially remodeled for a chapel. The lad had escaped the vigilance of the natives by the aid of a blind mestizo named Agustín Salazar. This blind man had been eavesdropping during the speeches of the Indian governor of Santa Fé, who had assured his people of their ability to overcome the enemy. Salazar then told Luján, and Luján dispatched the boy to Vargas. Don Diego promptly sent him back to gather more information. An hour later he returned to the general's tent with word of the arrival in the village of a Picuríes and Taos. These, hearing the clamor of Santa Fé warriors for the blood of the intruders, protested loyalty to the Spanish cause. His narrative was interrupted at this point by the dramatic arrival of blind Salazar, just escaped by ladder from the walled town, who delivered himself of significant details of the native plot. Salazar, who dwelt in a room in one of the former *casas reales*, had heard many Indians entering the square, some on horse. To spy upon them, he had wrapped himself in his cloak and in the darkness of night had mingled with the throng in the patio listening to the governor's speech. The gist of this was: "Arise, massacre the Spaniards!" When some remained hesitant, preferring for fear of hurt to their children to flee to the mountains, the chief cried out that it was no time to worry about children, but to fight till the enemy was routed. At the conclusion of his remarks some of the Spanish soldiers who were living in the villa left the patio posthaste for

Vargas' tent to report the imminence of an attack, since the natives had taken up their ladders.

Vargas immediately sounded the alarm by means of the trumpet and the war drum. The governor of Pecos was sent with two swift steeds for reinforcements from his pueblo, and there was no delay in sending for the families and soldiers living inside the villa. Some left all their belongings behind. Then the first spark flew: as Miguel Luján, who had been living in the whitewashed *estufa*, escaped with his wife and children, he was met by a storm of darts, clods, even stone hatchets, thrown from the walls, and accompanied by hideous and vengeful shouts. A flying squadron sent to examine the stronghold found its walltops already lined with warriors. When these caught sight of the approaching soldiers they put forth blood curdling shouts, interspersed with repellent blasphemy, and accompanied by a flight of missiles. For better protection the camp was quickly transferred to a flat, open meadow, directly in front of and an arquebus shot distant from the stronghold. Guards were stationed at strategic points. Then, with the *cabildo* and most of the soldiers, Vargas rode to the gateway of the walled city singing praise to the Blessed Sacrament.

On the walls above the doorway stood the rebel war captains and most valiant warriors, among them Antonio Bolsas. Vargas rode out ahead with Roque Madrid and his secretary, and from below harangued the rebels. But sweet words were of no avail. His order to quit the city brought out the mettle of the defenders. They were determined to defend their lands, and wished to hear nothing of the Blessed Sacrament and the Virgin Mary; they would fight, and all New Mexico was with them; the Spaniards would be either killed or enslaved. Remembering his tactics of the previous year, Vargas continued patiently with suave words, and Bolsas finally said that he would deliberate with the people and give an answer in the evening.

Vargas returned to his tent, but received no answer. Instead, as night fell, a chanting of war songs could be heard, which was drowned out from time to time in a din of hideous shouting. The delay worried the Spanish general, for it would give the confederates of the enemy time to come to their assistance. And so a ring of sentinels was placed around the city, and the whole camp kept watch.

At about seven o'clock next morning, December 29, 140 Pecos Indian allies came to the aid of Vargas. He sallied forth again to parley with the embattled rebels. Father Diego Zeinos gave a pious exhortation, followed by prayers and a blessing, after which the army formed and marched to the city. But Vargas had scarcely started to move forward, singing praise to the Blessed Sacrament, when the Indians began their hellish shouting. They cried out to the Spaniards that the whole countryside was against them, every Apache camp, as far west as Moqui. They would kill everyone except the missionaries, whom they would enslave. These fiendish boasts were followed by a storm of darts, arrows, stones, and other heavy missiles. "Santiago! Santiago! Death to these rebels!" cried out Vargas to his men, and the battle was on.

Most of the soldiers dismounted and charged rapidly in an effort to gain the walls, while others, with repeated volleys of gunfire, attempted to clear the way by shooting down those who were defending the walls from the trenches above. One group of Spaniards rushed the main tower above the gateway, scaled the walls by means of ladders, amid a hail of stones and darts glancing off their leather shields, and won the position. An attempt now was made to divert the enemy by attacking from many points, but they merely hid behind walls and houses. Vargas then ordered his men to batter down the principal and only gateway. When the axes did little damage to the sturdy wood, it was set on fire and burned, although in the process four Spaniards were wounded, one fatally. Through the open doorway rushed a squad of the front line soldiers, who forced their way through barricades and gained possession of the whitewashed *estufa* of the first square. By noon the Spaniards were in possession of the main gateway, the front square, the first communal dwelling, and the two towers above the doorway overlooking the first square. Half of the stronghold was already won. But in order to achieve complete victory the trenches on the surrounding walls had to be gained at great risk. Four ladders were made for this purpose. It would have been easier to burn the stronghold and thus exterminate the entire population; but looking to the safety of the women and children, Vargas decided otherwise. Don Diego was everywhere at once, urging his men on to great deeds of valor.

Suddenly, at about four o'clock in the afternoon, the sentinels saw a large troop of Indians, on horse and on foot, coming to the aid of the besieged. On seeing them the rebel defenders increased their shouting and fought with renewed vigor. They rained boiling water upon the soldiers undermining the walls. The new arrivals were attacked with such fury that five of them were killed in the first skirmish, and the others fled in bewilderment to a distant vantage point from which they were content to watch the spectacle. At sundown, however, they made a second sally. Four were killed and the others fled, never again showing their faces.

The watchword through the night was vigilance. Soldiers were stationed at all the strategic points already won, in the towers and in the first *estufa*, and others were placed about the pueblo where they could prevent escape or entry. The horses, mules, and livestock were formed in a circle around the camp. From minute to minute the Spaniards were ready for an assault which did not come. In the direction of the city all was quiet and darkness, save for the occasional flash and sound of gunfire from the first *estufa*, followed by an echoing crash, or telling thud. Vargas was on horseback all night.

Before dawn the soldiers hidden in the first *estufa* made a desperate attempt to scale the walls. In the light of a flint lock they took a ladder and gained control of the front walls. The surprised Indians offered little resistance; by dawn all the walls facing the first square were won. Once dominating the walltops running along the facade of the stronghold with its two towers, these crack soldiers soon captured positions covering the second square. From the barricaded houses and walls which separated the two squares, they looked down into the second square, where the fortified *estufa* was defended from within by a detachment of rebels. Shortly, from the first square was heard the cry "Praise be to the Blessed Sacrament!" as the second *estufa* was stormed and won.

Meanwhile, Governor José lay in his house writhing in pain from a broken right wrist, caused by a flying bullet. His fair city was being rent from the tribesmen foot by foot before his eyes, till scarce enough remained for him to stand on. Realizing that all was lost, José, in futile desperation, tightened a noose about his neck by means of a short iron bar, and took his own life.

By morning the city was won. The military leaders notified Vargas, who immediately had the royal banner placed upon the walls as a sign of victory, and a cross set over the main entrance. The Indians were asked to come out to obtain pardon. Most of the women and children complied, accompanied by the rebel Bolsas. The others stubbornly remained in hiding. Governor Vargas then entered the main square, accompanied by the *cabildo* and all the soldiers. Every house was searched from trapdoor to trapdoor, and from roof to cellar. Fifty-four men, women and children thus driven out of hiding were delivered to the guards. There were so many living quarters, including those that had been built over the *palacio*, or royal government buildings, that it took twenty soldiers and thirty friendly Indians the whole day to take a complete inventory. There were ample quarters to house the colonists.

The houses were well provisioned with maize, grain, and beans, which, under the supervision of the *cabildo*, were taken to a large *estufa*, newly swept. The *cabildo* set about distributing the grain to the families for food, and seed in order that the men might start planting. At about two o'clock in the afternoon, while the inspection tour was being made, and the rebels were being rounded up, the sentinels on the walls reported a large troop of Indians approaching. The colonists were taken into the city for protection. Eighty soldiers sallied forth to meet the enemy, who retreated without attacking. Vargas then ordered the people to take their lodging in the houses of the vanquished.

The fifty-four rebels first taken out of hiding that day, fifteen more found later, and Antonio Bolsas, the leading spirit of the uprising, were executed at the rear of the stronghold on the following charges: having stoned and destroyed a cross placed in the center of the square, broken a statue of the Virgin Mary, and committed treason against God and the Royal Crown. Those who had surrendered of their own free will, about four hundred of both sexes, were distributed among the soldiers and settlers in servitude for a period of ten years under the following provisions: they could choose their masters; they must be well treated; they should be instructed in prayer and religion by the missionaries; they could not be exchanged, as their masters owned only their services; they could not be removed from one locality to another. In Vargas' opinion this was within his powers as specified by royal cédula. After the ten year period, if sufficiently instructed in Christian doctrine and citizenship, they might return to a pueblo of their choosing. This action of Vargas was later confirmed by the viceroy and the Junta de Hacienda in Mexico City, even though the royal fiscal had previously reported that it was contrary to the Laws of the Indies.

As a result of the battle at Santa Fé, eighty-one rebels perished: seventy executions, nine battle deaths, and two suicides. Of the Spaniards, twenty-two had died of exposure during the two weeks' stay on the edge of the mountain, and one had died in battle. The Spaniards now had a solid foothold in New Mexico. But the effects of the conquest were widespread in the land. The executions at Santa Fé, considered by Vargas as a necessary war measure, angered the war captains and medicine-men of the surrounding pueblos. Recalling Tapia's story, they fortified their positions on the mesa-tops and remained hostile.

SUGGESTED READINGS

Jesse B. Bailey, *Diego de Vargas and the Reconquest of New Mexico* (Albuquerque 1940);

Oakah L. Jones, *Pueblo Warriors and the Spanish Conquest* (Norman 1966);

J. Manuel Espinosa, "The Virgin of the Reconquest of New Mexico," *Mid-America*, vol. XXIII (January 1941);

Espinosa, *First Expedition of Vargas into New Mexico* (Albuquerque 1940);

Atanasio Dominguez, *The Missions of New Mexico*, edited by Eleanor B. Adams and Fray Angelico Chavez (Albuquerque 1956).

6
Pueblo Auxiliaries

In the conquest of the New World, Spain quickly adopted a policy of employing Indian allies and of exploiting and fostering the traditional lack of Indian unity. The value of Indian auxiliaries was especially evident in Cortés' conquest of New Spain, and the Spanish continued to use them during the northward advance of the frontier. New Mexico was no exception to this general practice. During the long period of Spanish occupation, allies from several tribes were used against hostile groups, and they proved to be extremely important to the success of Spanish colonization.

Following the Pueblo Revolt in 1680, Spanish officials began to use friendly Pueblo Indians, who had accompanied the ousted settlers to the El Paso region, as scouts, guides, interpreters, messengers, and fighting men. These Pueblo allies were a vital force in the reconquest, and, as Spain solidified her control in the northern portions of the Rio Grande Valley in the 1690s and early 1700s, Pueblo warriors became an increasingly important element in the defense of the province. They were, writes Professor Oakah L. Jones, the bulwark of the defense of New Mexico.

Spanish officials employed Pueblo auxiliaries in a variety of ways. As scouts they provided the first line of defense and brought news of hostile invaders; as guides they led expeditions against hostile Apaches, Navajos, and Comanches; as soldiers they participated in defensive operations and offensive campaigns; and while at first they operated as a separate unit, Pueblo warriors were gradually integrated with Spanish soldiers and militia and often accounted for up to eighty percent of the force. At times, also, they conducted their own campaigns without Spanish assistance. Moreover, on almost all occasions they fought well, usually performing better than their Spanish counterparts. Although the use of Pueblo auxiliaries declined in the 1780s when greater reliance was placed on the newly allied Comanches, Pueblo warriors continued to play an important role in the defense of New Mexico throughout the eighteenth and nineteenth centuries. Their contribution to New Mexico history is described by Dr. Jones.

Spain spent a century after the beginning of the reconquest of New Mexico in the establishment of the security of the province from the widespread depredations of the *indios bárbaros*. The period from 1692 to 1794 was one of trial and error in the formation of her Indian policy for the Northern Frontier. Policies and practices were not developed rapidly; experience played a great part in the growth of a standardized policy for dealing with the aborigines who surrounded New Mexico. The use of Pueblo Indian auxiliaries was one of the earliest techniques developed and most consistently employed throughout the era.

Repeated raids by hostile bands necessitated extensive campaigning by Spanish forces to protect the settlements and to punish the marauders. The more significant of these punitive forays chronologically, indicate, as best as the records reveal, the use, recruitment, organization, leadership, and fighting qualities of Pueblo auxiliaries. It might now be appropriate to synthesize these aspects by reconstructing a hypothetical campaign in which the Pueblo warriors were enlisted. It must be realized, of course, that not all of the characteristics and practices to be discussed were developed at any given time or, indeed, within a short period of years. Evolving from an initial system, established to meet an immediate need during the reconquest, they developed with modifications throughout the course of the ensuing century.

What necessitated such a foray against hostiles and how did it commence? Generally, the campaign was either punitive or preventative in purpose, to discourage the continuous depredations of nomadic bands on the settled parts of the province. The root of the Spanish problem lay in the cultural and economic differences between the Spaniards and Pueblos on the one hand and the nomadic Indians on the other. The latter depended upon what the former produced or possessed, and obtained by plundering what it was unable to get by trading. From the Pueblos the "barbarians" took food, livestock, and captives; from the Spaniards, horses and firearms.

Friendly Pueblo informants, widely distributed over the province, reported these raids or the approach of the marauders. Sometimes they came directly to Santa Fe, and at other times they submitted their information through the local alcaldes. On occasion they even wrote directly to the governor. Once the complaint or report had been received in the capital, that Spanish official decided whether or not to call a *junta de guerra* to consider the report and to recommend what should be done to punish the offenders. Occasionally, prominent Pueblo leaders, such as the caciques and war captains, were invited to participate in these councils. Yet, the practice of consulting a junta was not followed religiously throughout the century. It was time-consuming and frequently did little more than endorse the governor's recommendations that the raid justified waging war on the offenders.

Once the decision to conduct a campaign had been reached either by the governor or the *junta de guerra*, the former instructed the *alcaldes mayores* as to the quota of men to be provided from each Indian jurisdiction, the number of weapons and horses required, the time and place of assembly, and the anticipated duration of the campaign. Generally, the governor led the presidial and militia forces from Santa Fe and collected other civilian militia and Pueblo auxiliaries along his route to the designated rendezvous point. The *alcaldes mayores*, acting through the individual pueblo governors, caciques, and war captains, recruited the Christian Indians and assembled the horses and arms which were regularly maintained within each jurisdiction to meet the governor's requirements. When the necessary warriors and equipment had been obtained at each village, they joined forces and marched together to the mobilization center, each pueblo led by its own alcalde, cacique, governor, or more frequently by its war captains. In the first half of the eighteenth century, the entire body of auxiliaries from a particular jurisdiction was under the over-all command of an Indian *capitán mayor de la guerra.*

At the designated assembly point the Spanish presidiaries and militia joined the Pueblo auxiliaries. Here a final muster was held as the governor reviewed his forces preparatory to the departure upon the campaign. The *plaza de armas*, or rendezvous point, was usually an Indian pueblo, particularly one near the enemy's last reported position. Thus, if the Comanches had created the immediate threat, the assembly point was usually at Pecos or Taos. If the punitive campaign was against the Utes, the assembly was at Taos, Abiquiú, or San Juan. Western campaigns against the Navahos or the Moquis departed from Jémez, Laguna, or Zuñi. Expeditions against the Apaches, however, were launched from a variety of locations, depending upon the particular band involved and their position at the time. Sandía Pueblo and the Bernalillo district served as assembly points for the campaign against the Faraones in 1704, but later in the century, after Comanche pressures had forced most of the resisting Apaches southward, Isleta became the leading rendezvous for the majority of the campaigns against the southern Apaches, although Laguna and Acoma were used occasionally for expeditions against the Gileños in the southwest.

The campaign itself usually involved a well-organized force. Until the latter half of the eighteenth century the expedition was divided into two basic elements: the Spanish soldier-settler unit as one body, and the Indian auxiliaries as the other. The combined force was usually preceded by a group, often quite large, of Pueblo scouts from the auxiliary element which maintained a position three leagues or so in front of the main column, frequently reconnoitering the advanced area as virtually independent bodies under the leadership of their own war captains.

The basic expeditionary force remained at all times under the over-all control and command of the provincial governor or his designated representative—either the lieutenant governor, an officer from the presidio, or the *maestre del campo*. During the early part of the century the horse herds, livestock, and warriors of the auxiliary force were not allowed to mingle with the stock of, or with the regular soldiers and militia. Separate camps were pitched at night for each of the major elements within the campaign force. In the latter half of the century, especially in the last two decades, this segregation seems to have been abolished. Perhaps the presence of other native allies necessitated such a change, since the placement of Comanches near Utes or the Pueblos without the presence of Spanish troops would undoubtedly have caused friction. At any rate, the expeditions of Anza and La Concha included auxiliaries integrated within a basic four-divisional organization. Each division included presidial troops, civilian militia, and native allies—Pueblos, newly pacified Comanches, Utes, Jicarillas, Navahos, and even *genízaros*. There were no longer any *capitanes mayores* in this period. Divisional officers were always Spaniards appointed by the governor, usually from among the officers of the presidial company, but occasionally from the prominent citizenry. Still, native war captains led their own forces within these basic divisions.

Pueblo auxiliaries performed a variety of services throughout these campaigns. Primarily, they constituted the principal quantitative element in the total force, usually over half the total number of men. On occasion, the proportion increased, especially as the century advanced, until it reached a maximum of 75 to 85 per cent of the expeditionary force. In addition to this major function, Pueblo allies also served as scouts, spies, messengers, and interpreters. Although no mention is made of it in the records, these natives must have performed also as guards for the horse herds and the droves of cattle and sheep which usually accompanied the expeditions.

Pueblo auxiliaries seem to have performed very well in all of the capacities in which they were employed. Their knowledge of both the terrain and the enemy made them invaluable as scouts. Their acquaintance with the languages of the hostile tribes obviously made them significant in parleys, conferences, and treaties. Most of all, however, they performed and fought well in actual engagements with the enemy. The Spaniards apparently never withheld them from battle nor relegated them to a subsidiary or rear-guard type of action. Instead, the opposite seems to have been the case, since Spanish commanders, upon encountering the enemy, had difficulty restraining the enthusiasm of the auxiliaries. Only when the expeditionary force was surprised, as at the Platte River in 1720, did the Pueblos, like all other elements of the force, behave improperly. Then, when the enemy warriors threatened to annihilate the entire expedition, the auxiliaries virtually disintegrated, retreating in utter confusion. In circumstances in which the Spanish authorities were in complete control, there was no reluctance to use the auxiliaries in any phase of combat. Both military and civil officials, and even the missionaries, frequently noted the loyalty, willingness to serve, and the over-all value of Pueblo assistance on these campaigns.

Why did the Pueblo participate so willingly and so extensively on these campaigns? The answer appears to be twofold. First, these expeditions provided the Pueblo with an opportunity to carry the warfare to his traditional enemy, to chastise him for his raids, and to prevent his further depredations. Second, they supplied the Pueblo with an opportunity to share in the spoils of battle. After the enemy had been defeated, the Spanish commander usually divided their possessions among the troops, and the Indian allies shared along with the soldiers and settlers, frequently receiving captive warriors, weapons of all types, horses, other livestock, and supplies of food. Not only did they recover their own animals but also some of their own people who had been captured by the marauding enemy. Profitable as these rewards for participation on Spanish campaigns may seem, there were still other incentives in the form of privileges, titles, and special recognition to the exceptionally valorous warriors and their leaders. Moreover, by the latter half of the century, the Spanish authorities made auxiliary service even more attractive by regularly distributing annual presents to the loyal allies.

When a campaign had been concluded and the spoils divided, the Pueblo auxiliaries were dismissed and returned expeditiously to their villages. This demobilization seems to have occurred either at the original *plaza de armas* or at the first pueblo encountered on the return route. The Spanish element, soldiers and militia, continued to Santa Fe or to their respective jurisdictions under the over-all commander of the expedition, whereas Pueblos were detached to return to their villages under their own native leaders. The arrival of the governor or his designated representative in the capital marked the conclusion of the campaign.

Pueblo Indian auxiliaries performed a major role in the Spanish reconquest and pacification of New Mexico in the late seventeenth and most of the eighteenth century. As the constant allies of the Spaniards, these loyal mercenaries contributed to the defense of the province in many ways. They served repeatedly on campaigns against the hostile tribes which surrounded the province. Also, they accompanied missionaries and Spanish officials on expeditions to aboriginal groups not yet converted to the Iberian way of life. They served as interpreters and informants, demonstrating both their knowledge of Castilian and their fidelity to the Europeans. In addition, they contributed to the sustenance of campaign forces, providing food, horses, and other livestock as needed. Their economic assistance was as valuable, perhaps as their military aid in the establishment of tranquility within the province.

Yet, one must remember that Pueblos were not the only auxiliaries used by Spain in the expansion of her authority in the Americas. The practice of relying upon Indian auxiliaries was widely employed throughout the Spanish colonial period in almost all of her kingdoms. Nor was this the only technique used in dealing with the natives encountered in the New World. The use of missionaries, the establishment of presidios, the extension of Spanish governmental institutions to Indian communities, the retention of native political structures under the control of designated Spaniards, and the employment of certain tribes, like the Tlaxcalans and Otomies, to colonize remote problem areas—all were practices resorted to by Spanish authorities in the control and assimilation of various aboriginal elements. The use of Pueblo Indians, although an important aspect of the reliance upon auxiliaries, is only an illustration of one commonly adopted technique in one restricted area of the Spanish Empire.

Was the system of employing Pueblo auxiliaries for New Mexico's defense a good one? Naturally, the answer to such a question must involve many factors, including an understanding of problems encountered and other means available to solve these difficulties *at that time*. Above all, it is necessary to weigh the strengths and weaknesses of the practice.

The greatest benefit Spain derived from her close affiliation with the Pueblos was the establishment of unity in a province formerly torn by internal dissension and native hatred for the conquerors. This early disunity, so prominent in the seventeenth century, ultimately resulted in the expulsion of the Spaniards from New Mexico for nearly a dozen years. Beginning with the reconquest, Pueblos gradually were attracted to the cause of the Iberians, thus forming a nucleus for future development and expansion. Without the unification of the Pueblos and their subsequent association with the Spaniards, Spain could not have controlled New Mexico with the limited resources she maintained in that area. Except for rare occasions in the early part of the period when conspiracies were reported, Spain in the eighteenth century never again had to worry about her Pueblo allies rebelling against her imposed authority.

To achieve this unity, Spanish authorities rewarded Pueblo Indians with titles, recognition, privileges, gifts, and the spoils of battle. Of singular importance in this regard is the Spanish permission for Pueblos to carry firearms and ride horses almost continuously throughout the century after the reconquest. Although there is no documentary evidence to indicate that these privileges were officially sanctioned by authorities in Spain, they were so widely recognized by governors, missionaries, military officers, and visiting officials that it became an accepted fact for Pueblos to be armed and equipped like the presidiaries and settlers of New Mexico. Therefore, the generally accepted statement that Spain prohibited natives within her empire from riding horses and carrying firearms is, indeed, not true for New Mexico.

Pueblo auxiliaries served as the most consistently reliable element in the pacification of hostile tribes and the defense of New Mexico during the eighteenth century. The presidial force at Santa Fe, numbering only eighty troops during the major portion of this era, was too small to control the province adequately by itself. Militia forces were unreliable, poorly equipped, and often untrained and undisciplined. From Vargas to La Concha, authorities complained of the reluctance of the settlers to serve in the defense of the province. At the same time they praised the loyalty, self-denial, and military preparedness of the Pueblos in fulfilling their obligations to defend the kingdom. Of unusual importance is the fact that both civil and religious authorities seemed to agree that the natives contributed greatly to the defense of the province.

Hostile tribes gradually joined the Spanish-Pueblo side. Attracted by the privileges granted to the Pueblos, the nomadic elements realized that they, too, could share in the benefits accruing to their traditional enemies. In addition, alliance with the Spaniards did not mean that these nomads must discontinue their warlike practices. Instead, it provided an opportunity to continue fighting, but on the side of the Iberians and Pueblos against a dwindling number of rebellious tribes. Toward the end of the century it is evident that Spain actually subsidized her allies, providing them arms, horses, and even cash payments for assistance rendered.

Another great strength of the Spanish system of employing Pueblo auxiliaries was the acceleration of cultural interchange between the two groups of people. The association of Spaniards with Pueblos on campaigns, visits, and inspections facilitated the assimilation of the Pueblos and the growth of a homogeneous population, basically devoted to agricultural development, throughout the province. Evidence of this trend is provided by the more rapid increase of the general population in the last three decades of the century, whereas Pueblo Indian numbers increased only slightly. Since immigration into the province was never very great, the only logical explanation for this increase lies in the expansion of the mestizo element. With the establishment and growth of such a society, New Mexico became a region where mixbloods dominated and the economic pursuits of both Spanish settlements and Indian pueblos closely resembled each other.

Nevertheless, despite these many strengths in the use of Pueblo auxiliaries, there were drawbacks to such a system. The greatest weakness may be observed in the relative lack of success experienced by individual campaign forces. Only in a comparatively few instances were these expeditions successful enough in chastising the enemy to compensate for their extensive preparations. The system of employing native auxiliaries in conjunction with presidiaries and settlers necessitated long delays in the execution of particular campaigns. It took time for all the elements to be advised, recruited, equipped, and assembled prior to their departure in pursuit of the marauding enemy. These delays of weeks, sometimes months, allowed the enemy to scatter, thus weakening the effect of the planned expedition to chastise them. Also, in the time so consumed, other hostile tribes struck elsewhere on New Mexico's frontiers, requiring diversionary efforts by Spanish-Pueblo forces and further delaying the expedition against the original enemy.

Pueblo participation on Spanish military campaigns probably intensified the hatreds of hostile tribes for the Spaniards. Traditional native antipathies of one tribe for another only increased when it was realized that Spanish authorities were using Pueblos against the enemy as a means for the enemy's reduction. Thus, the struggle may have been prolonged, rather than shortened, since Pueblos were allowed the spoils of battle after the nomadic tribes had been defeated, and rewards were offered for captives, heads, and ears. No doubt this practice led the enemy to choose resistance since the consequences of defeat were so severe.

Certainly, there were other weaknesses in the system of using Pueblo auxiliaries. Absence on campaigns injured the harvests and domestic pursuits of the sedentary natives. Likewise, it reduced the number of Indians left to defend the pueblos, thus exposing them to attacks by other tribes or even by the same enemy, should he be successful in eluding the original campaign force. All this military activity established a focus upon the pueblos since they were the rendezvous and provisioning points designated by the Spaniards. As a result, there was a continual drain on their agricultural resources and their stock-raising industry.

Like all mercenaries on campaigns, the Pueblos were often difficult to control. Their enthusiasm occasionally knew no bounds once the enemy was in view. In addition, once the Spaniards lost the advantageous element of surprise, it is obvious that the Pueblos were of no great value, fleeing in disorganized, full-scale retreat. It must be noted finally that the employment of Pueblo auxiliaries may have had an effect upon the social and political structures of their own villages. Naturally, duty as an auxiliary increased the prestige of individual native military leaders, enhancing their position relative to the traditional Pueblo chieftains. Thus, the positions of war captain and *capitán mayor de la guerra* became much more influential than those of the native governor, the cacique, or the Indian alcalde. It appears that the military and civil positions were sometimes combined as a result. On occasion, the overbearing attitude developed by auxiliaries seems to have been demonstrated within individual pueblos, further unbalancing the former social structure.

Even though there were identifiable weaknesses in the system of employing Pueblo auxiliaries, the technique was a highly realistic and practical one for the defense of New Mexico. Without the assistance of these allies, the province could not have been reconquered in the last decade of the seventeenth century. At that time only a portion of the Pueblo Indians served as the sole auxiliaries of the Spaniards. In the early decades of the following century these natives were first unified in support of the Spanish cause. Then they were organized effectively, after much experimentation and vacillation. Finally, near mid-century, Governor Vélez Cachupín integrated them into an over-all defensive concept for the province. Later they were combined with the nomadic tribes they had attracted, so that all could then serve as auxiliaries. By 1794 the Pueblos were only one of the many native allies employed by Spain in the defense of New Mexico, and their role in relation to the newer auxiliaries was in decline.

Throughout the period of 1692–1794, Pueblo Indians constantly contributed to the stabilization and pacification of the Spanish Empire in America. Their extensive support of the Spaniards in the remote province of New Mexico, especially through their service as Indian auxiliaries, helped to reconquer, control, and defend the province. Gradually they aided in pacifying this northernmost interior province, not only directly through their military aid but indirectly by attracting the resisting tribes to the Spanish-Pueblo alliance. This constructive contribution of the Pueblos has largely been ignored by historians and the general public. Instead, interest has been devoted to the destructive acts of the Pueblos in overcoming the Spaniards during the great rebellion of 1680. The loyalty, courage, constancy, and organizational ability of the Pueblo auxiliaries in the century following the reconquest are more notable aspects of their character, however, than their destructive tendencies in the expulsion of the Spaniards. Indeed, their aid was invaluable to the Spanish soldiers and settlers of the eighteenth century, and was a positive contribution to the defense and pacification of New Mexico.

SUGGESTED READINGS

Oakah L. Jones, Jr., "Pueblo Indian Auxiliaries and the Reconquest of New Mexico, 1692–1704," *Journal of the West*, vol. II (July 1963);
Jones, "Pueblo Indian Auxiliaries in New Mexico, 1763–1821," *New Mexico Historical Review*, vol. XXXVII (April 1962);

Donald E. Worcester, "The Navajo During the Spanish Regime in New Mexico," *New Mexico Historical Review*, vol. XXVI (April 1951);

Eleanor B. Adams, *Bishop Tamaron's Visitation of New Mexico, 1760* (Albuquerque 1954);

Alfred B. Thomas, "Governor Mendinueta's Proposals for the Defense of New Mexico, 1772–1778," *New Mexico Historical Review*, vol. VI (January 1931).

7
Spanish Indian Policy

The province of New Mexico, an isolated outpost on the northern frontier of New Spain, was an island of Spanish civilization amid tribes of wild Indians, and a main theme in the history of the region was relations with the Indians. The Indian problem was, in fact, one of the most difficult problems faced by New Mexicans, but it must be remembered that a similar situation existed in other sections of the frontier. New Mexico was just a part in an overall plan for defense of the northern frontier, and its relations with the wild tribes were controlled by a general Indian policy.

In *The Apache Frontier*, a study of Jocabo Ugarte's term as Commandant General of the Internal Provinces, an administrative organization for the defense of the northern frontier, Max Moorhead describes with great clarity the overall picture of Spanish defensive policy in this region. In 1768 Marqués de Rubí recommended a war of extermination against the Apaches, and while the Reglamento of 1772 fell short of Rubí's demands, it was the most brutal Indian policy ever sanctioned by the King. The Reglamento, however, did not entirely clarify the picture, for when Ugarte became Commandant General in 1786 he found at least six mutually inconsistent official guidelines for relations with the Indians. It wasn't until later in that year that the Instruction of 1786 synthesized these policies and eliminated the confusion. The Instruction was a compromise, Moorhead explains, between war of extermination and peace by persuasion and sought to spread discord and divide and conquer the Apache. On the assumption that a bad peace was better than a good war, peace would be accepted when offered no matter how frail it might appear. Trade was to be strictly regulated and was encouraged with peaceful Indians in an effort to accustom them to Spanish goods; the use of liquor was encouraged, and cumbersome muskets of poor quality were distributed in an effort to reduce the use of the more effective bow and arrow and to force the Indians to rely on the Spanish for ammunition and repairs.

Ugarte carried out this policy with considerable success although he was plagued by changes in the administrative structure of the Internal Provinces. Campaigns were waged against the Apaches while efforts were made to cement peace and mutual alliances with the Navajos, Utes, Comanches, and Jicarilla Apaches. It was, for example, during this general period that Juan Bautista de Anza campaigned effectively against the Navajos and Comanches and developed a vital alliance with the Comanches which brought them into the war against the Apaches. During Ugarte's tenure as Commandant General peace was made with most tribes, and the northern frontier was made more secure than it had been for some time.

Without doubt the most severe handicap under which Ugarte's frontier army operated was the absence of a well-defined Indian policy. For almost twenty years pronouncements from on high had attempted to formulate a uniform purpose and procedure in dealing with the hostile tribes of the north, but each successive official statement varied from its predecessor and each viceroy interpreted the policy differently. The most remarkable aspect of Ugarte's administration as commandant-general of the Provincias Internas was that he came as close as he did to achieving the complete pacification of the northern frontier amid such confusion of official thought and pronouncement.

A formula for dealing with the hostiles had been evolving from the very beginning. The crown had early made a distinction between the perennially hostile nomadic tribes and the normally peaceful and sedentary Indians, and it had even come to recognize nations that were essentially neutral. But any consistent policy for dealing with them, either separately or collectively, rested on shifting sands. The king himself was caught between the conflicting dictates of moral obligation and practical necessity, and even when humanitarian zeal did not collide with either imperial need or international commitment, there was always the embarrassment of budgetary consideration. The result was inaction or equivocation at the highest level. Moreover, provincial governors and garrison commandants had long acted in the interests of particular rather than general welfare, and so they had achieved little more in their independent military operations than the driving of the common enemy from one refuge to another and the gaining of an only temporary and local respite from the ravages of the marauding tribes.

Ugarte, as the supposed co-ordinator of these operations, was bound to some extent by at least half a dozen mutually inconsistent official guidelines. The first of these was the celebrated *Dictamen*, or recommendation, submitted in 1768 by the Marqués de Rubí. On returning from his inspection of the frontier presidios and consultation with the local commandants and provincial governors, Rubí had proposed basic changes in the heretofore haphazard strategy. In the past the frontier officials had attempted to attract the amorphous and predatory Apache bands to the tranquility of mission life. This, Rubí believed, had been a mistake. The Apaches had proved treacherous to all Spanish offers of peace and protection. Moreover, much more powerful Indian nations to the north of Texas were pressing down upon the missions and presidios of that province and driving the Apaches before them. These so-called Nations of the North were, along with the formidable Comanches, bitter enemies of the Apache bands, and their own attacks on missions and presidios stemmed not from any natural hostility toward the white man, but from resentment of the shelter that the Spaniards had given their historic foe. It had already been demonstrated that the Nations of the North and the Comanches could honor a peace treaty and enter into amicable trade relations—the former with Louisiana and the latter with New Mexico—whereas the Apaches had proved totally undependable. Therefore, Rubí felt, the Spaniards must pursue a more realistic policy. Harsh as it might appear, they must expel the Apaches from every mission, presidio, and settlement along the entire outer frontier and throw them back to their merciless enemies in the north. They should then attempt to cultivate and conciliate those more powerful nations, induce them to join in a combined offensive against the Apaches, and crushing these perfidious marauders between vise-like pressures from both north and south, bring about their total destruction. Without respite or refuge, Rubí believed, the Apaches would be forced to choose between extermination and unconditional surrender. If the latter, they should be admitted to peace and protection only in the widely-dispersed missions of the remote interior of New Spain, for it was only there that they might be Christianized, civilized, and assimilated among the already well-pacified tribes. Then, and only then, according to Rubí, would peace on the northern frontier be assured.

Although Rubí's opinions were not fully endorsed by the king, they did influence the thinking of some administrators. Ugarte, however, was more charitable toward the Apaches. Somewhat more to his liking, but still not completely palatable, was the *Reglamento de 1772*, which was based on Rubí's recommendations but tempered with the king's more humanitarian sentiments. Principally, the *Reglamento* redefined the duties of officers and troops and ordered the establishment of a new, outer line of presidios to ward off the invasions of hostile tribes, but one of its fourteen sections stated the king's Indian policy in rather definite terms.

In the first place, the *Reglamento* declared, the general objective of military operations on the frontier was peace, and the king's main concerns were for the welfare and conversion of the pagan tribes and for the tranquility of the northern provinces. Therefore, while the troops must wage an active and incessant war on the avowedly hostile tribes, carrying it even to their own lands, they were to observe good faith and gentle treatment toward those whom they conquered. Captured warriors were not to be abused (the death penalty would be imposed on anyone killing such a prisoner in cold blood). Rather, these captives were to be provided with rations and sent to Mexico City, there to be dealt with by the viceroy as he saw fit. Women and infants taken would be similarly well treated, but an attempt would also be made to convert and educate them.

Although kindness and good treatment of individual prisoners were to be encouraged, such were not to be guaranteed for entire nations, and most especially not for the Apaches. Under a variety of names, groups of these hostile savages had professed a desire for peace or submission whenever they were confronted with superior forces. But, interpreting Spanish clemency as weakness, they had abused the concessions at the first opportunity. Therefore, the Apaches were not to be admitted to peace except when they chose to subject themselves to the king's domination or when they offered strict guarantees and evidence that they intended to keep it; and even then the peace was to be provisional, merely a suspension of hostilities pending approval of the terms by the viceroy. In order to preserve life on both sides and possibly to arouse in the barbarous nations a humanitarian sentiment, the first condition for a truce was to be an exchange of prisoners, and in carrying out this stipulation good faith was to be required at all times. Whenever there was a well-founded expectation of achieving such an exchange, the troops were not to send their captives to Mexico City, but to intern them securely near the presidios.

As for the peaceful or neutral tribes, the best relations were to be maintained. The Spaniards were to overlook some of their faults and lesser offenses and endeavor by good example and persuasion to induce them to receive missionaries and to submit to the king's authority. If, as was their custom, these Indians should steal horses or commit other crimes that could not be overlooked, and if they should refuse to make restitution, force might be used, but only with the least possible injury inflicted on them. No bodily punishment was to be administered either in the field or after their apprehension, and in no case might those arrested be sent into servitude as had been illegally done in the past. Rather, they were to be treated in the same manner prescribed for prisoners of war, and any women or children taken were to be restored to their families so that all might recognize that the arrests had been made in the interests of law and justice rather than of hatred or selfishness.

Thus, the *Reglamento de 1772*, while recognizing the Apaches as unworthy of a general amnesty, ordering a vigorous war against them, and providing for the deportation of captured warriors to the interior, also insisted on humane treatment for those taken prisoner and left the door open for coexistence under treaties of peace whenever the enemy should enter into them with apparent sincerity. Meanwhile, all friendly and neutral nations were to be courted without reservation.

The next important royal pronouncement of Indian policy appeared in the king's instructions of 1776 to the first commandant-general of the now autonomous Provincias Internas. Croix was admonished to give his primary attention to the reduction of the numerous pagan tribes to Christianity and allegiance to the king, for this was uppermost in the royal mind when he established the independent command. To this end Croix was to avail himself of the gentle and efficacious means required by the laws of the Indies; that is, cajolery, good treatment, peaceful persuasion, gifts, and genuine offers of the king's sovereign protection. And in all, the articles of the *Reglamento de 1772* were to be strictly observed.

The pious intentions of the king were never totally disregarded, but Indian policy was also influenced by the recommendations of hard-bitten troop commanders on the frontier, who saw the problem in a colder light. Croix was guided during his early years in office as much by the resolutions adopted by his councils of war at Monclova, San Antonio, and Chihuahua as by royal policy. As these advisory juntas were made up of governors and military commanders, practical officers such as those whom Rubí had interviewed, they readily endorsed the harsh recommendations of that inspector. They again singled out the Apaches as the only truly implacable enemy, urged Croix to wage a war of extermination against them, and called for the enlistment of the Nations of the North to assist in this bloody project. As a refinement of their own they also recommended dividing the Apache tribes themselves and pitting them against each other. They especially urged Croix to cultivate the Mescaleros and turn them against the Lipanes, their rival kinsmen. By following this advice Croix managed to turn the tide in the Apache war. All that was lacking for the achievement of total victory, he reported, was the arrival of the additional troops he had requested. Instead of reinforcements, however, he received an order from the king requiring him to curb his offensive operations. Spain was about to go to war with England.

The royal order of February 20, 1779, was something more than a stopgap measure requiring stringent economies on the domestic scene in order to prosecute an expensive war abroad. It was also a reassertion of and an enlargement on a consistent royal policy of conciliating the hostile Indians and treating them as human beings. Although its reversal of the aggressive policy recommended by Rubí, the *Reglamento de 1772*, and Croix's councils of war was only temporary, its insistence on peaceful persuasion was neither new nor transitory. In short, the royal order of 1779, ostensibly born of economic and strategic necessity, was consistent with traditional royal attitude and would be basic to subsequent crown policy.

As the minister of the Indies expressed it, the king would prefer lesser conquests by gentle means to more formidable ones with bloodshed; he would rather be remembered as a humanitarian than as a conqueror. The royal order went on to explain that the kind of military campaigns that had been successful in European wars would never pacify, let alone exterminate, the kind of enemy that infested the northern frontier of New Spain. The numerousness of these hostiles, their dispersion over a vast area, the little they had to lose by attacking, and the facility with which they took refuge in the rugged terrain all had become unhappily apparent in the offensives already waged against them. Their own terrain, their agility, their very poverty and nakedness, and even their cowardice and lawlessness had given them an advantage over the troops; and the military operations, far from reducing their raids, had elevated the enemy from petty thieves to astute warriors. Worse, their numbers were increasing, not only beyond the frontier, but well within it, for they were now being joined by previously friendly Indians, even those who had been converted to Christianity and subjected to civilized life in towns. The enemy, like shot, now threatened to pierce the Spanish defenses in a thousand places, to wear down and annihilate the soldiers, to impede the advance of the settlements, and even to force the Spaniards to give up lands they already held. Apparently the king was not impressed by Croix's reports that victory was in sight.

To remedy the unhappy situation Croix was instructed to abandon his plans for a great offensive thrust against the Apache and confine his operations to purely defensive action. He was to concentrate on protecting the towns, ranches, and other settlements. By maintaining his troops under rigid discipline and accustoming them to the kind of fighting required to ward off Indian attacks, he was to present a firm and powerful resistance. He was authorized to launch punitive expeditions, however, for it was hoped that these would dishearten the hostiles and persuade them either to withdraw from the frontier or seek peace and friendship.

Those hostiles who might surrender and aspire to live in peace were to be treated with gentleness, humanity, charity, and good faith. Croix was not to force them to settle in the Spanish towns or even to form permanent villages of their own, but was to leave them in their just and natural liberty. According to the official reasoning, if these Indians were not oppressed, injured, or forced to serve the Spaniards, they could be converted from enemies to friends, and they would then see for themselves the advantages of the rational life of the white man and the aid that organized society could offer them.

To encourage this Croix was to provide such Indians with gifts, not only articles they normally desired, but also others, which would offer them new comforts, and which could be obtained only from the Spaniards. In this way they would little by little come to prefer Spanish commodities to their own. They would then begin to imitate the Spaniards in agriculture and handicraft, lose their own natural aversion to manual labor, and convert their camps into more permanent settlements. If some of the tribesmen could be induced to come into the Spanish towns voluntarily, others would follow, especially when they saw the piety and justice of law and order. Thus, without their realizing it, those still hostile would diminish in number and those friendly would increase. In time they would abandon their rude customs and insensate attitudes and would even cover their nakedness with regular clothing.

Having quietly inspired the savages to seek the comforts and luxuries of civilization, Croix was to encourage them to use Spanish firearms for their hunting and defense. It was hoped that they would thereby forget how to use or even manufacture their native arms. This, of course, was a reversal of past policy, which generally attempted to keep guns out of Indian hands.

It was hoped that by introducing Spanish food, clothing, and even firearms to the unconquered tribes, they could be made dependent upon the Spaniards. Provided with these necessities and treated humanely, the Indians would then desire to become Spanish vassals. Croix was to redouble his vigilance to see that they were not treated as slaves, as they had commonly been up to that time, for the king wished them to be cared for as children. The final step in their pacification would be their conversion to Christianity by the peaceful persuasion of the clergy, and Croix was to assist in these efforts.

Such was the reasoning of the royal order of 1779. For the present it merely frustrated Croix's plans for an all-out war on the Apaches, but in time it would be basic to the remarkably successful strategy of Jacobo Ugarte y Loyola. Initially, Ugarte was bound by the royal policy enunciated in both the *Reglamento de 1772* and the royal order of 1779, but shortly both of these pronouncements were superseded by the celebrated *Instrucción* of 1786.

The *Instrucción* of 1786 did not introduce drastic changes in the Indian policy, as some historians have intimated. Almost its only innovation was a synthesis of the policies of the past, principally Rubí's recommendations of 1768, the *Reglamento de 1772*, the instructions to Croix of 1776, the resolutions of the councils of war at Monclova, San Antonio, and Chihuahua of 1777–78, and the royal order of 1779. To anyone fully acquainted with these pronouncements the articles of Viceroy Gálvez's instructions to *Comandante General* Ugarte should have a familiar ring. Although revolutionary in some few details, the *Instrucción* of 1786 was extraordinary mainly in its clarity of statement and detail in specification. Now, for the first time, a policy was stated in its entirety, given the force of a royal ordinance, and (thanks to Gálvez's previous frontier experience) accepted generally by the presidial commanders as a practical rather than ideal prescription for the ills of the Provincias Internas. Along with the *Reglamento de 1772* it remained fundamental policy throughout the remainder of the Spanish period. In 60 of the first 116 paragraphs of his instructions to Ugarte, Gálvez spelled out the basic procedure for dealing with the *indios bárbaros* of the northern frontier.

In justifying his approach to the problem, the Viceroy recognized that the nomadic tribesmen of the north were warriors by profession; that they were skilled not only in the use of their native weapons, but of firearms as well; that they were better horsemen than the Spaniards themselves; that they fought with agility, cunning, and valor; that they seldom struck unless certain of victory; and that, when pursued, they could always find refuge in the fastness of the rugged mountains. Gálvez was convinced that since they were unable to supply their own primary needs from hunting and gathering and since their own surplus of seeds, wild fruit, and peltries was seldom sufficient to trade for the Spanish horses, guns, ammunition, and ornaments that they craved, they had either to plunder or perish. He recognized that they sometimes made peace in order to obtain these commodities, either as presents or in trade for their own goods. But he also realized that their love of liberty and idleness together with their hunger, or greed, often led them to break these pacts. Sometimes, leaving their families in perfect safety where they still kept the peace, they would go off to raid where they had no such agreement; and they saw nothing wrong in this.

To deal with such an enemy Gálvez provided Ugarte with a vigorous plan for pacification. It was brutal and deceptive in the main, but temperate and just in some important respects, a finely-drawn compromise between the war of extermination recommended by Rubí and the peace by persuasion ordered by the king. As had others before him, Gálvez recognized that the several Apache tribes constituted the most implacable enemies on the northern frontier. But, owing to the widely varying estimates reported from that quarter, he was unable to determine the total number of their warriors. He was sure that they would never submit to Spanish rule voluntarily, but he felt that they could be weakened by division and induced to destroy themselves. Accordingly, Ugarte was to exploit the existing discord between the Apaches and the Nations of the North and that among the separate Apache tribes themselves, reviving especially the bloody conflict that formerly existed between the Mescaleros and the Lipanes.

Ugarte was not only to divide and conquer; he was also to display alternately the feathers of the hawk and the dove. On the one hand he was to wage an incessant war on the heathen marauders, attacking them in all of the provinces, in their own lands, at all seasons of the year, and without respite. But, on the other hand, he was to accept their overtures for an armistice whenever offered, even without sincerity. In view of the inadequacy of the military forces on the frontier, a bad peace, as Gálvez put it, was better than a good war. He recognized that the northern tribes were fickle and often made peace only in bad faith, but, he pointed out, the Spaniards were guilty of the same insincerity. Moreover, even though the Indians might break the peace many times, they would seek it again whenever confronted by the renewal of a vigorous war. Ugarte must require the Spaniards to observe scrupulously the terms of each peace and compel the Indians to do likewise, punishing the latter for their serious breaches of the terms but overlooking their trifling violations. By waging a vigorous and incessant offensive against tribes that openly broke the peace, Ugarte would subject them to a constant pressure and deprive them of the advantages they had enjoyed under the terms. This, in turn, would incline them to seek peace again and make it more lasting.

In order to satisfy the requirements and desires of the savages, improve their way of life, and also reduce them economically to Spanish vassalage, Ugarte was to promote trade with those who made peace. Although such concessions were admittedly deceptive, Gálvez felt that they would be more fruitful than open warfare in achieving pacification. So that the Indians might not be cheated in the exchange of goods and thereby become antagonized, Ugarte was to provide strict regulations for such trade. Moreover, he was to expect losses rather than profits at first, for the Indians had little of value to offer. In the long run, however, this would reduce the number of hostiles, for the one-sided benefits of the exchange would provide the Indians with their needs and desires and eliminate the necessity for their plundering of Spanish settlements. The Spaniards would then be able to reduce their expenditures on military forces and eventually realize incomparable gains from such economizing. The savings thus effected, however, should be invested in presents for the peaceful tribes. Outright gifts were essential, Gálvez thought, because whatever the Indians could obtain in barter for their paltry trade goods was wholly inadequate to supply their needs and thus keep them at peace. Thus, whenever a band of Indians concluded an armistice, the local commandant was to reward the petty chief with from fifteen to twenty pesos worth of goods and provisions and issue each of the warriors one or two pesos worth of such supplies for himself and his family.

Even the implacable Apaches, once they were weakened by the internal dissension that Ugarte was to promote, could gradually be made dependent by accustoming them to Spanish foods, drinks, clothing, and arms issued as gifts or exchanged in trade. Perhaps they would even become greedy for the possession of land. It would not be easy to establish trade with the Apaches, Gálvez admitted, except for the Lipán tribe. The Lipanes had valuable furs to offer, and they had a craving for dried meat, raw sugar, maize, tobacco, brandy, guns, ammunition, knives, cloth, clothing, vermillion, mirrors, glass beads, and especially horses, mules, and cattle. If the Lipán Apaches could be induced to maintain abundant herds of their own, Gálvez thought, they would be less inclined to make raids on Spanish livestock.

In the past there had been a serious attempt to keep intoxicating liquor from the Indians, especially the hostiles, but Gálvez now reversed this policy. The French had introduced the liquor trade into Louisiana, and while he was governor of that province, he had seen it work to the advantage of the white man. He now believed that it could be practiced with the same effect in the northern provinces of New Spain. By encouraging the Indians to develop a taste for spirituous beverages, he reasoned, the Spaniards could gain and maintain their good will by supplying it to them. Furthermore, liberal indulgence in this new delight would induce them to divulge their secrets, forget about raiding, and, as habit made a necessity of this luxury, even become more dependent on the Spaniards.

Firearms had also been traditionally withheld from the Indians, except for a few presents to friendly chieftains and for those issued temporarily to auxiliaries and allies for campaigns against the hostiles. The royal order of 1779 had endorsed a freer dissemination of these weapons, but Gálvez now attacked the entire notion that they were more effective to the Indians as weapons than were bows and arrows. An Indian bow, he insisted, could discharge an arrow with force enough to pierce either a bullhide shield or the heaviest quilted leather jacket. While it was true that an arrow's range was less than a bullet's, the hostile Indians regularly kept well beyond gunshot distance whenever they were outnumbered, and when they had a numerical advantage they closed in for hand-to-hand combat. Furthermore, for each musket shot fired at them they were able to return many arrows with telling effect; and when their bowstrings became loose, they could tighten them more quickly than they could repair or even reload a musket. Thus, if the Indians could be induced to abandon the bow for the gun, Gálvez reasoned, they would be at a decided disadvantage. Guns were more difficult to obtain, repair, and operate effectively than bows, and so the Spaniards should be more liberal in trading muskets, powder, and ball to the Indians. However, he cautioned, the muskets should be long ones. These would be awkward for an Indian to use while on horseback. They should also have weakened barrels, stocks, and bolts, making them easily damaged and in continuous need of readjustment, repair, and replacement by skilled Spanish gunsmiths. Having accepted firearms, the Indians would abandon their native weapons, lose their skill with them, and become dependent upon the Spaniards for both the supply and maintenance of their new ones.

For one reason or another, probably because of the short supply of firearms for the troops and settlers themselves, this intriguing recommendation seems never to have been carried into full effect, at least during Ugarte's administration.

Having laid down these general guidelines, Gálvez got down to the specific problems of the individual provinces and the procedures that Ugarte should follow in resolving them.

The province of Sonora, beleaguered by the Gila Apaches from the north, was in a precarious situation. It was necessary to reduce the Seris and Tiburones, who were again in rebellion. However, Ugarte was instructed to wage no campaign against them unless he was certain of its success, for on the first signs of Spanish weakness the Gileño invasions from the north would deluge the province. The Sobaipuris and Piatos should be kept at peace and, along with the Opatas and Upper Pimas, used in campaigns against the hostiles. The Yaquis, Mayos, and Indians on the Río Fuerte, who were now living in mission towns, should be attracted to work in the mines. This would keep them busy and out of trouble, and it would also replace the workers who had abandoned the mines because of Apache attacks. The Yumas, near the confluence of the Gila and Colorado Rivers, were to be left alone, notwithstanding their treacherous massacre of Spanish settlers there in 1781. No action was to be undertaken against them until after the Seris, Tiburones, and Gileños had been conquered. When the Gila Apaches had been defeated, or at least chastised, Gálvez was confident that the other hostiles would fall more easily.

The Californias, isolated from the barbarous tribes by the high sierras and the Gulf of California, presented no such problems. Most of the Indians there were living at peace, either in their own communities or in mission towns. Ugarte was to see only that they remained at peace, that they not be allowed to use horses, and that their innocence be preserved.

Nueva Vizcaya, being immediately to the east of Sonora, was of major concern. This extensive province was frequently invaded—from the northwest by the Gila Apaches and from the northeast by both the Mescaleros and Lipanes. Although the Lipanes were supposedly at peace, they occasionally perpetrated robberies and attributed these violations to the Mescaleros. Gálvez, however, was especially apprehensive over the Tarahumaras, an interior nation that had long been reduced to mission towns. Although these Indians had not revolted openly since 1728, their loyalty had long been suspect, and Gálvez feared that the continuing Apache invasions would incite them to a general uprising. Many Tarahumaras had already fled their missions and reverted to heathenism, and some had gone over to the Apaches. Ugarte was to exercise great prudence to prevent further defection. Other Tarahumaras were being driven to despair by an all-too-vigorous prosecution for their alleged transgressions. Ugarte was to bring an end to this harassment, offer the Tarahumara renegades a general amnesty, provide those already imprisoned with an immediate trial, send those convicted to Mexico City without delay, remove all vagrants of other nations from their villages, and allow the magistrates, priests, and missionaries to handle all Tarahumara criminal cases locally and without notoriety. Some of the Tarahumaras had become acquainted with Gálvez when he was a military commandant in Nueva Vizcaya. Should any of these wish to present their grievances to him personally, Ugarte was to provide them with military escort and allow them to come to the viceregal capital to do so.

In New Mexico Ugarte was to maintain the long-standing peace with the Utes in the north and employ them against the Comanches to the northeast and the Navahos to the west whenever the latter two should become hostile. He was also to keep the peace with the Jicarilla Apaches in the northeast and court favor with the Comanches by conceding to both whatever they requested at the annual trading fair at Taos. He was to attract the Navahos by gifts and trade concessions and vigorously encourage the recent rift between them and their former allies, the Gila Apaches. He might allow the Apaches to the south (Faraones, Mimbreños, and Mogollons) to come to El Paso for trade, but he must keep these under skillful surveillance so as to prevent their raiding the settlements of Nueva Vizcaya. Finally, Ugarte was to keep Gálvez promptly informed on developments in the still apostate Moqui (Hopi) towns in the west.

Since the eastern provinces—Texas, Coahuila, Nuevo León, and Nuevo Santander—were being separated from Ugarte's command, the details for their administration were addressed to Colonel Juan de Ugalde. As *comandante de armas* of this division, Ugalde was to be subordinate to Ugarte, but he was also vested with authority to act first and report afterwards. Ugalde was to wage incessant war on the Mescalero Apaches, who were the only openly hostile tribe in the eastern provinces, and these campaigns were to be conducted at his own discretion. However, whenever the Mescaleros should sue for peace, they were to be granted it under prescribed terms. Although the Comanches, Nations of the North, and the Lipán Apaches all continued to keep the peace they had signed in Texas and Coahuila, they were not to be trusted. Yet, their friendship was to be maintained at all costs, for their employment against the hostile tribes was vital to Gálvez's over-all strategy. While the ancient and irreconcilable hatred between the Lipanes on the one hand and the Comanches and Nations of the North on the other was to be skillfully and discreetly promoted, Gálvez would hold Ugalde or any other officer involved strictly responsible for any unprovoked act that might result in war with either of these groups. Gálvez himself would reserve the right to determine whether or not war, even under provocation, might be declared. Ugalde was to exploit the enmity between the Mescalero and Lipán Apaches and keep them divided by any means he could devise, but he was to prevent the Lipanes from attacking the

Nations of the North or the Mescaleros, and the Nations of the North and the Comanches from attacking the Spanish settlements. Finally, Ugalde was to report regularly on the activities of the Borrados, or Chichimecos, in Nuevo Santander and recommend means to reduce these nomads, whose treason and bloody thievery had continued in spite of their armistices.

Summarizing his lengthy instructions for the conduct of Indian affairs, the Viceroy considered it possible to drive the openly hostile tribes from the frontier settlements or force them to make peace by means of incessant military operations; to attract those who sued for peace to a tranquil life and a dependence on the Spaniards by making trade concessions and presenting them with gifts; to induce those who broke the peace to seek it again by renewing the war against them; and to weaken those who remained hostile by exploiting their intertribal rivalries and baser instincts. In short, Gálvez was especially interested in promoting the self-destruction of the Apaches, since they were the avowed enemy of the Spaniards along the entire frontier.

In order to give lasting force to his comprehensive instructions to Ugarte, the Viceroy submitted them to the king's minister of the Indies for royal approval. In so doing he admitted that the detailed statement actually deserved more time than he was able to devote to it, especially for informing himself more fully on the true state of conditions in the frontier provinces. He had been obliged to dictate the instructions in the brief moments of respite that his illness and his infinite other duties allowed. He had drawn on his long experience in the Indian wars and on the advice of competent authorities whom he had convened for the purpose. The result was a formula, which established a basic system for the conduct of Indian affairs—one which linked the rigors of incessant war with both the benevolence of peace and the friendly ties of reciprocal commerce. Admittedly these pronouncements would not in themselves remedy the difficult problems of the frontier provinces, but they would open the way for other, more solid measures, which in time could bring nearer the longed-for general pacification. The king's approval of the *Instrucción* of 1786, giving it the force of a royal ordinance, was communicated to Ugarte on February 27, 1787.

SUGGESTED READINGS

Edward Spicer, *Cycles of Conquest: The Impact of Spain, Mexico, and the United States on the Indians of the Southwest, 1533–1960* (Tucson 1962);

Alfred B. Thomas, *Forgotten Frontiers: A Study of the Spanish Indian Policy of Don Juan Bautista de Anza, Governor of New Mexico, 1777–1787* (Norman 1932);

Thomas, *The Plains Indians and New Mexico, 1751–1778* (Albuquerque 1940);

Thomas, *Theodore de Croix and the Northern Frontier of New Spain, 1776–1783* (Norman 1941);

Marc Simmons, *Spanish Government in New Mexico* (Albuquerque 1968).

8
Land Grant Problems

The land grant problem is possibly the most persistent one in New Mexico history. It may also be the most volatile. During the nineteenth century certain individuals were able to absorb huge amounts of land, and Thomas B. Catron of the Santa Fe Ring was at one time probably the largest landholder in the United States. Fraud was common, and land grants sometimes grew overnight as owners managed to extend the boundaries of their grants. Land disputes, therefore, kept lawyers busy and provided political issues.

Dr. Myra Ellen Jenkins, state historian and the leading expert on the land grant question, points out that land grant problems were not limited to Anglos and Spanish-Americans. Indians also became involved in legal disputes as they struggled to preserve their lands, and, because of extensive land problems involving the Pueblo Indians, the Pueblo Lands Board was created in 1924.

Dr. Jenkins' study of the Baltasar Baca Grant provides an excellent case study of Pueblo land problems. In this case it was Laguna Pueblo which suffered encroachment on its lands. The dispute over the Baca Grant lasted for several centuries, and it was not until 1939 that the Indians recovered part of it. This selection describes the early years of the dispute.

In spite of the mass of legislation designed to protect the Indians in all the lands they used or occupied, the most serious problem of the New Mexico pueblos from the Spanish Colonial Period to the present century has been that of white trespass. The intent of a Spanish monarch and his Council of the Indies thousands of miles away, and the practices of officials in the new world were different matters. Governors often ignored the laws, and the special officials appointed for Indian protection paid little attention to their

---

Myra Ellen Jenkins, "The Baltasar Baca 'Grant': History of an Encroachment," *El Palacio*, vol. 68, no. 1, spring 1961, pp. 52–64.

duties or used their authority to exploit the natives. The office of *alcalde mayor* was probably the weakest link in the Spanish government of New Mexico. By the middle of the 18th century the region was divided into eight *alcaldias* each administered by an *alcalde mayor* responsible to the governor for the conduct of affairs within his jurisdiction. The alcaldes settled problems among the Indians, or between whites and Indians; notarized legal documents; investigated requests for land grants and placed grantees in possession; collected legal fees and tributes; and sometimes led forces against hostile tribes. They were, however, to obey scrupulously all the laws and decrees concerning Indian welfare and title.

Unfortunately, the laws were honored more in the breach than in the observance. The most influential Spaniard in the area was generally given the post of *alcalde mayor* for political favor and he in turn, especially if there were more than one pueblo in his jurisdiction, would appoint another member of his family or a close friend as assistant. The activities of corrupt alcaldes, and of those governors who abetted them, aroused the wrath of the Franciscan padres since these abuses interfered with Indian conversion. Confiscation of Indian supplies for the benefit of the alcaldes, forced labor, mistreatment of pueblo women and the appropriation of Indian land were major subjects of most 18th century Franciscan accounts. Prominent among the offending alcaldes in the Laguna area were Bernabé Baca and his son, Baltasar.

The antecedents of this Baca family are as yet unknown. Bernabé was apparently born in 1692, probably in Mexico, and resided in the Albuquerque region much of his life. As *alcalde mayor* of Ácoma and Laguna during the 1730's he was so unpopular with the Indians that they signed a complaint against him for extortion and other abuses on December 23, 1733. This was only the first of many Indian actions against Bernabé and his descendants for the next two hundred years.

Baltasar Baca, as alcalde of Laguna from about 1771 to 1774 was singled out by the Franciscans as one of those officials who most flagrantly mistreated the Indians as well as the priests who attempted to stop their abuses. In the spring of 1772, Fray Joaquín Ildefonso Rodríguez buried some forty-three Lagunas who had died "of the plague," probably small-pox, and noted that their suffering was made worse "with the plague of the alcalde Baltasar Baca." According to the account of Fray Joaquín de Jésus Ruiz, Baca had left Fray Rodríguez abandoned in the mountains for three days without food and exposed to inclement weather and hostile Indians. Fray Juan Agustín de Morfi, describing alcalde offenses in "Desordenes," mentioned Baltasar Baca, and his successor Pedro José Pino, as "among the ones that are most outstanding in these tyrannies."

More serious than these abuses, however, was the encroachment of the Bacas, and their close friends, the Pinos, on Laguna lands. Late in 1768

Baltasar Baca, on behalf of himself and his two grown sons, applied to Governor Pedro Fermín de Mendinueta for a grazing permit to a piece of land

> which is situated in the opposite direction from the Pueblo of Laguna, more than three leagues therefrom, a little more or less, and from the site of the Encinal about a league and a half, more or less, with which land I do not injure the said Encinal nor the ranches of the Ácoma and Laguna Indians, for they will forever remain secure, they nor I sustaining damage. The land is vacant, uncultivated, unsettled, and unappropriated, as I have ascertained, and the boundaries are: on the east to where the league of the Encinal may extend, on the west a mesa close to the Zuñi road, on the north the mountain, and on the south some white bluffs, the whole comprising somewhat more than a league and a half in width and about two and a half in length.

Governor Mendinueta, on December 16, authorized Laguna alcalde Antonio Sedillo to measure off a league of 5,000 Castilian *varas* westward from the site of the Encinal, and if there were no legal objections by any of the adjoining settlers, he was to place Baca and his two sons in control of the area. However, the governor specified definite restrictions on the grantees:

> And this grant I do make to father and sons in equal shares, for them and their successors, for the pasturage of their herds of stock, and not in any case for planting, and under the following conditions: that they do not abandon the residence they do now occupy; that they shall not sell the same to any ecclesiastical person; that they shall not injure the ranches and fields of the Indians of the pueblos of Ácoma and Laguna in that vicinity and much less the un-Christianized Apaches of the Navajo province.

Sedillo placed the Bacas in possession January 19, 1769.

In his application, Baca listed his residence as "the plaza of Our Lady of Belén," and from the terms specified by the governor it was obvious that Mendinueta intended that the Bacas should continue to live in that place. There is no indication that the land use grant was intended as anything other than a grazing permit, certainly not a title in fee simple, as Baca was not to plant crops nor to interfere with Indian use of the land.

Laguna Indians have long maintained that their ancestors grazed a large part of the land included in the permit, except during periods of Navajo encroachment. That the Spanish authorities were aware that both Lagunas and Ácomas were using part of the area, or land very close to it, is apparent from the wording of the restrictions. It would appear that even the grazing permit itself violated injunctions against Spanish herds being permitted to graze close enough to Indian lands to endanger crops. The site of the Encinal was a Laguna summer camp in the latter part of the 1700's, until the 1820's or 30's, when it became a settled village. Recent anthropological research of Professor Florence Hawley Ellis establishes various Laguna herding sites in the area, and Laguna pottery of the late 1700's and early 19th century were found at the site of the hacienda constructed by Marcos Baca in the 1840's. Furthermore, there is no indication in any of the documents or evidence introduced by descendants of Baltasar Baca in later litigation that he or his sons actually used the land for any purpose, or that any Baca claimant attempted to use it before 1846. Hence, even the grazing permit would have expired if the land had not been occupied for four years after the grant. Neither the relation of Fray Francisco Atanasio Domínguez in 1776, nor a report on the region sent to governor Juan Bautista de Anza to Mexico in 1779, nor the Fray Juan Agustín de Morfi account of 1782, report any Spanish occupation in the Encinal area, although de Morfi notes that there had once been "a ranch of Spaniards" there. He also stated that the Navajos were then using the land. From various 18th and 19th century narratives, as well as other documents, it appears evident there were a few Navajos in and out of the Cubero-Encinal area at different times. Their brief periods of occupation usually occurred during intervals when this tribe was on peaceful terms with the Spaniards, and for the most part they were friendly with the Pueblo Indians who did not oppose their presence in the region.

As Spanish colonial power disintegrated throughout the new world, before the independence of Mexico from Spain, the position of the pueblos grew even more precarious. Administration of the *Recopilación* virtually broke down in spite of an occasional conscientious official. The central government was too weak to curb abuses and non-Indian encroachment became more frequent. Joaquín Mariano Pino, in 1815, moved into El Rito lands east of the pueblo which the Lagunas had been permitted to use and occupy and, over the protests of the Indians and the alcalde, José Vicente Ortiz, Pino was given the land by Governor Allande. After the Cebolleta region, which Laguna was cultivating as late as 1779, was granted to thirty Spaniards from Albuquerque in 1800, trespass was constantly threatened from the north on the tract known as the Paquate. That the Pueblo of Laguna owned the Paquate before 1769 is clear from a statement made by alcalde Antonio Sedillo on May 15 of that year to the effect that he had settled a dispute among the Indians of the region involving a Pascual Pajarito "who had made a ranch within the limits of the land of the pueblo" and the Paquate family.

The southern boundary of the Cebolleta grant of 1800 was designated as "the Mesa del Gabilan which adjoins the rancho of Paquate." This mesa lies about two miles north of the Laguna village of Paquate. Laguna title to the region was respected by the Spanish authorities. When on July 14, 1808, alcalde José Manuel Aragón requested that the area be given to the

Cebolleta settlers, the request was refused because Lorenzo Gutierres, the alcalde from Albuquerque sent to investigate the matter, saw the document signed by Sedillo. A statement of March 13, 1813, of Laguna holdings also listed the Paquate as belonging to the pueblo.

The Cebolleta settlers, however, still encroached into the northern valleys of the Paquate, and in 1820 a Laguna delegation took its case to the Jémez alcalde, Ignacio María Sánchez Vergara, who was also Protector-General of the Indians of New Mexico for the Audiencia of Guadalajara. Sánchez Vergara determined that the region was Laguna's, "by virtue of the ancient possession of said lands to which the said natives refer, called the rancho of Paquate, acquired by legal title." At about the same time a Eusebio Aragón made a copy of the Sánchez Vergara decision for the Laguna delegation and listed specific boundaries for the Paquate which previous documents had failed to do:

> The aforesaid rancho and its boundaries in the direction of Cebolleta remained free with its ancient appurtenances as far as the Mesa del Gabilan, on the south to the cuesta, on the west to the Rita del San José, and on the east to the Cañoncito del Cojo.

Most of the land included in the Baca grazing permit clearly lay within these boundaries. Whether Laguna grant title to the Paquate originally extended as far west as the Baca permit cannot be determined, although the United States so held in issuing the Paquate patent to the pueblo a half century later in 1884.

Few changes were made in the legal status of New Mexican Indians by the treaty of Córdoba, August 24, 1821. Spanish land laws were continued and most officials exercised the same powers as before. Until 1824 New Mexico remained a *provincia interna,* administered by a governor in civil matters and the *comandante general* of Chihuahua in military affairs. From January 31 to July 6, 1824, it was joined with Chihuahua and Durango as the *estado interno del norte.* However, New Mexico became a territory on July 6, 1824, and remained in that status until 1837 when, under the domination of Antonio López de Santa Ana, Mexico adopted a centralist constitution and executive power was greatly increased. New Mexico then became a department and was divided into prefects. None of the Mexican constitutions provided a comprehensive form of government for the northern frontier. The national congress had legislative authority, but the central government was too busy with affairs at home to pay much attention to the northern territory. The chief executive of New Mexico, known as the *jefe político* until 1837, was appointed by the national government. The *comandante general* of Chihuahua had military control until 1839 when Manuel Armijo took over these duties as well. Until 1824 there was a provincial deputation of from four to six men. From 1824 to 1837 this body became the territorial deputation, but at no time did it have any real power and it functioned as an advisory council, rather than as a legislative body. It was usually composed of close associates of the *jefe político*. When Antonio Narbona was replaced by Manuel Armijo in May, 1827, less competent executives were chosen and a small native clique secured control of affairs.

The Pueblo Indians suffered even worse abuses under the Republic of Mexico, for now virtually all checks were removed. By the Treaty of Córdoba, Indians were granted citizenship and land rights were continued, but nothing was done to implement this provision by specific legislation or orders to the chief executives.

Narbona, however, made some attempt to prevent encroachment. On August 28, 1826, a Laguna delegation consisting of the governor, the cacique, and the war governor confronted him with their documents concerning the Paquate and petitioned that he make them safe in these holdings. Narbona saw the justice of this request and wrote at the bottom of the petition: "Let it be done as is asked, returning all to the interested parties for their use and convenience." He also endorsed their documents, including the Eusebio Aragón designation of the Paquate boundaries, with the following statement: "This document is approved so far as this government is concerned and legal and formal in its contents."

Trespass did not end, however, and in less than a year another Laguna delegation was back in Santa Fe with another complaint against the Cebolleta settlers. Unfortunately for the Indians, however, Narbona had been succeeded by Armijo less than a month before the delegation's arrival. The new *jefe político* had little interest in pueblo land rights and less concern for Indian justice and took no action. Narbona's approval of Laguna title to the Paquate with the boundaries cited in 1820 was not questioned in any litigation during the Mexican Period, although large areas of the Paquate, including the Baca permit, were occupied by trespassers.

The *alcaldes mayores* under Spanish rule had often been guilty of extortion, forced labor, and illegal use of land, but there were a few restraints on their activities. Once in a while a governor would send in an alcalde from another jurisdiction to investigate land claims if the resident official seemed to be partial, and sometimes the visiting alcalde would decide in favor of the Indians. Several governors had permitted the pueblos to expand their holdings when their areas were insufficient. The Indians could appeal to the Protector-General when their rights were flagrantly abused. The Franciscan padres were a deterrent to mistreatment although the offending officials often ignored their castigations. Now, however, the alcaldes were virtual dictators, except in the larger settlements, since they were the local law-enforcing officials and judges in criminal and civil matters. The *jefes políticos* usually paid no attention to their actions; there was no Protector-General to whom the Indians could appeal. The Franciscan missions were secularized after 1826 and many of the pueblos, including Laguna, were without a resident priest. The office of alcalde was usually bestowed upon a member of one of the same families who had profited from it in the days of Spanish control. Under these conditions it was but natural that the Bacas and Pinos would continue to control affairs at Laguna and further their own interests. Marcos Baca, like his great-grandfather, Baltasar, was one of the most notorious.

The record is not clear as to when Marcos Baca became alcalde of Laguna, but he held that office in 1830 when his mistreatment of the Indians was so flagrant that Vicente Romero, one of the delegation who had protested Cebolleta encroachment in 1827, took the pueblo's case against Baca and Joaquín Mariano Pino to Mexico City, and hired attorney Manuel Castañeda y Najero to represent the Indians before the Attorney-General. The complete *expediente,* including the testimony, is apparently not extant and some of the details are obscure. Castañeda y Najero submitted the complaint to Attorney-General José Ignacio Cobarruvias November 9, 1830, charging that Baca had illegally seized land from the pueblo, physically mistreated the Indians, levied illegal taxes, and compelled forced labor. The complaint asked that Baca be ordered off Laguna land:

> There is more than sufficient merit in this case as appears from the expediente in order to proceed with the investigation of the arbitrary and illegal conduct of the constitutional alcalde of the said pueblo, Don Marcos Baca. Your Excellency will be pleased to order that in justice the proper proceedings be instituted against the said alcalde and that he shall leave the vicinity of the said pueblo for a distance of six miles, all of which I will duly explain.
>
> The acts with which Baca is charged are public and notorious . . . . Baca has demanded cultivated lands which according to the customs of time immemorial should not be paid. Without hearing the parties he actually drew up necessary expedientes. He should not have exacted taxes for himself, although in justice they should be paid. However, he knowingly tramples under foot the laws without apparently hearing or without protecting according to law the unfortunate party which I represent . . .
>
> Contrary to law Alcalde Baca dares to beat the unfortunate Indians, he collects from them many fines by forcing them to do public work for the benefit and profit of a single individual. Knowing the wretchedness of the natives he has converted himself into a tyrant of the Laguna pueblo. Can his action remain unpunished? And shall the unfortunate Indian residents of the far away pueblos be abandoned by the supreme powers?

There is no evidence that the case was tried. However, Baca must have resigned or have been removed shortly thereafter, but he continued to live in the Laguna area. In 1833 his father, José, and some sixty-one other citizens of Albuquerque settled at Cubero, about nine miles northwest of the pueblo on lands used by both Ácoma and Laguna Indians. The land he was accused of having appropriated from Laguna in 1830 apparently lay east of the southern limit claimed by the Cuberos, since a document of May 12, 1841, allegedly settling a boundary conflict between Laguna and the Cubero residents, stated that the division should be:

> . . . on the south, two crosses raised on some rocks facing each other on both sides of a cañada, a distance of 674½ varas from the home of the citizen Patricio Chaves, and the same distance in varas from the aforesaid crosses to a juniper tree which was recognized and is recognized as the boundary of the citizen D. Marcos Baca. The said tract of land from the juniper to the crosses remained as the property of the Pueblo of Laguna, admitting as valid the deeds which under the accustomed formalities may have been made in favor of the citizen Marcos Baca by the members of the aforesaid pueblo.

Meanwhile, affairs in New Mexico continued to go from bad to worse. Jefe Político Albino Pérez, appointed in 1835, attempted to bring some competence into the government, but as he was not a native New Mexican the ruling clique constantly opposed him. His death at the hands of the rebels in the 1837 uprising resulted in the assumption of power by Manuel Armijo, probably one of the conspirators, whose venality went unnoticed and unrebuked by the authorities. In August, 1846, Armijo surrendered New Mexico to United States forces under Brigadier-General Stephen Watts Kearny without a struggle.

SUGGESTED READINGS

Herbert O. Brayer, *Pueblo Indian Land Grants of the "Rio Abajo," New Mexico* (Albuquerque 1938);

Victor Westphall, *The Public Domain in New Mexico, 1854–1891* (Albuquerque 1965);

Brayer, *William Blackmore: The Spanish-Mexican Land Grants of New Mexico and Colorado, 1863–1878* (Denver 1949);

William A. Keleher, "Land Law of the New Mexico Land Grant," *New Mexico Historical Review,* vol. IV (October 1929);

Clark S. Knowlton, "Land Grant Problems among the State's Spanish-Americans," *New Mexico Business,* vol. XX (June 1967).

9
The Significance of the Santa Fe Trade

When William Becknell, "father of the Santa Fe trade," opened commerce between Santa Fe and Missouri in 1821, he accomplished a goal that had eluded French and American traders for approximately a hundred years. Traders from the Mississippi Valley had indeed reached New Mexico during this period, but they had been unsuccessful in developing trade contacts with this outpost of the Spanish empire. Imperial regulations prohibited such trade with foreigners. However, using a route which had been traversed earlier by Pedro Vial while he was employed by the Spanish government, Becknell arrived in New Mexico immediately following Mexican independence and was welcomed by the New Mexicans who were now freed from the domination of Chihuahua merchants.

In *New Mexico's Royal Road,* Max Moorhead describes and evaluates the importance of the Camino Real—the old trade route between Chihuahua and Santa Fe on which New Mexico depended so long for its existence—and its extension to Missouri in 1821. American goods also flowed into Chihuahua by the old Camino Real, and this trade was important to Chihuahua and Sonora as well as to New Mexico and Missouri.

In this chapter on the significance of the economic connection between Mexico and the United States, Moorhead assesses its social, intellectual, and economic impact. The quarter century immediately following Mexican independence was the heyday of the Camino Real, and its commercial traffic "significantly altered the political and economic growth of the United States and, to a lesser extent, the social and economic growth as well." The most important result of this commerce was that Mexican silver had a stabilizing effect on the monetary system of the United States and particularly of Missouri, but in addition it stimulated various sectors of the economy, such as the mule industry, of the Mississippi Valley.

In New Mexico the commerce brought new and cheaper goods, raised the standard of living, and made the population increasingly dependent on the American trade. This dependence and the influence of American merchants who resided in New Mexico amounted to an economic conquest that prepared the way for the military and political conquest of New Mexico in 1846.

In 1848 the Treaty of Guadalupe-Hidalgo brought an end not only to the Mexican War but also to an era. Thereafter the Chihuahua Trail—although developing from a wagon trace into a stage road, into a railway, and ultimately into a paved automobile highway—was only one of several major inland trade routes between the United States and Mexico. Its principal rival was a shorter road through Texas. The heyday of the Camino Real was the quarter of a century immediately following the independence of Mexico from Spain. During that era its commercial traffic significantly altered the political and economic growth of the United States and, to a lesser extent, the social and economic growth as well. It also raised the standard of living of the New Mexicans, made them more dependent upon the Americans, and facilitated the military invasion which changed their very citizenship. These historical influences can readily be demonstrated, but the volume and value of the trade which wrought these changes can never be accurately measured.

The returns from Mexico were chiefly in specie and bullion—some gold dust but mostly silver bars and coin—but it is impossible to calculate how much they were worth from year to year. The traders were even more close-mouthed on this score than on their investment in goods, and so only fragmentary reports were publicized: $180,000 for 1824, at least $200,000 for 1829, $100,000 in 1832 from one company alone, and more than $200,000 in 1834 for another single company. Almost as incomplete and probably less reliable were the statistics reported by the New Mexican customs house, thanks both to official negligence and private evasion. During the fiscal year 1834–35, for instance, Santa Fé reported collections on the export of specie amounting to only $403 which, at the prevailing duty rate of 3.5 per cent would indicate that only $1,141 were exported in that season. For the calendar year 1842 collections were reported on only $49,656 worth of silver and for 1843 on only $46,950. Not all of the remainder escaped taxation, however, for the Chihuahua traders frequently returned by way of the Gulf of Mexico and cleared their money through Brazos de Santiago instead of Santa Fé.

In addition to the silver coin which the traders received for goods retailed, a considerable amount of money in silver bars was obtained from their wholesale operations and from purchases from mine operators. These bars, weighing between fifty and eighty pounds each and worth one to two thousand dollars, were assayed by authorized Mexican agents and were stamped with their proper weight and fineness, making them a convenient form of currency for large transactions. As they usually brought 10 per cent above their nominal value when presented at a United States mint, some traders in Chihuahua and Durango made special trips to the mines expressly to buy silver bars. On their return to the United States, they presented their bullion to the mint at Philadelphia. That of New Orleans was closer to their circuit of operations, but, as Gregg tells us, it had a bad reputation among the merchants of his acquaintance.

Probably the most vital influence of the overland trade on the economy of the United States was the stabilizing effect which this Mexican silver exercised, especially on the monetary system of Missouri. Before the beginning of the trade, Missouri, like other western states and territories, suffered acutely from a shortage of hard money, a rapid depreciation of "wild cat" bank notes, and a wide circulation of counterfeit paper bills, all of which embarrassed even the most ordinary business transactions. The influx of Mexican silver from the Santa Fé and Chihuahua trade admirably shored up this shaky monetary system. By the close of 1824, the Mexican peso had reached Missouri in such numbers and was circulating so freely that it was accepted by the federal land office in Franklin at par weight with the American dollar; by 1828 it was more common in the western counties of Missouri than the dollar itself; and by 1831 it constituted the principal circulating medium for the entire state. Although never legal tender in the strictest sense, the peso contained 374 grains of fine silver as compared to only 371.25 for the American dollar, and was therefore preferred at this time to the national coinage by most of the people in the western communities.

The abundant influx of Mexican silver made Missouri unique among the agricultural states in its popular preference for "hard" money, and it may well have influenced Senator Benton's own well-known proclivities for sound currency. More significantly, it enabled Missouri to weather more easily than other states the Panic of 1837 and the six-year depression which followed. When the crash came, Missouri was the only state in the Union without one or more state-incorporated banks, and only after the depreciated bank notes of neighboring states flooded it and threatened to drive out hard money did the legislature establish such an institution of its own. The Bank of Missouri, founded in 1837, gained a reputation as being one of the soundest state banks in the nation. Serving as a depository for the silver of returning traders, it was able to pay in specie from the very beginning, and its notes commanded a premium of 7.5 per cent over those of other western banks. During a "run" in 1839, it was saved from probable disaster by the timely deposit of $45,000 in silver by returning overland merchants.

Another branch of the American economy which the Mexican trade stimulated was the mule-breeding industry, especially in Missouri, where it reached a celebrated pre-eminence. As early as 1823, some four hundred jacks, jennets, and mules were brought to Missouri by a returning caravan; in 1824, over six hundred; in 1827, eight hundred; and in 1832, thirteen hundred. Many of these and their offspring were shipped to the southern plantations, where there was quickly developed a preference for mules over horses as draft animals. Until mid-century little breeding was done in Missouri itself, but it was an important center of the mule trade, which itself was a profitable enterprise during the early years. In 1829 jacks and jennets purchased in Chihuahua and Sonora at from seven to ten dollars a head brought sixty dollars in the United States. By 1840 they were selling at a sacrifice, and after the outbreak of war with Mexico, on account of the unusual demands of the American army, the New Mexican and Chihuahua prices were raised from forty to seventy-five dollars. Meanwhile, in the 1830's, the so-called Missouri mule made its appearance. The Mexican jack when bred with the American mare produced a larger and stronger mule than that raised in Mexico, and the offspring of an American stallion and a Mexican jennet was considered superior to the *macho*, its Mexican counterpart. However, all of the mules, jacks, jennets, and horses entering the United States for this industry did not arrive by way of the Chihuahua and Santa Fé trails. Virginia relied largely on jacks and jennets from Cuba; New Orleans and Natchez bought large herds driven from the Mexican state of Tamaulipas; and others were brought overland from the missions of California by the mountain men. By the 1850's, when Missouri became recognized around the world as a "mule kingdom," it produced an even larger animal than before. At that time most of the jacks came from Kentucky, where they were carefully bred from Spanish, Cuban, and Maltese stock. The Missouri mule soon won a preference over that of Mexico for farm work and wagon pulling, but the smaller Mexican animal found an important place in the pack trains of the United States Army.

Early attempts to introduce New Mexican sheep into Missouri were less rewarding. Sheep, the chief export of that province to the interior of Mexico, could be purchased from the poorer *rancheros* for from fifty to seventy-five cents a head, and wool, which brought fifteen cents or more a pound in Missouri, could be bought in New Mexico for from three to four cents.

It was inferior in quality to that produced by American sheep, however, and failed to compete successfully. The sheep of New Mexico were far more celebrated for their meat than for their fleece.

The intellectual and social influences of the inland trade are more difficult to assess. In an era of national expansion—"manifest destiny" as it was then known—it was only natural that the American public craved information and inspiration from the land to the west of the settled frontier, and it was likewise fitting that the letters, diaries, and memoirs of early adventurers in the new land should find their way into print. It was from these personal narratives that a new genre of American literature was born—the "western." But before the "dime novels," "penny dreadfuls," and other lurid fiction made their appearance—replete with Indian attacks on wagon trains, scalpings, stampedes, buffalo hunts, prairie fires, desert mirages, dark-eyed señoritas, half-breed villains, and fair-haired heroes—the factual raw materials had first to be reported. The Oregon Trail had its Francis Parkman, the Rocky Mountain fur trade its George Ruxton, and the Santa Fé trade its Josiah Gregg. Zebulon Pike's factual *Expeditions* (1810) must be considered the pioneer effort, and George Kendall's graphic *Narrative of the Texan Santa Fé Expedition* (1844) an important complement, but Gregg's *Commerce of the Prairies* (1844) was the finest and fullest description. It was an adventure story, nature study, historical treatise, travel guide, and handbook for traders, all rolled in one. Other memoirs of traders and travelers on the Chihuahua Trail which caught the public fancy and were forerunners of the "western" were James O. Pattie's *Personal Narrative* (1833), Ruxton's *Adventures in Mexico and the Rocky Mountains* (1847), and John Taylor Hughes' *Doniphan's Expedition* (1847).

The social influences of the trade stem not only from the widespread effects of this literature but also from the first-hand contacts of teamsters and traders with the people of northern Mexico. And the attitudes which they developed demonstrated that international contact in itself does not always promote international harmony. Although some of the veteran traders such as the Magoffins became tolerant of the striking cultural differences between their hosts and the people back home, most of the Anglo-Americans showed a prejudice against the Spanish culture as deep and bitter as that of their ancestors in Elizabethan England. By declaration or intimation they pictured the Mexican as superficially polite and generous, but more often undependable, treacherous, dishonest, and addicted to gambling, inebriation, promiscuity, and other vices which were frowned upon, although practiced none the less, in their own homeland. The Roman Catholicism of the Mexican was extremely abhorrent to the predominant Protestantism of these frontiersmen. Although they were hostile toward such prevalent Mexican forms of amusement as the bullfight, cockfight, and rodeo in its original form, they fully enjoyed the *fandangos* and card games. The Mexicans, on the other hand, looked upon the *americanos* as political expansionists, economic materialists, religious heretics, and cultural barbarians. Yet a most striking result was the frequent intermarriage of the two nationalities. Most of the resident American merchants married into Mexican families, learned the Spanish language, and remained on good terms with the people of the country even after the outbreak of the war.

As has already been demonstrated, the main political influence of the inland trade was in paving the way for the American "bloodless conquest" of New Mexico. A quarter-century of New Mexican association with American traders had not only brought about an economic dependence on them, but also a measure of respect and admiration, especially for their ability to deal effectively with hostile Indians. The influence of James Magoffin and Henry Connelly in dissuading Governor Armijo and Colonel Archuleta from resisting the Army of the West has already been discussed, as have the services of the Trader Battalion to Doniphan's column. Of perhaps equal importance was the fact that when New Mexico was annexed to the United States and made an organized territory, a surprisingly large number of American traders became the political as well as commercial leaders of the new commonwealth. Had they not done so, and had new faces appeared from the East to govern it, the Spanish-speaking population might have received a much less sympathetic treatment and have been slower to accept the new order.

The influences of the trade on Mexico itself were much more pronounced. The most significant change was the reorientation of New Mexico's trade. Previously its commerce was entirely with Chihuahua and the other cities to the south. Unfavorably balanced, it drained away New Mexico's short supply of gold and silver coin and thus compounded the poverty of the province. The overland trade from the United States, while adversely affecting the internal trade of central and coastal Mexico, was a boon to the frontier. Now, thanks to greater competition among the merchants, lower taxes, and fewer losses to Indian raids, the expensive imports from the south were more cheaply obtained from the east. Especially after the passage of the Drawback Act of 1845, the overland caravans brought, at prices much lower than those of Veracruz and Mexico City, not only the domestic manufactures of the United States but also the superior products of Europe. The resulting loss of profits to Mexico importers and freighters constituted a corresponding gain to the New Mexicans. Now they were able to buy immense quantities of imported dry goods and hardware and sell them to the interior in competition with those entering from Veracruz, Tampico, Mazatlán, Guaymas, and Acapulco. Moreover, the New Mexicans were now in a position to demand specie from the south for these wares, and the imbalance of their interior trade was thereby reversed.

By 1839 several wealthy New Mexican merchants were taking their own trains to the United States to buy at wholesale for the Mexican market. Less is known of these traders than of those of Missouri, but their importance was fully as great. Most of the *ricos* of the province—the Chávez, Perea, Ortiz, and Otero families—became merchants as well as feudal lords. José Chávez y Castillo, who became acting governor of New Mexico in 1848, purchased eleven wagonloads of dry goods in the United States in 1840 and a large consignment of English goods in New York in 1846. Mention has already been made of Antonio José Chávez, who was robbed and murdered on the Santa Fé Trail in 1843. His brother, Mariano Chávez, of Padillas, sent $26,474 worth of imported goods from Santa Fé to Chihuahua in 1844, and during the same season several other New Mexicans carried American goods to the south, principally to Chihuahua, Durango, Zacatecas, and Aguascalientes. Among these were the brothers José and Juan Perea with goods valued at $25,128, Antonio J. Ortiz with two consignments ($17,878 and $2,102), Antonio José Otero with another two ($2,341 and $2,385), Manuel Antonio Otero ($2,326), Santiago Flores ($5,837), José Salazar ($892), Governor Manuel Armijo ($10,309), and Ambrosio Armijo ($18,049). The Governor was buying goods from the United States at least as early as the summer of 1841, when he lost over $18,000 worth of merchandise being shipped from St. Louis to Independence. By 1845 he had run up an outstanding debt of $6,000 and nineteen ounces of gold with P. Harmony, Nephews and Company of New York.

Even more important than the enrichment of the merchants of New Mexico was the elevation of the standard of living of their customers, which was brought about by the large-scale introduction of both necessities and luxuries at lower prices. Before the trade from Missouri was developed, the New Mexicans, except for the *ricos*, were not only virtually without real money but also without almost any kind of clothing except leather and homespun, and almost without iron or steel tools of any kind. There was not a single printing press in the province, and there was a deplorable scarcity not only of books but also of paper. Medical supplies other than native herbs and potions were equally rare.

Within a few years after 1821, however, most of these needs were available in quantity. The market was soon flooded with textiles of almost every kind: broadcloth, cotton prints, shirting, drills, muslin, bandana, cords, denim, flannel, taffeta, calico, percale, cambric, pongee, velvet, velveteen, nankeen, lawns, linen, silk, and cashmir. Almost every conceivable article of clothing and personal adornment became readily available. And by the 1840's the women of New Mexico and Chihuahua were aping even the styles set in Paris. Curiously enough, the fashion leader in

New Mexico was not one of the provincial aristocracy but Gertrúdiz Barcelo, a notorious *monte* dealer.

Little imagination is necessary to visualize the effect on domestic industry of the wholesale introduction of tools. Now there were iron and steel implements for carpentry, housekeeping, farming, and hunting. There were also the common drugs of the day: alum, Seidlitz powders, Epsom salts, cologne, saffron, cream of tartar, sulphur, balsam, spirits of nitrate, cathartic salts, bicarbonate of soda, emetic tartar, and assorted pills for various ailments.

The new trade brought in comforts to the mind as well as the body. Books, although not in great quantity, began to make their appearance in Santa Fé assortments. Josiah Gregg, for instance, brought in 1,141 books in one year (1834). Although several of these were for his own use to while away the winter hours at his Santa Fé store and only 30 of them were in the Spanish language, over 700 were designed for use in primary schools. William Hooke introduced 22 books that same year; Hiram Smith, 10; and Philip Houck, 24. New Mexico's first printing press fully equipped with type was also imported from the United States in 1834, by Gregg and his partner, Jesse B. Sutton. It was entered duty-free and was almost immediately put to use by Father José Antonio Martínez of Taos, who during four weeks of the same year published the province's first newspaper, *El Crepúsculo.* This publication lapsed after Martínez's election to the national congress, but the press continued in operation and produced several primers, catechisms, and loose-leaves.

The introduction of American wagons was another boon to northern Mexico. Previously the only vehicles available to the ordinary people were the homemade oxcarts fashioned entirely of wood whose wheels were so irregular, axles so ill fitting, and total construction so unwieldy that two oxen were required to pull a load easily drawn by one in a conveyance of American manufacture. Since the American traders returned to the east with little cargo, they needed only a few of their wagons and sold the others with their regular goods. The native merchants were eager buyers, but so were those from the south, for in 1843 there were more than one hundred American wagons owned and operated by the citizens of the state of Chihuahua.

American wagons were veritable fortresses on wheels and, together with superior American firearms and the undaunted confidence of American traders and teamsters, gave their caravans something of an immunity against Indian attack on the Camino Real. Real security from Indian raids had never been provided by Mexican authority, either local or national, and Mexican trains, large or small, were forever the victims of marauding Apaches and Navajos. Such was the reputation of the caravans from

Missouri that Mexican traders often delayed their departures until they could accompany American merchants, and the provincial governments sometimes availed themselves of the same protection for important mail and money shipments. Samuel Magoffin's wagons were chartered by the government at Chihuahua to carry the Santa Fé garrison's pay roll in 1842, one Mexican sergeant and five soldiers constituting the "official" escort. To some extent, then, the well-armed American caravans served to patrol the highways and keep the hostile tribes in check.

The annexation of Texas in 1845, the temporary occupation of Nuevo León, Coahuila, and Chihuahua during the next two years, and especially the acquisition by the United States of additional Mexican territory in 1848, reoriented the trade of northern Mexico once more. North of the Río Grande ford the Camino Real was now an American road, and El Paso del Norte replaced Santa Fé as the Mexican port of entry. However, with Texas now a recognized part of the United States, many of the American traders now took a short cut through that state. The Chihuahua Trail of Texas stretched from Indianola on the western shore of Galveston Bay through San Antonio and the Davis Mountains to El Paso. From San Antonio, other wagon roads took a more southerly direction, crossing the Río Grande at Del Río and Eagle Pass and reaching Chihuahua by way of Monclova and Guajoquilla. These routes were well established by 1851 and flourished until superseded by the Galveston, Harrisburg and San Antonio Railroad in 1877 and the Southern Pacific shortly thereafter.

The Santa Fé Trail remained the most important route linking the Mississippi Valley with New Mexico until the completion in 1880 of the Atchison, Topeka and Sante Fe Railroad from Chicago to the Río Grande. This line, curiously enough, by-passed Santa Fé itself, but in the same year the Denver and Rio Grande Western completed a track from the north which passed through the city and connected with the Santa Fe line at Lamy.

The Chihuahua Trail was superseded by rails in 1882. In that year the A. T. and S. F. extended its track from Santo Domingo on the upper Río Grande to El Paso, Texas, where by crossing the river it connected with the just completed Mexican Central Railroad. The latter, originating at Mexico City, followed the old Camino Real all the way north through Chihuahua to Ciudad Juárez, the former El Paso del Norte.

In summary, the Chihuahua Trail exerted several significant influences on a strategically important region. The wagon trace blazed by Oñate's emigrant train at the close of the sixteenth century from the mining camps of northern Mexico to the Pueblo towns on the upper Río Grande proved to be not only the most feasible route thither but also the very life line of a new frontier civilization. Over this trail passed the mission and merchant caravans which kept New Mexico alive in the seventeenth and eighteenth centuries. By means of a near monopoly of this traffic, the merchants of Chihuahua impoverished the province, but their stranglehold was broken by merchants from Missouri early in the nineteenth century. At first these so-called "Santa Fé traders" exchanged only the produce of Missouri for that of New Mexico, but within a few years they were buying better goods more cheaply in the distant Atlantic seaports of the United States and Europe and, by following the Camino Real beyond Santa Fé, were selling in the larger and richer cities of the Mexican interior.

By availing themselves of larger wagons, sturdier draft animals, greater capital, longer credit terms, and more effective government protection, they developed a complex and far-flung business whose volume and value increased almost annually. By resorting to contraband and connivance, they subverted the restrictions imposed on them by the Mexican government. By underselling the merchants of the interior, they provided New Mexico with sufficient necessities and luxuries to raise its standard of living and weaken its dependence upon central Mexico. By taking payment in silver, they bolstered the economy of their homeland. And by recording and publishing their exciting experiences in the West, they helped give birth to a new genre of American literature.

During the war between the United States and Mexico their road to Chihuahua facilitated the American invasion, and their own influence over the people and governments of northern Mexico was turned to American military advantage. After the war many of them participated actively in the administration of the conquered territory, and by so doing rendered less difficult and painful to both sides the pacification of New Mexico. Finally, their historic wagon road between Santa Fé and Chihuahua was not forgotten in the onward march of civilization, but remained instead essentially the route still followed by the most modern means of transportation.

SUGGESTED READINGS

Josiah Gregg, *Commerce of the Prairies* (Norman 1954);
Jack Rittenhouse, *The Santa Fe Trail, A Historical Bibliography* (Albuquerque 1971);
Noel M. Loomis and Abraham P. Nasatir, *Pedro Vial and the Roads to Santa Fe* (Norman 1967);
Leo F. Oliva, *Soldiers on the Santa Fe Trail* (Norman 1967);
France V. Scholes, "The Supply Service of the New Mexico Missions," *New Mexico Historical Review*, vol. V (January, April, and October 1930);
Max Moorhead, "Spanish Transportation in the Southwest, 1540–1846," *New Mexico Historical Review*, vol. XXXII (April 1957);
Robert M. Utley, "Fort Union and the Santa Fe Trail," *New Mexico Historical Review*, vol. XXXVI (January 1961).

10
Conquest of New Mexico

From the moment that the first shot was fired, politicians and historians have been debating the causes of the Mexican War. They have made studies of public opinion, party and sectional attitudes, and the motivation of President James K. Polk and suggested that Manifest Destiny, commercial interests, and Mexico's refusal to negotiate contributed to the conflict. Despite the controversy surrounding the Mexican War, which has recently been compared to the war in Vietnam, there is little doubt that Polk was determined to use this opportunity to acquire California and New Mexico for the United States. Almost immediately Stephen Watts Kearny, an experienced frontier officer, was placed in command of the Army of the West.

As the army marched toward Santa Fe, agents were sent forward to convince the local population to accept American control; a bribe was apparently offered to Governor Manuel Armijo, and Kearny repeatedly promised to protect the lives and property of the inhabitants. "Not a pepper, not an onion, shall be disturbed or taken by my troops without pay or by the consent of the owner," he said; and he also promised to give protection from the Indians. Those who resisted, however, would be hanged.

Ralph Twitchell, author of several useful works on New Mexico history, describes the conquest of New Mexico, and although he does not deal at length with the reactions of the people to United States control, he does describe conspiracies which developed after Kearny departed for California. He also describes the rebellion of 1847 that erupted in parts of northern New Mexico and resulted in the death of Governor Charles Bent and other leading figures. Historians have not, however, analyzed the depth or extent of opposition to American rule, nor have they explained whether New Mexicans were opposed to

American rule from the beginning or whether the rebellion was the result of resentments that developed following the conquest.

On the 24th day of April, 1846, the Mexican general, Arista, informed General Zachary Taylor, in command of American forces on the lower Rio Grande, in Texas, that "he considered hostilities commenced and should prosecute them." On the same day, a party of dragoons, sent out by General Taylor, became engaged with a superior force of the Mexican army in which sixteen Americans were killed and the others captured. On the 13th day of May following, President Polk, by proclamation, announced the existence of war with Mexico. Volunteers were called for by the governors of several of the states and the president asked congress for authority to call for troops and for means to carry on the war.

The United States immediately began the formation of plans for the invasion of New Mexico, Chihuahua, and California. An expedition, called the Army of the West, was organized and its command given to Colonel, afterwards Brigadier-General, Stephen W. Kearny. The command consisted of two batteries of artillery, Major Clark; three squadrons of dragoons, Major Sumner; 1st regiment of Missouri cavalry, Colonel Doniphan; and two companies of infantry, Captain Angney. The march across the plains from Fort Leavenworth to Santa Fé was commenced in the latter part of June, 1846. When concentrated upon the Arkansas, near Bent's Fort, the entire command consisted of 1,558 men and sixteen pieces of ordnance. The exact point of concentration is not known, but it is said to have been at a point nearly nine miles below the fort. It was here that the expedition was joined by Francis P. Blair, Jr., afterwards named by Kearny as district attorney for New Mexico. On the 31st day of July, at Bent's Fort, General Kearny issued the following proclamation, which was distributed as the army proceeded: "The undersigned enters New Mexico with a large military force, for the purpose of seeking union with and ameliorating the condition of its inhabitants. This he does under instructions from his government, and with the assurance that he will be amply sustained in the accomplishment of this object. It is enjoined on the citizens of New Mexico to remain quietly at their homes, and pursue their peaceful avocations. So long as they continue in such pursuits, they will not be interfered with by the American army, but will be respected and protected in their rights, both civil and religious. All who take up arms or encourage resistance against the government of the United States will be regarded as enemies, and will be treated accordingly."

At this point Kearny despatched Lieutenant De Courcey, with twenty men, to the Taos valley, for the purpose of ascertaining the disposition of the inhabitants in that portion of New Mexico, with instructions to report to him en route. This officer joined the column August 11th, on the Poñil, a stream in Colfax county, bringing in a number of prisoners who gave exaggerated accounts of the Utes and other Indians joining the Mexicans in opposing the American advance.

On August 2d, Captain Philip St. George Cooke, of the 1st dragoons, with twelve men, was sent to Santa Fé, nominally as an ambassador, but really for the purpose of escorting James Magoffin, who was the real emissary on the part of the American government, as he was entrusted with a secret mission and having full instructions from the president of the United States.

Captain Cooke and his party arrived safely at Santa Fé on the 12th of August where he was hospitably received by General Armijo, the governor of the territory. Armijo had been advised by the alcalde at Las Vegas, Juan de Dios Maes, that Cooke was on his way to Santa Fé, having sent a messenger over the mountains by a short route to the capital. Although Armijo informed Captain Cooke that it was his opinion that "the approach of the army was rather sudden" he concluded to send a commissioner to General Kearny in the person of Dr. Henry Connelly, with whom on the following day, Captain Cooke set out on his return to meet the army.

If we may predicate our judgment by subsequent events Magoffin proved himself a very astute and convincing emissary. On the 8th of August General Armijo had published and sent into all parts of the territory his proclamation, couched in bombastic terms, calling his people to arms to meet the invader, and still, though the response to this call was very flattering, Armijo, when the crucial moment arrived, deserted his post at Apache Pass and fled to Mexico.

The fact that the government at Washington, even to this day, refuses to disclose the contents of the papers filed by Don Santiago Magoffin, in which it is believed that Magoffin "itemized" his expenditures, lends color to the general belief that the same means which had theretofore purchased favors for the Santa Fé traders enabled Magoffin to convince General Armijo that it was best for him that he abandon the idea of making any defense at the Apache Pass, a point on the route to Santa Fé which might have been held by a very few men of spirit and bravery. One hundred men, fairly well armed, behind the entrenchments which Armijo had prepared, with the cannon which he had, could have successfully commanded the pass and compelled the American army to take another course in its march to Santa Fé.

It was not so easy a matter, however, to compromise and conciliate some of the officers of the army, but in this the customary Hibernian wit, coupled with his known plausibility, enabled Magoffin to arrange matters with Archuleta, the second in command. He called this officer's attention to the proclamation of General Kearny in which the general only claimed the territory *east of the Rio Grande*, and suggested to him that by proclamation he might secure for himself all of western New Mexico. By thus appealing to Archuleta's ambition, the American "ambassador" succeeded in securing an open road to Santa Fé.

On the 13th of August the army had arrived at the Sapello river, where Kearny was advised that the Mexican forces were assembling at Apache canyon, about fifteen miles from the city of Santa Fé; that the pass was strongly fortified and that Kearny had best go around it by way of Ojo de Vaca and Galisteo. The day following the American general received word from Armijo that he would meet him on the plains near Las Vegas, the message being delivered by an officer of lancers, accompanied by a sergeant and two privates. At this point the army was joined by Major Swords, Lieutenant Gilmer, and Captain Weightman, who brought with him and presented to Kearny his commission as brigadier-general. These officers had heard that a battle was to be fought the following day near Las Vegas and had ridden sixty miles in order to participate in the engagement.

On the morning of the 15th of August, 1846, precisely at eight o'clock, General Kearny and staff galloped into the plaza of Las Vegas, where he was met by the alcalde, Don Juan de Dios Maes, and a concourse of people. Pointing to the top of an adobe building, one story in height, and located on the north side of the plaza, General Kearny suggested to the alcalde that if he would go to the top of the building, he and his staff would follow, and from that point, where all could see and hear, he would speak to them, which he did as follows:

> "Mr. Alcalde and People of New Mexico: I have come amongst you by orders of my government, to take possession of your country and extend over it the laws of the United States. We consider it, and have done so for some time, a part of the territory of the United States. We come amongst you as friends, not as enemies; as protectors, not as conquerors. We come among you for your benefit, not for your injury.
>
> "Henceforth I absolve you from all allegiance to the Mexican government, and from all obedience to General Armijo. He is no longer your governor [great sensation in the plaza]; I am your governor. I shall not expect you to take up arms and follow me to fight your own people who may oppose me; but I now tell you, that those who remain peaceably at home, attending to their crops, and their herds, shall be protected by me in their property, their persons and their religion; and not a pepper, not an onion shall be disturbed or taken by my troops without pay, or by the consent of the owner. But listen! He who promises to be quiet and is found in arms against me, I will hang!
>
> "From the Mexican government, you have never received protection. The Apaches and the Navajós come down from the mountains and carry off your sheep, and even your women, whenever they please. My government will correct all this. It will keep off the Indians, protect you in your

persons and property; and I repeat, will protect you in your religion. I know you are all great Catholics; that some of your priests have told you all sorts of stories; that we would ill-treat your women and brand them on the cheek, as you do your mules on the hip. It is all false. My government respects your religion as much as the Protestant religion and allows each man to worship his Creator as his heart tells him is best. Its laws protect the Catholic as well as the Protestant; the weak as well as the strong, the poor as well as the rich. I am not a Catholic myself; I was not brought up in that faith, but at least one-third of my army are Catholics and I respect a good Catholic as much as a good Protestant.

"There goes my army! You see but a small portion of it; there are many more behind; resistance is useless.

"Mr. Alcalde, and you two captains of militia! The laws of my country require that all men who hold office under it shall take the oath of allegiance. I do not wish for the present, until affairs become more settled, to disturb your form of government. If you are prepared to take oaths of allegiance, I shall continue you in office and support your authority."

The captains did not protest but looked with downcast eyes upon the earthen roof upon which they were standing. Noticing his attitude, General Kearny said to one of them, in the hearing of all the people: "Captain, look me in the face, while you repeat the oath of office!" The oath was administered through the interpreter, Robidoux, and the general and his staff descended, mounted, and galloped away to the head of the column.

The sun was shining brightly; for the first time since leaving the Missouri river, the guidons and colors of each squadron, battalion, and regiment were unfurled. The trumpeters sounded "to horse" with spirit and the rocky hills to the west multiplied and re-echoed the call.

Leaving Las Vegas, it was expected that the troops would meet with some opposition at a point a few miles distant, but nothing occurred and the command moved on toward Tecolote where Captain Cooke and Dr. Connelly were met. Here and at the next town, San Miguel del Bado, the general made the same character of address as had been made at Las Vegas.

At every step reports came to the general that Armijo had collected a formidable force and would oppose his passage at Apache canyon. When the command reached the ancient town of Pecos, Kearny was notified by a Mexican coming from the direction of Glorieta that Armijo and his army had ingloriously fled.

On the morning of the 18th of August Kearny had reached a point twenty-nine miles from Santa Fé. Not a hostile arrow or rifle was now between the Army of the West and the ancient capital of New Mexico. The general determined to make the march in one day and raise the American colors over the ancient palace before sundown. Fifteen miles from Santa Fé the column reached the point deserted by Armijo. It is a gateway, which, in the hands of a competent engineer and one hundred resolute men would have proved a second Thermopylae. As has been said, had the position been defended with spirit and ability, General Kearny would have been compelled to turn it by taking the road by way of Ojo de Vaca and Galisteo. On the way to Santa Fé Kearny was met by the acting secretary who brought a letter from Vigil, the lieutenant governor, which informed the general officially of the flight of Armijo and of his readiness to receive him in Santa Fé with the hospitalities of the city.

The advance of the American column arrived in sight of the city of Santa Fé at three o'clock in the afternoon of the 18th of August, 1846; by six o'clock the entire army was at the confines of the capital. The general and his staff, and some other officers of the army, were received at the old palace by Lieutenant-governor Vigil, assisted by about thirty representative citizens of the city. Refreshments were served by Governor Vigil and as the sun sank behind the far-distant Jemez and Valles mountains, painting the clouds which overhung the lofty ranges with a glorious combination of saffron, opal, purple, and golden color, the American flag was hoisted over the ancient palace and a salute of thirteen guns from cannon planted on the eminence, afterwards known as Fort Marcy, declared the conquest of New Mexico complete.

Kearny and Doniphan had no sooner left the territory than rumors of intended revolt among the natives were constantly being circulated. These could be traced to no authoritative source. It was also believed that Mexico intended sending a substantial force from Chihuahua for the purpose of regaining the territory. This belief was entirely shattered when news came of the battle of Brazito. General Price had nearly two thousand men with whom he felt fully able to keep the territory in subjection, although many of these were on the sick-list. The main force was stationed at Santa Fé. Small detachments were stationed at other towns, notably Albuquerque, on the Mora and another at Cebolleta, on the Navajó frontier. But with all their belief in their ability to handle the situation, Santa Fé came near proving a Capua to the American soldiers. Frequent altercations occurred between the Mexican inhabitants and the soldiers; the natives, naturally, were jealous of foreign interference; many of the disbanded militia which Armijo had called out lingered in the vicinity of Santa Fé, ready to be employed, if opportunity presented itself; the civil officers who had been displaced viewed Governor Bent, Secretary Vigil, and the other appointees under the newly established government, with emotions of hatred and ill-will. The Pueblos were violently hostile and some of the most prominent and influential citizens in the territory, led on by the clergy, as is well known, labored to foment the disaffection which was rapidly gaining ground. News that an insurrectionary movement was on foot and apt to be launched at any moment came to General Price through Secretary Vigil. Don Diego Archuleta, who considered that he had been cheated, owing to the representations made to him by Santiago Magoffin, was a leader in the movement. He was ably assisted by Don Tomas Ortiz and others. When Price was notified he immediately caused the arrest of those supposed to be implicated and an investigation was had, in the course of which it appeared that a plan had been formed for a general uprising on Christmas eve. The principal leaders, Ortiz and Archuleta, escaped in the direction of Chihuahua, the project was further frustrated by the arrests which had been made and in a few days the alarm entirely subsided.

The leaders of this revolution were men of restless and unsatisfied ambition. Their inactivity lasted but a brief period. A second and still more dangerous uprising was plotted. The experience gained in the failure of the first attempt prompted the most absolute secrecy in the formation of the plans for the second. Everywhere in the northern counties the people secretly began to arm and equip themselves; this was not known to the military authorities, and on the 19th of January, 1847, the rebellion broke out in several parts of New Mexico. On the 14th of January, Governor Bent had left Santa Fé to visit Taos; five days later he was foully assassinated in his own residence in that village. Early on the morning of the 19th of January, the insurrectionists, led by Pablo Montoya and a Taos Indian, known as Tomasito, entered the city, joined the resident members of the revolutionary movement and began the attack. The houses of the resident Americans were destroyed. The Indians, under the leadership of Tomasito, visited the house of Governor Bent, and firing through the door, wounded him in the chin and stomach; the door was next broken down and his body pierced with arrows. Amidst the fiendish yells of the Indians he was scalped.

Intelligence of the murders committed at Taos and elsewhere reached Santa Fé on January 20, and circulars written by the revolutionists, calling upon the people of the *Rio Abajo* for aid, were also intercepted. The lower order of Mexicans of the Taos valley and of the small towns in the vicinity rose en masse and joined with the Pueblo Indians in the work of pillage and murder. They organized themselves into a revolutionary army, appointed leaders, and sent circulars to different parts of the territory inciting the people to rebellion. All the towns in the northern part of the territory except Tecolote and Las Vegas declared in favor of the insurrection. At the last named place an attempt to incite the population was defeated by the timely presence of Captain Hendley, of Lieutenant-Colonel Willock's battalion, with a portion of his grazing detachment. At Arroyo Hondo, some twelve miles from Taos, at Turley's mill, eight men were attacked and seven killed on the same day as the massacre of Governor Bent.

SUGGESTED READINGS

Albert K. Weinberg, *Manifest Destiny* (Baltimore 1935);
Frederick Merk, *Manifest Destiny and Mission in American History* (New York 1963);
Otis Singletary, *The Mexican War* (Chicago 1960);
Justin H. Smith, *The War with Mexico* (New York 1919);
David Lavender, *Bent's Fort* (Garden City, N.Y. 1954);
Dwight Clarke, *Stephen Watts Kearny: Soldier of the West* (Norman 1961);
Ralph E. Twitchell, *The Military Occupation of New Mexico, 1846–1851* (Denver 1909);
E. K. Francis, "Padre Martinez: A New Mexican Myth," *New Mexico Historical Review*, vol. XXXI (October 1956).

II
Failure of the Confederate Invasion

Although Americans have shown an undying interest in the Civil War, few authorities have been attracted by events of the 1860s west of the Mississippi River. Certainly the West did not seem important in April 1861 when Confederate cannons opened fire on Fort Sumter, but fighting did occur in the West, and in 1861 Confederate forces invaded New Mexico providing a potential threat to Colorado Territory and California.

After Lt. Col. John Baylor occupied the southern portion of New Mexico and created the Confederate Territory of Arizona in the region south of the 34th parallel, Brigadier General Henry H. Sibley, a former U.S. officer who had been stationed in New Mexico, was authorized to conquer New Mexico, probably as a first step toward acquiring part of California and making the Confederacy a sea to sea power. Sibley invaded New Mexico in February 1862, fought briefly with Union forces at Fort Craig, and continued north to Santa Fe. At Glorieta Pass, however, the Confederates met resistance. Although technically the battle was a Southern victory, it was the turning point of the war in New Mexico since the Confederate supply train was destroyed by Colorado troops under Colonel John Chivington. Sibley, therefore, began a retreat marked by intense suffering.

In this selection Professor Martin H. Hall evaluates the campaign, describes the condition of the returning invasion forces, and discusses the response in Texas and Richmond to this defeat.

Though the exact number of Confederate casualties resulting from the campaign is not known, the toll was, nonetheless, very heavy. At least eighty had been killed outright on the several battlefields, while some of the over two hundred wounded later died of their wounds. Diseases such as smallpox

---

and, particularly, pneumonia carried many to the grave. The three hospitals left behind in Santa Fé, Albuquerque, and Socorro were filled with sick and wounded, and all along the line of retreat the Confederates had abandoned those too ill to continue. Over 100 Texans had been captured at Apache Canyon and Peralta. In addition, the Federals had taken a number of stragglers. It is probably not an exaggeration to estimate that, either because of battle or disease, around 500 Confederates had lost their lives during the course of the campaign. If such was the case, Sibley's casualties amounted to 1,000 men. Consequently, of his invading force of nearly 2,500 men, only about 1,500 formed the army which straggled back to the Mesilla Valley at the close of the disastrous venture to capture New Mexico. Of the large train which had accompanied the army, only seven wagons remained. With the exception of the six guns captured at Valverde, all the artillery had been buried, captured, or destroyed. To say the least, the campaign had left the Army of New Mexico in a shattered condition.

After establishing temporary headquarters at Fort Bliss, Sibley wrote the adjutant general a brief, but full account of his campaign. Far less exuberant than he once had been, Sibley reluctantly expressed the conviction, "determined by some experience, that, except for its political geographical position, the Territory of New Mexico . . . [was] not worth a quarter of the blood and treasure expended in its conquest." This, of course, was not startling, since most Confederate expansionists from the first had viewed New Mexico solely as a means to an end, namely a stepping stone toward a port on the Pacific.

Sibley maintained that lack of supplies alone had necessitated his evacuation of New Mexico. He had found, as expected, that the land could not be relied upon for food or other goods. But, unexpectedly, he had failed to capture great stockpiles of Federal war matériel. Rather than admit he had underestimated the ability of his opponent, Sibley blamed lack of specie for his failure to obtain adequate supplies. Since Captain William H. Harrison, the brigade paymaster and quartermaster, had never left San Antonio, the General pointed out that he had had to wage his entire campaign "without a dollar" in the quartermaster's department. Hard money was virtually nonexistent, and one thousand dollars was all he could raise for the use of his hospitals and secret service. Sibley noted that adequate supplies could have been purchased in Mexico, but since the merchants there refused to accept anything but specie, the Army of New Mexico consequently from the beginning had been hindered by lack of war matériel of all kinds.

In summing up his operations, Sibley toned down the true condition of his army. Undoubtedly he was reluctant to give a thoroughly accurate picture lest he suffer loss of prestige in Richmond or, worse still, be severely censured and reduced in rank. His men, having suffered intensely during the campaign, naturally manifested a "dogged, irreconcilable detestation" of New Mexico and her people. The troops were eagerly awaiting only the time when they would take up the line of march for San Antonio.

When Sibley had been retreating down the Río Grande, the Confederacy had been suffering reverses elsewhere. The month of April witnessed the bloody battle of Shiloh and the fall of New Orleans. Even with these great disasters attracting his attention, General Paul O. Hébert, commander of the Department of Texas, had not forgotten the New Mexican campaign. When he received Sibley's urgent pleas for reinforcements, he ordered two regiments of cavalry which had been intended for service in Little Rock to march to his support. But communications were slow, and Hébert had not received notice that Sibley had already evacuated New Mexico.

In faraway Virginia, McClellan had begun his Peninsular campaign and was pressing upon Richmond. On the very day of the opening of the Battle of Seven Pines, May 31, 1862, Robert E. Lee, general in chief under the President, informed Hébert that Jefferson Davis had received reports of Sibley's destitute and critical condition and had approved his sending the two regiments of reinforcements. Lee advised Hébert to send at once all the supplies he could for Sibley's use. In this matter, he suggested that the departmental commander call upon the governor of Texas for assistance.

The first news of reinforcements came to Sibley through unofficial channels. During the latter part of May the week's mail brought information from several reliable persons that the government intended to send Sibley one or more regiments. In fact, Colonel X. B. Debray was supposedly already en route. Hamilton Bee, commander of the Western District of Texas, reportedly had announced that New Mexico and Arizona were to be held at all costs. All this was exceedingly distressing, for neither Sibley nor his men were desirous of engaging in another New Mexican campaign!

In a determined effort to forestall the sending of reinforcements and thus the renewal of the campaign, Sibley hastily wrote Bee a far more accurate account of the condition of his army than he had presented in his report to the adjutant general. Sibley pointed out that he had evacuated New Mexico because his provisions, forage, and ammunition had been completely exhausted. He warned that any force sent to operate in New Mexico could not expect to rely upon the country for supplies. In the vicinity of the Mesilla Valley and Fort Bliss, Sibley found himself but little better off. Having confiscated all spare supplies in the Mesilla Valley, he now ordered his foragers to secure all available provisions and transportation from the villages below Fort Bliss. Sibley's troops were in desperate straits, and were presently subsisting on a limited supply of poor meat and bread. Such luxury items as coffee and sugar were virtually nonexistent. With clothing stocks gone, the men were clad in rags—many were almost naked. Only about a hundred rounds of ammunition remained for the heavy guns. The army's sick and wounded were suffering from lack of medicines and other necessities. To be sure, with specie, supplies could have been purchased on the Mexican side of the river. In the area now held by Sibley's men, Confederate currency was selling at the rate of twenty cents on the dollar, and large amounts could have been bought for less had there been any purchasers.

Sibley lamented that he had sent report after report to his superiors during the recent campaign, but had not received a single line of acknowledgment or encouragement. In the absence of all official communication, he had been forced to rely entirely upon his own judgment. Since he now believed that the safety of his army depended upon its moving to a base of supply, he informed Bee that he had already given the order for the bulk of his forces to withdraw to San Antonio. As far as Sibley was concerned, the New Mexican campaign was at an end. This view was shared by the rank and file as well. As one officer expressed it: "We are all tired of this country, we are all anxious to return to the sunny land of Texas, to behold for a short time the faces of the loved ones at home, and then renewed and invigorated we can meet the invaders of our soil, consoled by the reflection that we are 'striking for our altars and our fires' and not throwing our lives away in endeavoring to obtain possession of a country which is not worth the life of one good man, of the many who have breathed their last upon its arid sands."

The evacuation began on or about May 20, when Major Pyron, in command of the battalion of the Second Regiment Mounted Rifles, left Fort Bliss for San Antonio. Though the bulk of the Confederate forces were evacuating, Sibley ordered Colonel William Steele, who was then at Doña Ana, to remain behind with his "fresh" force of about four hundred men to hold the Territory of Arizona. Undoubtedly Sibley meant this to be a rear-guard holding operation. Surely he could not have seriously entertained the thought that Steele could have held the territory for long against Canby's impending invasion from the north. With the withdrawal of the greater part of the army, all hope for the conquest of New Mexico and the West, temporarily at least, came to an end.

Though Sibley's men had endured a great deal during the New Mexican campaign, their suffering was far from over. Lack of adequate transportation and food, as well as the run-down condition of most of the men, would make the long journey back to San Antonio a most difficult one.

A woman riding on the stage from El Paso noted, as she passed by the various detachments of the Fourth Regiment, that "The men were suffering terribly from the effects of heat; very many of them are a-foot, and scarcely able to travel from blistered feet. They were subsisting on bread and water, both officers and men; many of them were sick, many ragged, and all hungry; but we did not see a gloomy face—not one! They were all cheerful, for their faces were turned homewards. 'We are going home!' " She maintained that two-thirds of the suffering endured by the soldiers was due to the merchants of El Paso del Norte, Mexico, who would not accept Confederate currency for their foodstuffs and other merchandise.

From early July until the latter part of August, the various detachments of the Army of New Mexico began arriving in San Antonio. On July 10, the Valverde Battery came into town and was honored with an eleven-gun salute. During the middle of July, General Sibley and his staff, though apparently having traveled most of the way with the Fifth Regiment, proceeded ahead to San Antonio to the welcoming boom of cannon. Green's regiment left Fort Bliss around June 19, and reached town during the first week of August. The first battalion of the Seventh was reportedly due in from the West within a few days. All soldiers received sixty-day furloughs, though they were still subject to call at a moment's notice. While enjoying the pleasures and comforts of home, the men were under orders to remount and reoutfit themselves. As the San Antonio *Herald* of July 19, 1862, commented, "The men have seen hard times, but they are nothing daunted." Though the campaign in New Mexico might have come to a close, the war was far from over for the Sibley Brigade.

Confederate public opinion concerning the New Mexican campaign was confined almost exclusively to the state of Texas. For while Sibley's small army was engaged in distant New Mexico, the attention of the rest of the nation was held by the spectacle of far larger armies clashing in great bloody conflicts close at home. Among those who were aware of Sibley's efforts in the Southwest, and concerned about them, opinions were often widely divergent—not especially as to the conduct of the campaign, but as to the sagacity of having attempted the conquest of New Mexico in the first place.

The bulk of the rank and file of the Sibley Brigade were highly disgusted, and felt that they had been led on a wild-goose chase. Most believed that even if they had been successful in taking the territory, the results would have been nil, for as far as they were concerned, New Mexico was totally devoid of any value whatsoever. Almost to a man they had come to detest the area most vehemently. As one participant disgustedly commented: "The Territory of New Mexico is utterly worthless. It never will be the abode of civilized man . . . The naturalist is the only character that could be benefited by travelling" there. And what had the New Mexican campaign accomplished? Another soldier caustically commented that "We have brought down 6 pieces of cannon, the Valverde trophy, and fed ourselves for over 2 months on Yankee provisions; that is all the good we have done for our country, and if you balance that against the loss the farming interest on the Rio Grande has sustained, the odds will be considerably against us." This prevailing opinion among the troops was not surprising—in fact, it was to be expected. After all, few soldiers took into account the important over-all aspects of the campaign and the importance it might have held if victory had been achieved. Homesick, and in a relatively desolate region, their viewpoints were products of bitter personal experiences.

On the other hand, what was the attitude of those who tried to view the New Mexican campaign from the standpoint of national perspective? The editor of the Austin *State Gazette* opined that Sibley and his men had been "chasing a shadow" in a barren wilderness. Although performing great deeds of valor, even defeating the enemy in two pitched battles, they had been "compelled to abandon the country from the sheer want of something to eat." What a fruitless sacrifice of gallant Texans! The editor, though apparently completely oblivious to any advantages which would accrue from possessing the Southwest, did display a true grasp of the military situation. He minced no words in condemning President Davis' policy of trying to "defend the Confederacy by posting a few thousand men at every assailable point." To him the only way to bring the war to a successful conclusion was for the Confederacy to concentrate its armies and then deliver knock-out blows against those of the enemy. Erroneously, he assumed that that was to be Davis' new policy. As such, he hoped that "the brave remnant now toiling their way back [from New Mexico], fighting against those worst of enemies hunger and thirst, yet [will] have the opportunity of meeting and conquering . . . [the enemy] somewhere within the bounds of civilization, where the soil is not sand, and water the essence of bitterness, towns hovels in mud, the comforts fleas and rattlesnakes, and the people cayotes [sic]." Once the concentrated armed might of the South had defeated the main enemy armies then, the editor implied, if New Mexico was important enough to become a part of the Confederacy, it could be obtained at the peace conference. In retrospect, it seems unfortunate for the Confederacy that Davis did not heed the advice of this editorial from faraway Texas.

An article in the Houston *Telegraph* took a somewhat different attitude toward the campaign. Its author, too, noted that New Mexico had been conquered and "relinquished," not because the Texans had been defeated, but because the army had failed to find adequate provisions. He praised Sibley by saying that his plan of conquest was "well calculated." Unfortunately, the many unforeseen delays Sibley had experienced in the organization of his army and his getting it into field had given the enemy ample notice to be prepared to meet him. Under the circumstances, Sibley and his men had done all that it was possible for them to do. But, mused the author, "The expedition has proved in no sense a failure because it reached there too late to capture the forts, . . . [for] it has 'sloshed about' where it pleased and captured everything else it wanted." Though admitting that, except as a boundary, New Mexico was not worth having, he patriotically maintained that "all the officers and men have done nobly, and have upheld well the glorious name of Texas, as well as added lustre to its character in the field and in the march." In other words, Sibley's western venture might have been a failure as far as its objective of capturing New Mexico was concerned, but the distinguished bravery displayed by the Texas troops during the campaign was adequate compensation! Unfortunately, to win the war, bravery alone would not suffice.

Most of those composing the militant "manifest destiny" school feared that if the Confederacy failed to occupy New Mexico, or at least hold Arizona to the war's end, the South might be denied those territories at the peace conference. This would be a crippling blow to those who dreamed of a Confederacy stretching from coast to coast. This view was clearly stated in another article in the Houston *Telegraph* berating those who criticized the "extravagance of sending an army a thousand miles to conquer a country not worth having." New Mexico, according to the author, was invaluable, because it would serve as an area for the extension of slavery and as a stepping stone to the Pacific coast. To win independence without New Mexico would leave the South surrounded by a cordon of free territory which, in effect, would "let slavery sting itself to death." It was to prevent this that President Davis approved Sibley's New Mexican plan of campaign. The writer presumed that neither Davis nor Sibley expected a Confederate army to be welcomed with open arms by the native New Mexicans. But that was irrelevant, for New Mexico had to be conquered or "our liberties would be but half won with our independence acknowledged. Nor is this all. The conquest of New Mexico opens the way to the portion of the Pacific coast that affiliates with us in sentiment. It is the entering wedge to the breaking off from the United States of all that coast we desire. It also is the opening scene for our manifest destiny."

Colonel William Steele, who had been ordered to stay behind with his force of four hundred men to hold the Territory of Arizona, found himself in a highly unenviable position. He had formerly been at Doña Ana as Sibley's rear guard, but he now moved his headquarters to Fort Fillmore. From a purely military standpoint, his condition was critical. He had less than thirty days' supply of food, his ammunition was low, and his transportation facilities were inadequate. If something was not done soon, his men would be faced with starvation. Steele had been sick for several days, and though scarcely able to be about, he wrote Sibley asking that some of the supplies which Green and Hardeman had taken with them be left on the road for the use of his men. Obviously, Steele was planning to evacuate, rather than try to hold Arizona. To compensate Green and Hardeman, he suggested that supplies be sent from San Antonio to meet them on the way. Though the country would soon be producing flour and cornmeal, Steele knew that he would not be staying in the Mesilla Valley long enough for the crops to be harvested.

Of great concern to Steele also was the native Mexican population of the valley. After Sibley had left with the bulk of the army, the Mexicans correctly reasoned that Confederate tenure was "frail and uncertain." As such they were unwilling to sell anything for Confederate currency. Since Steele had no specie, he was compelled to authorize his men to seize needed supplies from the natives and force them to take scrip as payment. Food, wagons, and draft animals were the main items requisitioned. These foraging operations, which were even more thorough than Sibley's had been, aroused greater ill feeling. The Mexicans, having little interest in the present war between the states, were concerned solely with their own welfare. When the Texans began seizing their goods, they naturally attempted to defend their property. In many instances they offered armed resistance. In the various skirmishes which took place, one captain and several men of the Seventh Regiment were killed. It is, indeed, not difficult to understand the attitude of the Mexicans. While it had been Sibley's policy to treat the natives with kindness and justice, many of the soldiers from the beginning had acted otherwise. Since the days of the Revolution, Texans in general had held Mexicans in low regard. When the whole brigade was stationed in the valley, the natives had been powerless to resist. Against Steele's small force, however, they were able to express in deeds their hatred of the "Tejanos."

Steele was also troubled by the attitude of his own men. They were completely disgusted with the campaign and were anxious to return to Texas as had the other units of the army. So strong was this feeling that, on several occasions, the soldiers had been on the point of open mutiny. Unless they were speedily marched back to San Antonio, Steele feared his men would take matters into their own hands.

Since Canby considered the California Column adequate to pacify and reoccupy all of Arizona, he discarded his former offensive plan. After taking the precaution of leaving a large force at Fort Craig to support Carleton if necessary, he shifted a thousand men to Fort Union to guard the supply line from the east.

Colonel Steele feared that with the coming of the seasonal rains Canby would soon be able to march across the Jornada del Muerto to invade the

Mesilla Valley. He had learned from spies that the Federals had been reinforced by 500 more volunteers from Colorado, as well as by 250 soldiers and six rifled cannon which had accompanied the paymaster from Kansas. Not counting these additions, and even after leaving sufficient garrisons behind, Steele was certain that Canby would be capable of placing a three-thousand-man army in the field against him. From the captured dispatches, the Confederate commander also knew that the California Column consisted of fourteen hundred men and would shortly set out from Tucson. With two armies poised to close in upon him, Steele lost no time in making preparations to evacuate the Territory of Arizona.

Since the actions of the Texans—particularly the foraging operations—had caused such great feelings of bitterness on the part of the Mexican population, Steele was afraid they might take their wrath out on the Americans who were remaining behind. All those who had sided with the Confederacy had either left with Sibley or were preparing to leave with Steele. The Americans who were staying, some of whom had families, had taken no part in the struggle between the Confederacy and the Union. But to insure their safety, the Texas commander entered into a covenant with the principal Mexicans of Mesilla, who bound themselves to protect them. The consideration was the release of a certain Domingo Cebeno who was Steele's prisoner "under circumstances which would ordinarily cost him his life." Before leaving the area, the Colonel addressed a letter to the Federal commanding officer informing him of the arrangement. "For the sake of humanity," Steele hoped that the Union officer would "inquire into the manner" in which the agreement had been kept.

Confederate government in the Territory of Arizona naturally received a death blow with Steele's decision to leave. Sibley's abortive campaign in the north had already been reflected in the court record: "in consideration of the disturbed condition of the County," the regular session of the court which had been scheduled for May, 1862, was adjourned until the following June.

When Steele abandoned Fort Bliss, the northwestern frontier of the state of Texas and its line of military posts was left exposed to the oncoming Federal forces. Confederate military operations in extreme West Texas, Arizona, and New Mexico had come to an end.

If Trevanion T. Teel's postwar statement is correct, Sibley looked upon the taking of New Mexico as merely a means to an end, the real goal being the conquest of California. If this was the case—and many Unionists staunchly believed that it was—then the New Mexican campaign takes on added significance. In supposition that Sibley had succeeded in New Mexico, what would have been his chances of success in capturing California?

To have conquered New Mexico would have meant the fall of Fort

Union and Canby's subsequent capitulation at Fort Craig. Undoubtedly before Canby and his subordinate at Fort Union surrendered their posts, they would have destroyed the bulk of their war matériel to have kept it from falling into the hands of the Confederates. Sibley's condition, then, would have been just as critical as before. Consequently, in order to have properly supplied his haggard army—especially in regard to ordnance—he would have had to receive supplies from Texas, or else be forced to evacuate New Mexico. It is to be remembered that Texas had been unable to supply Sibley adequately in the first place!

But supposing that Sibley had captured a large amount of supplies from both Fort Union and Fort Craig, how long would he have been able to hold his conquest? The evidence indicates that his tenure would have been short at best, for two Union armies were preparing to converge on him. To be sure, Sibley was to receive reinforcements in the form of two regiments, and, perhaps, additional men could have been recruited from Utah and Colorado. But would this have been enough? Part of the volunteer force raised in California was on the way to attack from the west. Composed of "green" troops, not great in number, the California Column might have suffered defeat at Sibley's hands. The road to California would then have been open, but it was a long road through a vast desert. By the time Sibley would have arrived in the vicinity of Fort Yuma, the bulk of the Union forces of California would have concentrated to challenge his further advance. Could Sibley have counted upon a revolt of Confederate sympathizers in southern California? This seems unlikely, for that minority element had already been quieted and thoroughly overawed by the might of Union troops. But even if Sibley had conquered the California Column, his attention would not have been turned toward California, but toward the northern part of New Mexico. While the Confederates were preparing to advance upon Fort Union, a force of five thousand men was being outfitted at Fort Riley, Kansas, for service in New Mexico. There can be little doubt that Sibley would have been overwhelmed by this Federal army. And even if he had been successful, the Union would have renewed its efforts with even greater vigor—not because the Federals considered New Mexico so valuable, but because they feared Confederate designs on California and northern Mexico. The South and Texas, in particular, were extremely limited as to the number of men and supplies they could send to Sibley. In comparison, the Union was well manned and generously supplied.

If the capture of New Mexico by the Confederates would have rendered the conquest of California probable, then the New Mexican campaign of 1862 should be viewed as one of the most important military operations of the war. But for the reasons already advanced, Confederate success in New Mexico would have been of such an ephemeral nature that California would not have been seriously endangered. A much more meaningful evaluation of this situation indicates that had Sibley been successful in conquering New Mexico, a much greater part of the war would have been fought on far-western soil.

The New Mexican campaign was a gallant, but essentially impractical, effort to accomplish a great objective with woefully inadequate resources. Though the evidence is overwhelming that Sibley's plan for the West had no chance of success, nevertheless, like the whole Confederate adventure, it might have succeeded!

SUGGESTED READINGS

Loomis M. Ganaway, *New Mexico and the Sectional Controversy, 1846–61* (Albuquerque 1944);
Ray C. Colton, *The Civil War in the Western Territories* (Norman 1959);
Max L. Heyman, *Prudent Soldier: A Biography of Major General E. R. S. Canby, 1813–1873* (Glendale, Calif. 1959);
William A. Keleher, *Turmoil in New Mexico, 1846–1868* (Santa Fe 1952);
W. H. Watford, "Confederate Western Ambitions," *Southwestern Historical Quarterly,* vol. XLIV (October 1940);
Charles S. Walker, Jr., "Causes of the Confederate Invasion of New Mexico," *New Mexico Historical Review,* vol. VIII (April 1933).

12
The Long Walk

During the Spanish and Mexican periods the Navajo and other tribes raided at will, and by the 1860s the Americans also had demonstrated their inability to guarantee peace and security to the people of New Mexico. The withdrawal of regular troops with the outbreak of the Civil War and the disruption caused by the Confederate invasion of New Mexico encouraged Indian raiders while the extermination policy of Lt. Col. John R. Baylor of the Confederate Territory of Arizona simply antagonized the Indians. Therefore, when General James Carleton, commander of the California Column, assumed control of the Department of New Mexico, he decided to solve the Indian problem.

Carleton warned Indian leaders that if the tribes did not make peace they would be punished, and when raids continued, he dispatched Colonel Kit Carson and other field commanders against the Mescalero Apache and in 1863 against the Navajo. Carleton's orders were simple: all Indians were considered hostile, and soldiers were not to negotiate with them without specific authority from the departmental commander. During the Navajo campaign relatively few Indians were killed. Their means of livelihood, however, was destroyed, and the Navajo surrendered and were taken on the Long Walk to Fort Sumner in the Pecos Valley to join the Mescalero who had already been located there under the watchful eye of the military.

The removal of the Navajo to Fort Sumner was an experiment which Carleton hoped would not only solve a military problem but which would also train the tribe to become farmers so that they could settle down and support themselves. As Frank Reeve demonstrates in this selection, which is one of a series of articles in the *New Mexico Historical Review* on Federal relations with the Navajo, the experiment failed. Rivalries between the War and Interior departments and between Carleton and Michael Steck, the Indian Superintendent, disrupted

Reprinted by permission. By Frank D. Reeve; first published in the *New Mexico Historical Review*, vol. XIII, no. 1 (January 1938), pp. 14–35.

the program as did crop failures, raids by Plains Indians, conflict between the Mescalero and the Navajo, and lack of food, clothing, and fuel. In addition there was opposition from politicians and individuals who were interested in opening the Pecos Valley for settlement.

Because of these difficulties, some of which are discussed by Dr. Reeve, and because of the immense expense of maintaining the experiment, the government finally decided in 1868 to permit the Navajo to return to their homeland. The sojourn at Fort Sumner was, in many ways, disastrous for the Navajo, and events in Navajo history are now described as occurring before or after the Long Walk. However, it also apparently taught them the futility of continuing the old practice of raiding, for the tribe remained at peace after 1868.

The change in superintendents temporarily removed the troublesome opposition in the Indian service in New Mexico toward the Bosque Redondo experiment, for the new incumbent favored the project. The harmony of views between the military and Indian officials was further strengthened by a clearer definition of their respective jurisdictions, a troublesome question that had persistently raised its head from the outbreak of the Navaho war in 1858. The superintendent and agents were advised

> that where Indians are hostile, the civil authority is to be held in abeyance until the measures taken by the military authorities for quelling the outbreak have been concluded; that where the Indians are generally quiet and peaceable, but require prompt action to quell disorders among themselves, or to prevent unlawful interference of white persons with them, the military are to render assistance when appealed to by the agents; and at all other times the military are not to interfere with the civil control of the Indians.

The Navaho, of course, did not fit readily into this arrangement because Superintendent Steck had refused to accept formal responsibility for them. The current arrangement, therefore, was continued for the time being: for dispensing funds for clothing, implements, and the purchase of sheep they were under the control of the agent; for subsistence and general control they continued as prisoners of war under the military.

But the harmony between the Indian service and the military solved no fundamental problem. The future of the Navaho loomed as a great question mark to those in positions of responsibility, and the seed of discord planted through Steck bore abundant fruit in the next three years. In the fall of 1865 the commissioner of Indian affairs wrote that

> In regard to the Navajoes . . . the accumulated testimony is so conflicting, derived from sources equally entitled to credit, and from persons who should have, and, so far as appears, have had but one object in view—the

> best interests of the government and of the Indians, that I am reluctant at present to express a decided opinion in regard to the permanent policy to be adopted.

For the time being, he recommended that the Indians be left at the Bosque Redondo because they were there and were at peace. This acceptance of the *status quo* illustrated the difficulty of the problem; however, it was only a temporary acceptance, since measures had already been taken along two lines to solve it: a congressional investigation had been instituted in the spring and a special investigator for the Indian bureau had been appointed in the summer.

Under a joint resolution of March 3, 1865, a committee of seven was appointed to inquire into the condition of the Indian tribes west of the Mississippi. Messrs. Doolittle, Foster, and Ross were assigned to work in Kansas, Colorado, Utah, New Mexico, and the Indian Territory. They collected their New Mexico data during the summer, and it was far from being clear and conclusive. Those who testified at the hearing agreed that a reservation removed from the settlements and protected by a military force was the *sine qua non.* In the second place, the Navaho should be made self-supporting by being induced to cultivate the soil after the example of the Pueblo Indians. This idea was strengthened by the fact that they had raised some crops before their removal to the Bosque Redondo. But where the reservation should be located was the moot point.

The proponents of the Bosque Redondo contended that there was no area sufficiently large in the Navaho country upon which the tribe could be located and made self-sustaining. Furthermore, the troops could not keep them on the reservation, and if they were allowed to scatter, trouble would develop with the New Mexicans as formerly. This argument was countered by the proposal that the Navaho should be located in several groups or pueblos in various parts of their old country which would make it possible for a few troops to keep them on their reservations. Additional arguments for the Bosque Redondo were that it contained good farm land and that the presence of the Navaho there was a *fait accompli* and should be continued. Various other points were advanced pro and con; it was cheaper to feed them at the Bosque Redondo than to fight them in their own country; fewer troops were required to control them; a grazing country in northwestern New Mexico had been opened to the white man; and the route to Arizona was safe; on the contrary there was a scarcity of wood around Fort Sumner, the country belonged to the Comanche, the area of farm land was insufficient, the Navaho were self-supporting in their own country, there were no mines to attract the whites into the northwest, the Navaho and Apache could not live together, and the Bosque Redondo entailed immense cost to the government.

Among those consulted by the committee, Carleton was perhaps in the most certain frame of mind about the matter. He had formed his opinion about placing Indians on reservations which

> will be Islands: and as time elapses and the race dies out, these Islands may become less and less, until finally, the great sea [of white men] will engulf them one after another until they become known only in history, and at length are blotted out, of even that, forever.

Since the Bosque Redondo would serve the purpose of an "island" very well, there was no need to seek further for a location. The committee, however, did not decide the issue.

The second line of inquiry into the situation in New Mexico was due to the unsatisfactory condition in the Indian service. The appointment of Delgado as superintendent had been looked upon with misgivings by some of the citizens in the Territory. Neither he nor three of the new agents could keep their accounts or report to their superiors in the English language. This handicap made necessary the employment of assistants, sometimes in relation to business of a confidential nature. The importance of party politics could hardly permit such weak points on the battle front. As the chief justice of the Territory pointed out, "Much, therefore will *rest* upon the *integrity* and *good faith* of the *clerks* or *friends* who may be trusted in a confidential *relation* with the officers in this portion of the Indian affairs." Furthermore, Delgado did not furnish satisfactory reports about conditions in New Mexico and the Washington office felt at a distinct disadvantage in discharging properly its responsibility in the Territory.

Before taking any action the commissioner of Indian affairs appointed Julius K. Graves in August, 1865, as commissioner and special agent to investigate the general situation in the superintendency. He was instructed to report on the sufficiency of the Bosque Redondo as a reservation for both the Navaho and Apache, the cost of surveying the reservation for the purpose of allotting the land in severalty, the character of the personnel in the Indian service, and the practice of slavery. The expenditure of the congressional appropriation of March, 1865, was placed in his hands.

Graves made a thorough and detailed series of reports in the spring of 1866. He philosophized about the status of the Indians, condemned the practice of slavery or peonage, recommended a shakeup in the service, and favored the Carleton policy of keeping the Navaho at the Bosque Redondo. His sympathies were distinctly with the Indians, but he did not accord them a particularly favorable place in the affairs of this world. He thought the star of the red man was setting while that of the white man was rising. God had so willed, and history could prove,

> That the Indian under an all wise dispensation of Providence was created for a specific purpose, should mark his gradual decline seems evident from their past history.

"They are fading—they are fading
In solemn gloom away
Like mists upon the mountain
At dawning of the day."

He echoed a rather common charge that most Indian troubles were precipitated by actions of the white man, and stated that the reservation plan by separating the two groups was the proper solution to that problem.

The practice of enslaving Indian captives in New Mexico was almost as old as the length of the white man's occupation. There were about 2,000 of them worth from $75 to $400 each. Their treatment varied with the owners; some were occasionally abused, others were adopted and treated as members of the family. The custom had long been recognized as one of the chief causes of the chronic warfare with the Navaho. The Indian bureau had made no effort to end the evil on the ground that it lacked jurisdiction. Since the leading office-holders in the Territory held such slaves, they naturally were not interested in operating the machinery of local government to their own loss. But the situation was incompatible with the results of the Civil War, and some steps had been taken to remedy it. President Johnson issued an order on June 9, 1865, for the suppression of the practice, and the Freedmen's Bureau had been approached without success to take charge of the captives. Since these efforts had resulted in little change, Graves recommended that Congress take action, which it did in due time.

The question of reorganization in the service occasioned a slight disagreement. The removal of Delgado had been urged upon the commissioner of Indian affairs by Delegate Francisco J. Chaves, on the ground of "total incapacity" to perform his work. This charge must be discounted a bit because Chaves and Delgado were on opposite sides of the political fence, but in addition to the language handicap, other grounds were found for Cooley to recommend that the superintendency be placed in the hands of Governor Mitchell. The governor held certain military powers which it was considered would be an aid in the management of Indians, and the fusion of the two offices would eliminate one salary cost of $2,000.

Graves vigorously opposed combining the two offices because "The Indian service in this quarter *imperatively* demands the *constant* and *unremitting* efforts, care and attention of a thorough going, practical and energetic man—the whole time . . ." But he did recommend a general shakeup for various reasons: Delgado should be removed because of his language handicap; Diego Archuleta, who had been reappointed to the Abiquiu agency, was accused of having a bad reputation for honesty and integrity; Manuel Garcia was not earning his salary, and M. S. Salazar of the Ute agency was a zealous official but lacked judgment and capacity. The Mexican agents in general had friends and relatives who "hang on to the agency" and who appropriated the Indian goods. Theodore H. Dodd of the Navaho agency was rated as competent. The traditional hostility with the Indians was pointed out as a bar to the use of Mexicans as agents. He condemned the practice of political appointments, and, with the instinct of the reformer, he recommended permanent tenure on good behavior and salaries adequate to attract competent men.

The Bosque Redondo, he believed, was a satisfactory place for the Navaho, but not in company with the Apache because of their traditional hostility; the water was all right (despite former complaints to the contrary); piñon wood for fuel as a substitute for the dwindling mesquite could be secured about twenty-five miles to the north; the Pecos valley provided excellent pasturage; the location was remote from the mountainous retreats of the Indians; and the mineral wealth in the old Navaho country could be exploited. In short, the prisoners should not be returned to their former homes. Their fear of dwindling away in their new environment was merely a superstition. In attributing the visitations of measles to the unhealthy location they failed to recognize that epidemics of that sort were "the divine visitation of God for his own good purpose." Finding about 2,000 acres under cultivation, and that fruit trees and vines had been set out, he believed that the experiment of Carleton on the whole was successful.

The recommendation of Graves for a change in the personnel was promptly carried out. Colonel A. Baldwin Norton was commissioned superintendent in February, 1866. Delgado went through the formality of resigning his position, complaining of not having received the proper financial support nor recognition during his tenure of office; in fact, Graves had practically superseded him in the control of financial matters. Before the new incumbent arrived, Archuleta was suspended in April on the ground of misconduct in office, and Dodd was reaffirmed in May as agent to the Navaho.

Dodd had come to New Mexico with Doolittle in the summer of 1865 as agent for the Navaho, but his commission had been withheld temporarily because he disobeyed instructions to visit Washington before proceeding to the scene of his work. Carleton was troubled at that time by the usual delay in forwarding goods for his charges. He therefore sent Dodd back East "to see personally after these important matters in which the health and comfort of 9,000 Indians—*entirely dependent upon the Government for everything*—are concerned." Despite his exertions to hasten matters the train of goods started across the plains too late in the season to complete the trip, so it wintered at Fort Zarah, Kansas; however, necessary farm equipment for spring planting was sent through by mule teams.

The Graves report, far from settling the Navaho question, seemed but the prelude to the working of diverse forces which ultimately led to the abandonment of the Bosque Redondo. The question of transferring the

Indians to the control of the department of the interior was debated, the military advocated their removal to the Indian Territory, and internal affairs on the reservation went from bad to worse.

The expectations of Carleton that the prisoners would be self-supporting within a year by farming had not been realized. The cost to the department of war of subsisting them for the eighteen months period from March 1, 1864, to October 1, 1865, was $1,114,981.70. This of course did not include the expense of transportation nor the sums appropriated by congress and expended by the Indian bureau. Since the army estimates for the year 1866–1867 were not based on the continuation of this extraordinary expense, the commissary general of subsistence, A. B. Eaton, raised the issue of transferring the Navaho to the civil department. Secretary Harlan was not adverse, of course, to the plan. The main plea for not assuming responsibility when the first party of captives arrived in September 1863, had been the lack of money to provide food for them. The remedy for that difficulty simply lay in congress appropriating the necessary funds and having the civil officials do the spending.

The system of double jurisdiction was also unsatisfactory. The military fed the captives, stood guard, and superintended the farming operations; the Indian bureau provided clothing and equipment. The Bosque Redondo was not a military reservation, but was officially a reservation for Indians. In cabinet discussion, Secretary Stanton urged that the prisoners be transferred to the control of the department of interior on the grounds that they would then be under the proper jurisdiction, the military could resume their primary duties, and stricter accounting and economy could be enforced. Any requisitions that the agent might make on the army subsistence department could be paid for. This meant a return to the usual condition where the military aided the Indian service in emergencies, with the expectation of being reimbursed. The commissioner of Indian affairs heartily concurred in the opinion of the secretary of war, expecting of course, "the cordial co-operation of the military authorities, if their aid should be necessary."

The order for the transfer of the Navaho to the control of the department of interior was issued on December 31, 1866, but, for several reasons, the actual change was delayed until November 1, 1867. Superintendent Norton was absent from New Mexico for several months because of illness and no one was officially designated to act in behalf of the civil department. Upon the return of Norton to his duties in the summer, the new commander of the District of New Mexico, Major General G. W. Getty, was not aware of the existence of the order of December 31, 1866. When he discovered it on September 30, the final step was delayed until the next regular date for issuing rations. Agent Dodd then accepted control of 7,111 Navaho from Major Chas. J. Whiting and the military were finally relieved of their four year burden.

Superintendent Norton assumed the additional responsibility reluctantly. He had estimated the cost for the support of the Navaho at $600,000. Congress saw fit to appropriate only $100,000 "for subsistence and for the purchase of sheep, seeds, agricultural implements" and a like sum for "relief," with the proviso that the department of war should furnish no more rations after July 1, 1867. Obviously, in the light of past experiences, the appropriation would last for only a short time. Yet, the new task was taken in hand and the lucrative contract for feeding the Navaho was awarded to Elizah Simerly who assigned it to Perry Fuller & Co. of Lawrence, Kansas.

The heyday of military domination of Indian affairs in the Territory of New Mexico had now passed. The star of Carleton had set and his experiment in civilizing the Navaho on the Bosque Redondo reservation was doomed. Despite his early irritation at the failure of Steck to take care of the prisoners, he now feared that the transfer of control would result "in great injury to, if not in the positive failure of, the important measure of fixing forever the Navajo tribe of Indians upon a reservation." However, the fundamental cause of the defeat of his project was not to be found in the change of jurisdiction, but in the internal conditions at the Bosque Redondo.

In addition to the controversy between Steck and Carleton, there were four main reasons for the failure of the policy of locating the Navaho on the banks of the Pecos: insufficient wood for fuel, crop failures, inadequate financial support, and hostility of the Comanche Indians. The mesquite had been relied upon as the fuel supply, but for 7,000 or more users it proved to be insufficient. This possibility had been foreseen by Carleton, and among his early instructions was the order to plant trees against the day of the disappearance of the natural growth. From December 7, 1864, to April 30, 1865, the Indians, under military supervision, planted 12,068 trees. This measure, however, did not produce soon enough. By 1867, the Indians were traveling five to eighteen miles away to secure fuel, carrying it home on their backs. A one "man" load lasted but a short time during the cold months; consequently, it was a constant race to secure enough fuel to prevent suffering from the cold and even freezing to death. The Navaho complained about this situation and requested animal transportation to better enable them to cope with the problem; the situation became increasingly serious to the point that the superintendent finally wrote: "God knows what these indians will do for fuel this winter—God only knows—It becomes scarcer and farther off daily."

The failure of the crops was particularly discouraging because the success of the colonization scheme was based upon the theory of turning the Navaho into a farmer. The first season the corn crop was almost entirely destroyed by worms, and grasshoppers occasionally bothered the other crops. Some of the land was too alkaline for cultivation. Hailstorms at times and insufficient water added to the troubles. The lack of water was partly due to the difficulty of turning the river into the irrigation ditches, the sandy bottom of the Pecos being a treacherous foundation for a diversion dam; a flood might sweep away such a structure at a time when the need of water was greatest.

The problem of managing the farming activities was also troublesome. In place of employing a sufficient number of experienced farmers to direct the labor of the hundreds of Indian workers, a military officer was detailed to superintend the work. This proved to be unsatisfactory, either because of his lack of experience for such work or because of a lack of interest; and, of course, some Navaho were not inclined to work. To solve this difficulty, Dodd recommended in the summer of 1866, that the farm land be divided into ten acre plots with a practical farmer and assistant in charge of each division. The Indians who desired to work would be settled on the edge of these plots with a permanent home and personal garden plot. This proposal was in keeping with the current idea of allotting the land in severalty. The plan was followed in certain respects the next year, but without appreciable results:

> 2367 acres were carefully ploughed and planted . . . This farm was divided into three sections, and each section was subdivided into ten-acre fields. Over each of the three divisions a non-commissioned officer, with four private soldiers as assistants, acted as superintendent, and eighteen Indians performed the labor; the soldiers instructing and assisting them . . . Lieutenant McDonald had entire control over all farming operations.

What with crop failures and a parsimonious (or dishonest) master, the Navaho were never adequately supplied with food or clothing. In spite of the efforts to make them self-supporting, they were absolutely dependent upon the government for subsistence. This was a prime factor in keeping them on the reservation. As Carleton wrote, "The great magnet which really holds the Navajos fast to the Reservation is the food which they get once in two days. . . . They cluster around the commissariat like steel filings around a loadstone . . . Now I believe they have no disposition to run away," except for a few vagabonds. He was probably wrong in his estimate of their disposition, but it was a long way to their old home and the military were prompt in the early years in pursuing large parties that left.

The ration issued to the Navaho varied from three-quarters to one pound of meat per day for each person and a like amount of bread-stuff. The Indians were counted and ration cards issued as they filed through a gate into a corral. The cards at first were made of card-board. They were sometimes lost and often forged. Stamped metal slips were next used, but the clever Navaho craftsman made dies and again forged them. At one time there were about 3,000 extra ration tickets in existence. The situation was finally changed by securing them from Washington with an intricate and special design that could not be copied.

In regard to clothing, the well-known ability of the Navaho in the art of weaving was not utilized for their benefit. Instead of supplying the prisoners with flocks of sheep in place of those taken as part of the spoils of the roundup, cheap shoddy blankets, which provided but little warmth and were quickly worn out, were purchased in the East or Middle West and transported at considerable expense to the reservation. Sometimes they were picked to pieces and rewoven into a better article. In addition to the poor quality, there was a lack of quantity. Granting that congress was generous in appropriating money for clothing and farm implements, whether the whole of the proceeds would be spent in the interest of the Indian was another question. And, as a matter of fact, it was not.

The final reason for the failure of the Bosque Redondo experiment was the plains Indians. The Navaho had been located on the western edge of the Comanche country. These nomads (Comanches) had long been a source of trouble to the white man, especially along the Texas frontier, which was their special field for depredating. They found a ready market for some of their spoils, particularly cattle, through trade with the New Mexicans in the eastern part of the Territory. Through this channel they received guns and ammunition, or hoop iron for making arrow heads, and sometimes whiskey. The trade assumed extensive proportions at times; about 700 traders were in the field in 1867 due to the practice of subletting licenses and the loose manner of issuing the permits. It was suspected that some of them who did not favor the Bosque Redondo reservation incited the Comanche to attack their new neighbors.

Various steps were taken by the government to solve this problem, not only for the sake of the Navaho but as a part of the general attempt to control the Indian tribes. In the summer of 1866, Norton revoked all permits for trading. This proved to be only a temporary measure. The following year he sought an agreement with the Comanche for the protection of the Navaho. A conference was held in Santa Fé in September between representatives of the two groups, but it produced no results. Two months later, when Agent Labadie made a trip to the Texas Panhandle for another interview, "They indignantly refused to make any terms of peace with the Navajos, and manifested their natural hatred toward them, saying that they would always fight that tribe . . ."

While the trials and tribulations at the Bosque Redondo were testing the courage of those in charge and wearing out the patience of the Navaho, a movement was started for their transfer to some other locality. The use of the reservation had been severely criticised from the beginning of course, but in 1866 General Pope made a vigorous proposal that it be abandoned. In his opinion it was a mistake to locate Indians on reservations in their own country because of friction with the incoming tide of white immigrants. This difficulty was illustrated, he thought, in the conflict of opinion that had raged around the Bosque Redondo. He proposed that the Navaho be moved farther east to the Indian Territory or to some other permanent location in that general direction. This would result in reducing the cost of subsistence due to the shorter distance to the source of supplies, it would bring the Indians under a more civilizing influence, fewer troops would be required to guard them, and the frontier would be opened for settlement. He considered the Bosque Redondo to be the best location at the time selected because it was the farthest point east that Carleton was then able to take his prisoners.

Pope's idea of Indian country in regard to the Navaho was certainly broad. The Bosque Redondo was a long way from their old home. However, this assault on the reservation met with a cool reception in the department of interior, although it found a ready welcome in the ranks of the military. General Sherman passed the responsibility for deciding the issue on to Washington with the remark, "This is a matter of some importance, and is most costly. I think we could better afford to send them to the 5th Avenue Hotel to board, at the cost of the U. S." The lateness of the season when the matter was discussed in Washington delayed any immediate action, but the stage was set for a change. The President instructed Secretary Browning to mature plans for disposal of the Navaho, to be carried out as soon as conditions would permit. The idea of seclusion from contact with the whites, so common at the time, influenced his opinion, and he recommended their removal to the Indian Territory, stipulating, however, that it should be done "with the consent of the removed." The idea of "consent" was to play an influential part in the final decision that was yet to be made.

The proposal to transfer the Navaho to the Indian Territory was in keeping with a general plan to form one large reservation south of the Arkansas River and concentrate all the southern Indians on it. The northern Indians were to be concentrated north of the Platte River. This scheme was designed to open the country between the two rivers to white travel and the construction of a transcontinental railway.

The officials in New Mexico differed in their views and with those of their superiors in Washington. John Ward, one-time agent for the Navaho under Collins, recommended that they be returned to their old home. A line of forts should then be constructed from the San Juan River through Fort Wingate to Fort Craig. A bi-weekly patrol between the posts would constitute a military barrier to restrict the Navaho west of the line and would prevent the illegal entry of white men into the Indian country. Getty, on the other hand, was of the opinion that the Indians could be made self-supporting at the Bosque Redondo under certain conditions that had not been provided in the past, but he suggested that they be located in the country east of the Sacramento mountains, the home of the Mescalero Apache. A prime factor in his opinion was a supply of fuel.

Superintendent Norton held a conference with eleven Navaho chiefs in September, 1867. They reiterated their complaints, making it clear that they were not satisfied with the Bosque Redondo. Events now began to move rapidly toward a crisis. That same month the Comanche raided and killed nine Navaho, besides capturing two women. The soldiers failed to catch the marauders, and the Navaho were not properly armed to punish them decisively. This episode on top of their accumulated woes developed a strong spirit of unrest among them. A party estimated from 200 to 250 deserted the reservation on the 26th and 27th. Norton immediately sought permission from Washington to issue 4,000 Mexican blankets to quiet the others, a step that was promptly approved by wire.

The quick action of Norton in meeting the delicate situation in September was only a stop-gap, and the crucial question of what to do with the Navaho was yet unanswered. He strongly favored the policy of removal: "Justice, humanity, Christianity, and the welfare of the Indians. The safety of the whites, and the *pecuniary interests* of the government all demand the change." But where? He analyzed the proposals of Ward and Getty. If removed to their old country they could be made self-sustaining within one year, while it would take four years at an estimated expenditure of $700,000 to accomplish the same result if the proposal of the military commander was followed. The immediate pecuniary advantage of the suggestion of Ward was outweighed finally by the belief that the Fort Stanton area would make possible a much sought after goal; namely, the protection of the whites against the Indians for all future time because of its remoteness from the settlements, a rather unsound argument.

The spirit of Carleton still hovered over the office of Indian affairs. Perhaps the Bosque Redondo experiment could be carried on to success under the management of the Indian bureau with proper support from congress. And by no means should the Navaho be allowed to return to their former homes where the old game of hide-and-seek with the military would have to be played again. The "good of the Indians, the safety of the white settlers in their vicinity, and the general prosperity of the Territory . . ." forbade such a move. This view was clinched with the stock argument that it was cheaper to feed them than to fight them.

While the officials were proposing, other forces were disposing. The Navaho owning horses planned to steal away during the winter. In the month of January, 1868, 250 to 300 were estimated to have left. Contemporary with this movement, the Indian Peace Commission was recommending to congress that a treaty be made with the Navaho, or their consent obtained in some other way, for their removal to the southern Indian district "where they may soon be made self-supporting." Their proposal carried force because the cost of feeding the Indians weighed heavily with congress and that will-o'-the-wisp, "self-support," might yet be attained if prompt measures were taken:

> We are paying now for the subsistence of seventy-five hundred Navajo Indians in New Mexico. We have for the last five years issued to them rations costing us $750,000 per year, and it is likely to cost us that amount of money again this year unless we remove the Indians somewhere.

Congress followed the advice of the commission and intrusted it with the task of settling the Indians on some permanent reservation, the earlier instructions of President Grant becoming the basis of the plan. Inspector-General R. B. Marcy had been requested by Sherman to render a report on the country lying between the 98th and 101st parallels, the Canadian River on the north and the Red River on the south. Marcy selected a site for a Navaho reservation between the Wichita Mountains and the Red River. The Indians could become self-supporting there within two or three years, he believed. Sherman doubted that a reservation in their old country could be permanent because of the rising tide of miners pushing into western Colorado and northwestern New Mexico; so, "with the light now before me, I would prefer their removal to a point north of the Red River, west of the Chickasaw line and east and south of the Wichita mountains."

The commission empowered Sherman and Tappan to proceed to New Mexico and negotiate a treaty with the Navaho for their removal. The two delegates left for the Territory in May with the idea in mind that there was no use in moving the Indians unless they were located east of the 98th parallel. But at Trinidad, Colorado, Sherman dispatched a note to Getty to meet with them at Fort Sumner and "to bring with me [him] one or more who are familiar with the old Navajo Country, west of the Rio Grande."

The two commissioners to the Navaho surveyed the scene at the Bosque Redondo and consulted with Getty, Dodd, and others. On May 29 and 30 they held councils with the Navaho. Three propositions were laid before the Indians as the basis of the discussion: they could settle anywhere as citizens in the Territory of New Mexico, remove to the region of the lower Canadian and Arkansas rivers, or discuss the advisability of returning to their old country. Needless to say, the last one was seized upon as the choice, which was in keeping with their attitude for the past year. They had refused to plant crops and had petitioned their agent to return them to their old home until Dodd was convinced that they would never be contented elsewhere. Several other factors influenced the commissioners to satisfy the longings of the Indians: the secretary of interior had been lukewarm toward the proposition to move them farther east; peonage had been abolished in New Mexico, thus removing a chronic cause of war with the Navaho; their old country "is unoccupied, is utterly unfit for white civilization, and towards which they yearned as the Swiss for their native mountains;" and "Without absolute force they will not remain here or immigrate further east.

As the military had moved the Navaho from their tribal home to the Bosque Redondo, the military moved them back. In both cases action was taken under the war powers. Without waiting for the formality of treaty ratification by the senate, Sherman issued the order for their removal on June 1: "Until congress makes provisions to carry out the terms of our treaty, as the military commander on this frontier, I authorize and instruct you to put these people in motion for their own country. But where the removal under the direction of Carleton had been based on the will of the white man, the action of Sherman and Tappan was based on the desires of the Indians. In both cases there were people who questioned the wisdom of the decision. In anticipation of criticism of the action now taken, Tappan vigorously pointed out that the Navaho

> have been prisoners of war to all intents and purposes, and the person who for selfish pecuniary and political purposes is responsible for such inhuman treatment of these Indians as that of keeping them for nearly four years upon such a reservation deserves the condemnation of the people, the severest and most ignominious penalties of violated law. To have compelled them to remain "would have forced upon them the horrors of Andersonville and rendered our government infamous . . . Navajoe men, women, and children were compelled in mid winter, to travel on foot over a bleak plain, from twelve to thirty (12 to 30) miles to dig from a hard soil, the mesquite root and pack it on their shoulders back to prison . . ." Sherman acted promptly, with judgment and humanity as military commander in a crisis "when as commissioners we were powerless—not hesitating to assume responsibility." It was a most infamous crime ever to have removed them.

In contrast to the unwilling trek eastward under duress, with a past history of war and depredation, they now returned westward willingly with the desire to live in peace with their white neighbors. Five years of enforced restraint at the Bosque Redondo had impressed upon them more strongly the wisdom of adhering closely to some of the demands of their conquerors. They even acquired a reputation of having destroyed and stolen less on the return march than a column of soldiers of like number would have done. Only one complaint was registered against them; the thief was punished by order of Barboncito, being tied to the end of a wagon and forced to walk.

Major Whiting was placed in charge of the Navaho migration, a ten-mile long procession moving westward to Albuquerque by way of San José and Tijeras Canyon. Seven days were spent in crossing the Rio Grande. They arrived at New Fort Wingate on July 22 after a trip of thirty-five days. Dodd then assumed charge and the Indians eventually spread back into the hills and mesas of their old home. The government spent about $56,000 on the removal from Fort Sumner, but the dream of Navaho self-sufficiency was not yet attained, many more dollars being yet to be spent in the next decade.

SUGGESTED READINGS

Ruth Underhill, *The Navajos* (Norman 1956);
William A. Keleher, *Turmoil in New Mexico* (Santa Fe 1952);
Robert M. Utley, *Frontiersmen in Blue: The United States Army and the Indian, 1848–1965* (New York 1967);
L. R. Bailey, *The Long Walk* (Los Angeles 1964);
Frank Reeve, "The Government and the Navaho, 1846–58," *New Mexico Historical Review*, vol. XIV (January 1939).

13
The Santa Fe Ring

In the years after the Civil War the Territory of New Mexico was dominated politically and economically by a group of men known as the Santa Fe Ring. It is with considerable justification, then, that Howard Lamar uses the Ring and its operations to relate the history of the territory during 1865–85, for the Ring and its members were involved in every important area of the economy and dominated the political life of the territory. Lamar describes the flexible Ring and gives capsule portraits of leading members such as "Smooth Steve" Elkins, who eventually left New Mexico to become a senator from West Virginia and later Secretary of War, and Thomas B. Catron, who was the dominant figure.

"A logical and sometimes brilliant combination of able men," the Ring included merchants, lawyers, judges, and local politicos from both parties although it relied heavily on Republican patronage for its success. The membership was involved in business, in railroads, in ranching, in mining, and above all in land grants which acquired "Indian rubber like qualities" as individuals and groups managed to stretch them far beyond the original boundaries. The Ring was involved in the dispute over the Maxwell Land Grant which led to violence in Colfax County; and, through relations with the Murphy-Dolan faction in Lincoln County, it was also indirectly involved in the Lincoln County War of the 1870s.

Eventually the Ring developed factions and declined in significance, but while it lasted it was "a sophisticated combination of the eighteenth-century speculator and the nineteenth century businessman." As Lamar explains, the members of the Ring reflected national business trends and political practices and ethics. It is also evident that the impact of their land grant manipulations continued beyond their life-spans as the current discussions regarding land grants demonstrate.

After the Civil War many young veterans found the docile life of their home towns so unattractive that they headed West in search of new careers and new excitement. Some, having learned to command men, knew they were destined for bigger things. Others could not shake off acquired habits of violence. The conflict had made still others so psychopathically bitter that they continued to wage a private war against the world long after the surrender at Appomattox. The border state of Missouri, which had already dotted the Far West with mountain men and traders, now seemed to have just such a surplus of restless and ambitious veterans. Out of the counties of southwestern Missouri in the postwar decades rode the Coles, the Youngers, the Jameses, and scores of obscure drifters and gunmen hunting their destiny in the wide-horizoned West. Their doings made West Texas a land for tough men only; they brought notoriety and death to a score of Kansas cattle towns, and for a time it was literally true that there was "no law West of the Pecos." Always drawn to a region where society was in a developmental stage, such a large number of these men came into Lincoln and Colfax counties in New Mexico that Ralph Twitchell has called that area "catch-basins for the reckless and criminal element." Southeastern New Mexico in the twenty years after the Civil War, wrote Emerson Hough, was "as dangerous a country as ever lay out of doors."

Not all the immigrants were from Missouri, had a gun at their side, or possessed an itchy trigger finger. Members of Carleton's California Column remained in the Southwest, to find a livelihood after their service had ended. Colonel W. L. Rynerson, future political leader of southern New Mexico, was one of those who stayed. Major Lawrence G. Murphy, attracted by cattle ranching and the profitability of stores in army towns, became a trader at Ft. Stanton and a rancher and political boss in Lincoln County as well. Other able young men, in pursuit of one of the professions, continued to drift down the Santa Fe Trail. Among these were two graduates of the University of Missouri who were members of the class of 1860. After they had parted company at graduation, Stephen Benton Elkins, the more openly brilliant and urbane of the two, joined the Union Army, while the other, Thomas Benton Catron, crusty, blunt, energetic, and domineering by nature, sided with the Confederates.

Elkins and Catron made no great reputation in the Civil War and, unlike half their political colleagues in New Mexico, did not assume the title of major or colonel after the fighting was over. By 1864, in fact, Elkins had left the Army for the troubled town of Mesilla, where he became a lawyer. An attractive personality and a quick mastery of Spanish won him a seat in the New Mexican House of Representatives the next year. Later he was advanced from the territorial attorney general's office to become the United States district attorney for New Mexico. Only twenty-six years old, he seemed to be a second Henry Clay in the making, and both his admirers and detractors referred to him as "Smooth Steve" Elkins.

Elkins' meteoric rise persuaded his college chum to join him. The ever-practical Catron loaded two wagons with flour in 1866 and set out for Santa Fe. The sale of the flour would pay the cost of the trip. Undoubtedly warned by Elkins and others that he was coming into a new culture, Catron doggedly memorized a Spanish grammar on the trail and deliberately lived with a Spanish-speaking family for a few months after his arrival, until he was fluent in the language. After studying law with Merrill Ashurst and clerking for Chief Justice Kirby Benedict, the boss of a wing of the Republican Party, Catron was appointed district attorney for the third judicial district in 1867.

Then the intertwining of two famous legal and political careers began. In 1869 when Elkins was United States attorney, Catron was the territorial attorney general. By now they had pooled their resources as the law firm of Elkins and Catron, an office that was to carry the names of half the attorney generals or chief justices to serve in New Mexico. In this firm and its branches in Albuquerque and Las Vegas, much of the political history of territorial New Mexico was to be made. Both partners dreamed of reaching the United States Senate one day, and when Elkins discovered that statehood was not imminent for New Mexico, he moved his fortune and his career to West Virginia. An important figure in national Republican circles, he became Benjamin Harrison's Secretary of War in 1891 and served as senator from West Virginia from 1895 until his death in 1911. Catron, however, once having identified himself with New Mexico, remained there for the rest of his life and became, as William A. Keleher has accurately observed: "the one man, who more than any other, dominated New Mexico's political and business affairs for fifty years."

As Elkins and Catron looked about their adopted territory, it was obvious that aside from Indian affairs, five things preoccupied the thoughts of business and politically minded New Mexicans: the land-grant question (details of which Catron learned in Merrill Ashurst's office), statehood, open-range cattle ranching, railroads, and mining. With the possible exception of statehood, all problems were clearly related to land and its control. As attorneys their concern was to associate their careers with these five questions. Their methods and activities helped make the political and economic history of New Mexico for the next three decades.

From the time of the Taos Rebellion until 1854, when Washington finally appointed a surveyor general for New Mexico, the title to all property in the territory had lain in uneasy status. The United States, by the treaty of Guadalupe Hidalgo, had promised to respect New Mexican holdings, but these were enormously complicated by the existence of three kinds of grants: one to a community, usually for grazing purposes; a second to an individual for some outstanding service, such as defense against wild Indians or as a reward for settling a new area; and a third to the various Indian pueblos. As has been demonstrated elsewhere, there were further complications, because such grants had been variously awarded by the King of Spain, the Republic of New Mexico after 1822, and the provincial governor—particularly Manuel Armijo—in the five years before American conquest. There were even more refined distinctions between grazing and irrigated land grants, individual and common grants, and Pueblo and white grants.

When Surveyor General William Pelham arrived in Santa Fe in 1854, he must have been dismayed at the task facing him. Over one thousand claims awaited settlement, of which 197 involved large private grants. Moreover, many of the private holdings overlapped one another. Outside of California and possibly French Louisiana, Americans had never before dealt with such complicated land questions. At the same time, Congress had given Pelham such elaborate and burdensome instructions that he was actually hampered rather than helped by them. One clause, for example, written into the act which created his post, declared: "Until final action of Congress on such claims, all lands covered thereby shall be reserved from sale or other disposal by the government."

This was the equivalent of denying the existence of a public domain in New Mexico, while at the same time it guaranteed that long legal battles climaxed by acts of Congress would characterize the history of the New Mexican land system. A paradise for lawyers and politicians had been created. Commented William A. Keleher: "The claims approved by Congress were generally those with the most persistent influence on the outside and the most powerful political influence on the inside." And as if to clinch the necessity for lawyers in land settlement, the grants in their wording were so extraordinarily vague that a claim could be stretched to include an estate of almost imperial size.

Despite many difficulties, including faulty, hasty, and fraudulent surveys and the refusal of many distrustful Spanish-American grantees to cooperate, a number of grants had been confirmed by 1857. In the process, however, the legal profession of Santa Fe had become involved in securing title for their clients. They were men whom Governor E. G. Ross described as "sharp, shrewd Americans . . . possessed of some local lore and with a large amount of cheek and an unusual quantity of low cunning and astuteness." The first chief justice, Joab Houghton, erstwhile builder of the capitol, was also an attorney for twelve claimants, among them Ceran St. Vrain. Hugh N. Smith, the "delegate" to Congress elected by the extralegal statehood forces of 1849, was concerned with at least ten land grant clients. Later in the fifties Judge John S. Watts told a Congressional committee that he was handling forty-three cases. Other pioneer lawyers such as Merrill Ashurst, Theodore Wheaton, and Spruce M. Baird were also engaged in the land-title business.

In the rush to clear title Carlos Beaubien and Gaudalupe Miranda, two of the largest claimants, decided to take no chances. They hired three lawyers: Houghton, Wheaton, and Smith. The old Taos merchant's dream of empire seemed to come true when Congress confirmed the grant in 1860. In doing so, however, Congress was guided by the Mexican Colonization Law of 1824, which limited the size of a grant to eleven square leagues for each claimant. Had Congress stuck by this ruling, the solution of the New Mexican land question would have been relatively simple. But there were too many other Spanish and Mexican laws contradicting the 1824 statute. Shrewd lawyers began to stretch their clients holdings on this basis until, as Governor Lionel A. Sheldon later remarked, the grants took on remarkable "India rubber qualities."

The history of the scores of land-grant cases and their role in New Mexican history might be epitomized by a brief account of the most famous and notorious of all tracts, the Beaubien-Miranda claim, which came to be called the Maxwell Land Grant. When Carlos Beaubien died in 1864, his enterprising son-in-law, Lucien Bonaparte Maxwell—husband to Luz Beaubien—bought the grant from his in-laws and purchased Guadalupe Miranda's part as well. Maxwell's was a princely domain. At his house in Cimarron scores of guests and dozens of retainers mingled in an atmosphere of luxurious frontier hospitality. Kind-hearted and affable, he was loved by Indian and white alike. But Maxwell was also a businessman. He had made money selling cattle and grain to Indian agencies and to the Army. Now that title was secure—or so he thought—he saw a chance to sell the grant for a fantastic price. He had been made aware of the possible great value of the grant when gold was discovered on the land in 1867 and prospectors and investors had swarmed onto the grant regardless of his claim to ownership. Maxwell also knew that his neighbor at Mora, the elderly Ceran St. Vrain, was negotiating with Colorado financiers for the sale of the huge Vigil and St. Vrain tracts.

In 1869 Maxwell asked for a new government survey and learned that by the 1824 Colonization Law his claim was 22 leagues or, roughly, 97,000 acres. By now Maxwell's name, already known and liked all over the Southwest, became familiar to frontier businessmen and speculators as well. In Colorado, Jerome B. Chaffee, a wealthy mine owner and future senator, made overtures to Maxwell for the purchase of the grant. At Chaffee's side was George H. Chilcott, former land register for Colorado—who had doubtless gathered details on the New Mexican grants, since parts of several of the large grants had been included in Colorado when it was created a territory in 1861. And in the background was ex-Governor William Gilpin,

Colorado owner of the Sangre de Cristo grant, who had been interested in St. Vrain's and Beaubien's land activities for over twenty years.

The importance and the extent of the interest in New Mexico land grants becomes obvious when it is realized that the Colorado contingent was but one of four groups interested in Maxwell's land. In New Mexico itself Stephen B. Elkins, Thomas Catron, Governor William A. Pile, ex-Delegate Watts, and Miguel A. Otero (the wealthy partner of Otero, Sellar and Company) were among the purchasers. And, as always, the current surveyor general was a party to the scheme. After some negotiations, in 1869 Maxwell agreed to give Chaffee and Elkins an option to buy. A year later the purchase was concluded for a paper price of $1,350,000. The buyers called their acquisition The Maxwell Land Grant and Railroad Company. At the same time Elkins, who never did things by halves, bought various Colorado mines on Chaffee's recommendation and persuaded Maxwell to use part of his money to found the first regular bank in New Mexico—the First National of Santa Fe. The bank, in turn, was chiefly interested in handling the Company's securities.

The men who purchased Maxwell's Grant had even larger plans than Beaubien, St. Vrain, or Lucien Maxwell had ever envisaged. Acutely aware of the vagueness of the grant, they hired W. W. Griffin, United States Deputy Surveyor of New Mexico, to survey the grant as a 2,000,000 acre plot—in contrast to the 97,000 acres to which Congress and Secretary of the Interior Cox had limited it in 1869. The results of Griffin's report were filed in Washington; and without waiting for confirmation, Wilson Waddingham, an English rancher connected with the new company, went to London and sold the grant to English purchasers.

The London firm constituted the third group interested in the Maxwell Grant. In a maneuver that looked suspiciously like passing the buck, the English company persuaded a fourth party, Dutch financiers in Amsterdam, to handle the mortgage. Stock was then issued for $5,000,000. The company then elected an Anglophile American Civil War general, William Jackson Palmer, as its president. At the time, Palmer was superintendent of the Kansas Pacific Railroad; Stephen Elkins, the leading lawyer in New Mexico, was to be the resident director and local attorney of the company; while Governor Pile, M. A. Otero, and Judge Watts were to be vice-presidents. Full knowing that its claim to 2,000,000 acres was quite shaky, the ambitious firm eventually got the opinion of a half-dozen leading lawyers—among them William M. Evarts and Judah P. Benjamin—that the enlarged grant size was the valid one.

So far, things had gone remarkably well for these bold American and British speculators. Then in 1871 the new Secretary of the Interior, Columbus Delano, once again ruled that the grant covered only 22 leagues or 97,000 acres. Unless the company, now busily selling $5,000,000 worth of stock on the European market, could suspend this ruling, its fate would be that of other great frontier land schemes like John Law's Mississippi Company or the Scioto Land Company in Ohio.

Too much was at stake to give up now. Already the company was making overtures to Kansas Railroad men to extend their lines into southeastern Colorado. General Palmer had undoubtedly accepted the presidency with the idea that the Kansas Pacific would traverse the northern edge of the grant, and from that point one branch would run northwest to tap the rich town of Denver, while another branch would follow the Santa Fe trail through New Mexico to the Pacific. To Palmer, Elkins, Chaffee, and their far-flung associates, the Maxwell Grant—and other grants as well—promised to be a modern Bent's Fort through which the riches of Colorado and the Southwest could be filtered, while their railroad would replace the Santa Fe trail. If their plans were to succeed, they could control the economy of Colorado and the entire Southwest, just as Bent, St. Vrain, and company had done thirty years before.

To circumvent the 1824 Colonization Law and hostile Secretaries of the Interior, the Company resorted to court action and Congressional influence. Fortunately for the firm, Chaffee was elected delegate from Colorado in 1870, and two years later "Smooth" Steve Elkins—now president of the Company in Palmer's place—ran for the delegateship from New Mexico on an irresistible ticket: he promised his constituents that he would settle all land claims and at the same time secure statehood for New Mexico.

Elkins' proposals were political strokes of genius. The land issue was a question in which many prominent New Mexicans and every American lawyer was interested. Statehood was what the old states-righters and anti-American conservatives—for the most part Democrats—had wanted since Padre Martinez had first declared for admission in 1849. There had been a new movement for statehood in 1872, in fact, led by the archconservative Tomas Cabeza de Baca and *el antiguo revolutionario,* Diego Archuleta. A constitution was written, and an election held; but while the results were favorable, they were not strong enough to impress Congress. Elkins' platform, then, appealed to frustrated Democrats and ambitious Republicans alike. Aided by promises, money, pressures, and fraud at the polls, he was elected by a majority of 4,000! This was an incredible margin in a territory where nearly every delegate election was so close that it was contested.

As urbane and diplomatic as Delegate Elkins was, his efforts to get Congress to accept his proposals for settling land grants (and that of Maxwell in particular) were in vain. The company was becoming desperate, and in its distress, several factions appear to have formed. The investors were demanding returns on their money; the Amsterdam financiers were questioning the claim, and local speculators in Colorado and New Mexico were determined not to let go. To keep Elkins in Washington where he was needed, his supporters secured his re-election in 1875, although Elkins himself was in Europe the whole time selling company stock. In an effort to corner more votes, his partner, Catron, reputedly used 600 pending land-case indictments as weapons to get at least that number of votes. The territory was well aware of the stakes, for the *Las Cruces Borderer* said during Elkins' first campaign that it was "the honest people of New Mexico against a foreign company of Monopolists and its attorney."

Despite all that could be done, the company was in bankruptcy by 1875, but the legerdermain practiced by the New Mexicans interested in the company now became more subtle than ever. Having secured a state of bankruptcy from a friendly judge, the company's claim in 1877 was sold to cover a tax debt. It was bought by M. W. Mills, a Colfax county attorney, who sold it a few months later to Thomas Benton Catron, Elkins' old friend and law partner. In reality bankruptcy appears to have been a means by which the company could escape its creditors and at the same time remain under the direction of its original New Mexican promoters, but the Dutch bankers managed to regain control at the last minute.

The question still remained whether the grant was 97,000 or 2,000,000 acres. This time the company took the tack of seeking confirmation of its enlarged survey. Rather than appeal to a new Secretary of the Interior—and especially to a reformer like Carl Schurz—they persuaded Land Commissioner James A. Williamson to establish the precedent that court decisions based on a surveyor's recommendation would henceforth determine the size and validity of a claim, regardless of the 1824 Law. The Maxwell case was reopened and a new survey ordered. Again the company tried to rely on the expanded vision of Surveyor W. W. Griffin, but Secretary Schurz wisely ruled him out as an official surveyor. The company then gave the contract to two engineering innocents: R. T. Marmon and J. T. Elkins, the latter a brother of "Smooth" Steve. After a swift and almost meaningless survey lasting only twenty-two days, they filed their reports, declaring that the grant was indeed nearly 2,000,000 acres in size. On May 19, 1879, a ten-year battle ended because of favorable court decisions and land-office rulings, and Land Commissioner Williamson issued patents of ownership for 1,714,764,094 acres of land. While many grants remained unsettled until the 1890s, the Maxwell Company had made old Carlos Beaubien's dream of empire come true with a vengeance.

The schemes and successes of the Maxwell Company had many important consequences for the political and economic makeup of New Mexico Territory. It became obvious that to succeed in settling land questions,

Elkins needed a machine to back him, made up of lawyers, judges, politicians, businessmen, and a friendly press both at home and in Washington. Out of such a need grew the first so-called Santa Fe Ring. Many legends surround its purpose and its membership, but it was essentially a set of lawyers, politicians, and businessmen who united to run the territory and to make money out of this particular region. Although located on the frontier, the ring reflected the corporative, monopolistic, and multiple enterprise tendencies of all American business after the Civil War. Its uniqueness lay in the fact that, rather than dealing in some manufactured item, they regarded land as their first medium of currency.

The famous Santa Fe Ring was a logical and sometimes brilliant combination of able men. Besides Elkins and Catron, both declared Republicans, Henry L. Waldo, another law partner of Elkins also belonged. As open, trustworthy, and frank as anyone in the territory, Waldo was a Democrat who was respected by friend and foe alike. Other members were the current surveyor general and the wealthy New Mexican merchant, A. Staab. The ring also found it useful to ally the county probate judges with the organization. Particularly valuable were the services of Dr. Robert H. Longwill, probate judge of Colfax County, in which a large portion of the Maxwell Grant was located. Among the federal judges, Chief Justice Joseph G. Palen—and, later, Judges Samuel B. Axtell and L. B. Prince—were counted as members of the ring. From the late 1860s until 1885, nearly every governor appears to have been a member, as well as other federal officers.

Further requirements for success were a strong press and contacts in Washington. The ring found the former in a superb team, William Manderfield and T. J. Tucker, who began publishing the Santa Fe *New Mexican* about the time the Beaubien-Miranda grant was purchased from Lucien Maxwell. The paper gave the Maxwell Company and the ring open support, and so able and powerful a paper did it become that it remained the leading newspaper throughout the territorial period.

Elkins, the ring, and even the *New Mexican* would have experienced great difficulty, nevertheless, in maintaining their preeminent positions had not the Republican Party been in power in Washington in the key years from 1865 to 1885. Unbroken patronage flowing from the nation's capital sustained all three. Nor could the ring have survived without excellent Eastern connections. Elkins and Chaffee were well known in New York business circles. Among those interested in New Mexican speculation were Senator Stephen W. Dorsey, who developed a giant ranch in Colfax County, and George M. Pullman, builder of sleeping cars and a friend of Chaffee. Prominent lawyers and public men, such as William Evarts and Senator Thomas F. Bayard, were friends of the company, as were several New York, Philadelphia, and Providence bankers.

Finally, the ring survived because it was realistic enough to accept within its circle any cooperative or useful official, so that every five years the personnel changed somewhat. In a similar way the ring changed its economic interests as the economy of New Mexico altered: after the heyday of land grants, they were more interested in ranching, mining, and railroads. This sort of flexibility gave them a reputation as monopolists and for having economic and political omniscience.

The last characteristic that made for success was its nonpartisan view of able men. Though it was a Republican ring, it had many Democratic adherents, among them the chairman of the Democratic Party between 1884 and 1889! "A well formed Ring," wrote Governor L. B. Prince, "embraces members of both parties and the New Mexican one is remarkably well formed. They seem to fight when in reality they are pulling together." Governor Edmund Ross also observed that each combination had a Republican and Democratic lawyer "for prudential reasons, so that whichever side might come uppermost, the dominant party was represented, and there was an average of one lawyer to every ten Americans."

In the realm of the remaining land grants the methods and successes of the Maxwell Company triggered other claimants and speculators into action. At the same time that the Maxwell purchase was being made, Colorado speculators were buying the Las Animas (originally Vigil and St. Vrain) grant in southeastern Colorado. The Sangre de Cristo grant (Narciso Beaubien, and Lee) was being sold to William Blackmore, an English investor with extensive holdings in the Southwest. In less than a year the suspect Gervacio Nolan grant went to still another British investor. Once bitten, Blackmore became interested in the Cebolla and Conejos grants and the Canon de Chama claim. And by 1872 negotiations for the purchase of the Beck, Cucilla, San Cristobal, Cinequilla, Mora, and Los Luceros grants were being carried on.

To interest Eastern and European investors, impressive brochures were printed providing a résumé of the documents relating to the grant, its possibilities, and the opinion of some prominent attorney. Typical of these was a pamphlet issued in 1879 which carried General Benjamin F. Butler's legal opinion that the Vigil and St. Vrain grants of 1843 were valid. All the owners needed, he cautioned, was to find the "missing document" in which Governor Armijo had been given the power to suspend the eleven-league limitation of 1824. Butler succumbed to his own eloquence and bought up a portion of the Mora grant a year or so later.

In the decade from 1875 to 1885, the remaining unconfirmed grants continued to stretch impressively. When George W. Julian took over the surveyor general's duties in the latter year, he was shocked to find that the Cañada Ancha grant, which had originally been for 130 acres, was now a claim for 375 square miles of territory. Others were even more spectacular:

the Canon de Chama grant of 184,000 acres was increased by the claimants and preceding surveyor generals to 472,000 acres; the Tierra Amarilla grant was by then some 932 square miles, while the Mora claim was for a mere 1,400 square miles. Counting the Maxwell grant, some thirty-four claimants alone declared their holdings to be over 100,000 acres each! It was patent that here was the territory's largest industry.

Naturally the lawyers of Santa Fe exacted their fees for clearing titles. Being paid in land, they themselves gradually acquired ownership of the largest grants and became, as it were, their own clients. Eventually over 80 per cent of the Spanish grants went to American lawyers and settlers. Most impressive of all were the accumulated holdings of Thomas B. Catron. Never a modest man, on June 23, 1893, he listed his estate as being:

50,000 acres of the Mora Grant
80,000 acres of the Beck Grant
2/3 of the 78,000 acres of the Espiritu Santo Grant
1/2 of the 21,500 acres of the Tecolote Grant
7,600 acres of the Juana Lopez Grant
24,000 acres of the Piedra Lumber Grant
11,000 acres of the Gabaldon Grant
15,000 acres of the Baca Grant
a portion of the Tierra Amarilla Grant
8,000 acres in patented homesteads

Not even these told the whole story. A year later the Santa Fe *New Mexican* estimated that he was interested in seventy-five grants, owned nearly 2,000,000 acres, and was part owner or attorney for 4,000,000 more.

Perhaps the most significant consequence of the land-grant speculations and of ring rule was that Elkins and Catron and their colleagues had discovered a method by which New Mexico could be profitably exploited by Americans, whether it was in land, ranching, mining, or railroad development. The country that once seemed worthless to Kearny's soldiers was now an item in the stock exchange and a topic of interest in a dozen investment houses in Europe. Wrote Governor E. G. Ross irately:

> From the Land Grant Ring grew others, as the opportunities for speculation and plunder were developed. Cattle Rings, Public Land Stealing Rings, Mining Rings, Treasury Rings, and rings of almost every description, grew up, till the affairs of the Territory came to be run almost exclusively in the interest and for the benefit of combinations organized and headed by a few longheaded, ambitious and unscrupulous Americans.

Ross also observed that each combination had a Republican and Democratic lawyer:

> Thus the Santa Fe Bar became to all intents and purposes a close corporation, and the syndicate it represented and controlled, came to be and has for many years been known as the Santa Fe Ring, a great combination which included all the less Rings, and dictated at will the legislation and general conduct of the affairs of the Territory, with branches here and there in the lesser towns, but all subservient to the Central head.

A brilliant frontier technique of exploitation, reminiscent of the Holland Land Company and of the Ohio Associates, had been revived, modernized, and given the trappings of the corporation and of the post-Civil War political ring common to the era of Ulysses S. Grant. The Santa Fe Ring was a sophisticated combination of the eighteenth-century speculator and the nineteenth-century businessman.

Of equal significance was the Ring's political power. To succeed, it had to control the territorial and local governments, and to do that required some control over the exhausting factionalism that characterized New Mexican politics. After the arrival of Elkins and Catron, the seesaw rise and fall of delegates and the frequent coming and going of the governors, surveyor generals, and judges was no real indication of change. A local bureaucracy, as it were, continued to run things as they saw fit and made the necessary federal official a part of their schemes. Thus Governor Pile (1869–71) was a willing member of the Maxwell Land Grant Company, and as early as 1872 Governor Giddings (1871–75) was described by the Las Cruces *Borderer* as a "tool" of Elkins. Governor Lew Wallace (1878–81) sarcastically remarked that the office of governor had so little power that his only function was to count sheep and people for the annual report to Washington. Governor Sheldon (1881–85) found that the territory ran itself and willingly let a member of the ring, Attorney General Breeden, virtually assume all gubernatorial duties. Governor Ross aptly summarized the ring's role in politics when he remarked: "For years its rule was imperious and unquestioned. . . . It elected Legislators and Delegates to Congress. It had the ear of the Administration at Washington, and could build up or pull down men at its pleasure."

The Santa Fe Ring's attempt to control both the economy and government of New Mexico did not come without its full share of excitement, violence, and fraud. And the two "catch-basins" of the reckless element, Colfax and Lincoln Counties, came to be apt illustrations of such activity. The Maxwell Company claims, for example, encroached on the lands of scores of settlers who had innocently settled in the lovely Cimarron country, little knowing that they were trespassers on private property. As early as 1870 great bitterness was evident in the relations between the settlers and company representatives. By 1876 even the Indians residing at the Cimarron Agency were declared trespassers and were forced out.

The issue was complicated by the presence of two other groups. In 1867 gold had been discovered on the grant and a sizable community of miners, estimated at one time to be 10,000 persons, lived at Elizabethtown and in surrounding camps. The saloon element—gamblers, drifters, and robbers—naturally followed the miners there to clip their share of the coin. Simultaneously Texas ranchers, eyeing the fine grasses of Colfax county, pushed their herd across the boundary and established ranches on what they called the public domain. With this latest Texas invasion came the inevitable rustler and cowboy gunman.

To complicate matters even more, two local factions fighting for control of the Maxwell Company appeared on the scene. One of these was headed by a young lawyer named Frank Springer, who opposed Santa Fe control of the company during the early 1870s. The other group was composed of the Santa Fe interests, led by Doctor Robert Longwill, Probate Judge of Colfax County and a member of the ring in good standing. Given so many unstable elements in Colfax County and the company-squatter issue, it was inevitable that violence would result.

Although these factions shifted back and forth in their loyalties, and a general confusion existed as to who stood for what, by 1873 the real lines were eventually drawn between the company and squatters. A squatter club was formed at Cimarron that year to protect settlers' rights, while in nearby Raton two groups, both anti-Grant, organized. One wanted to shoot it out with the company, while the other determined to wage a press campaign against its monolithic enemy. The anti-Grant groups were encouraged by a new Interior ruling in 1874 which stated the Grant was a part of the public domain.

The first victim of the many-faceted feud, ironically, was a man of God, the Reverend T. J. Tolby, a strong-willed, outspoken Methodist minister. In September 1875, a few days before he was mysteriously killed on the road to Elizabethtown, he had declared to Judge Joseph G. Palen, a member of the ring, that he intended to expose Palen. Suspicion pointed to two New Mexican toughs, Cruz Vega and Manuel Cardenas. When apprehended by a mob, Vega said that Cardenas had committed the murder after having been hired to do so by one Pancho Griego and one Donahue, a mail contractor against whom Tolby also had damaging evidence of fraud. Vega's statement did not help his own predicament; the mob hanged him just in case he might have been guilty.

Manuel Cardenas then came forward with the story that Dr. Robert Longwill and M. W. Mills, a local attorney for the company—along with Donahue and Griego—had hired Cruz Vega to murder Tolby. In a tortuous sequence of events stretching over two years, Vega was hanged by a mob, Pancho Griego was shot by a Texas gunman and rancher named Clay Allison, Dr. Longwill fled—first to Fort Union and then to Santa Fe

—in fear of his life, and Cardenas and Donahue were committed to jail. When Donahue's trial finally opened, excitement was at a high pitch. But before the accused could testify, Cardenas was killed from ambush while going from the jail to the courtroom, and Donahue, out on bail, joined Dr. Longwill in exile at Santa Fe.

Onto this troubled scene came a tragicomic figure, another Methodist minister, the Reverend Oscar P. McMains. A cantankerous fire-eating crusader against the Maxwell Company and at times editor of a local paper, he became the self-appointed sleuth to track down Tolby's murderer. McMains himself was such a violent personality that he was tried in 1877 for leading the mob that killed Cruz Vega. His attorney on this occasion, paradoxically, was Frank Springer, solicitor for the Maxwell Company. Although he was acquitted a year later for lack of evidence, McMains was to carry on his private war throughout the coming decade, despite the fact that the Company finally had its patent validated by a Supreme Court decision in 1887.

Obviously the Colfax County troubles and the hopeless confusion in northeastern New Mexico did not take place in a vacuum. They agitated the officials at Santa Fe and particularly the new governor, Samuel B. Axtell, (1875–78) a former California congressman who had also been territorial governor of Utah for a brief time. A man of strong feelings and great dignity, Axtell seemed determined to solve the Colfax troubles. After Cardenas was killed, the Governor declared that Cimarron was in a state of "riot and anarchy" and sent troops from Fort Union. This proved no solution, for many of the soldiers were Negroes, whom the Texans refused to respect. Within two weeks of their arrival two of them lay dead by bullets from Clay Allison's gun.

It was not long, however, before the Santa Fe Ring recognized in Axtell an exceptionally able man and useful official. They persuaded him that it would be unfair to return Dr. Longwill for trial under such hostile conditions and in such a violence-ridden community. To secure a just trial and to bring order to Colfax, Axtell, on January 14, 1876, attached Colfax to Taos County for judicial and administrative purposes. This meant that cases concerning the Cimarron trouble would be held in Taos, where Longwill, Donahue, and others might easily be declared innocent.

Frank Springer, then a leader of the anti-Santa Fe wing of the Maxwell Company, was quick to feel that Axtell was an enemy. In eloquent pleas he and his faction demanded return of their courts, charging that most of the Taos jurors were Penitentes and that the boss of Taos was a member of the Santa Fe set. While this open attack was occurring, the Company also spread the rumor that Axtell was a Mormon bishop, whose secret policy it was to declare the grant public domain and settle Latter Day Saints thereon. At the same time, a contradictory rumor spread that ex-

Senator Dorsey and Axtell were speculators themselves and were intriguing to buy the Una de Gato Land Grant in the county. Although Longwill was acquitted and local courts were returned to Colfax County, the Cimarron feuds continued into the 1890s with frequent outbreaks of violence.

What is the significance of the Colfax County troubles? Why should violence erupt in a territory now some thirty years under American rule? First of all, it is obvious that Colfax and the Maxwell Grant region represented the coming together of three American frontiers in one place. The mining center of Elizabethtown was a small echo of the California and Colorado mining camps, with their usual boisterous and often criminal society; second, the Texan and local ranchers reflected the booming Great Plains cattle frontier, of which Colfax County was the western edge; and, third, there was the transportation and land speculation frontier, which wanted to develop and exploit northeastern New Mexico and southeastern Colorado as a multi-faceted big business enterprise. Here for the first time in New Mexico was an area which resembled other American frontiers. In the fight for the spoils, however, the heritage of large private land grants, the absence of a public domain, and the existence of the Santa Fe Ring immensely complicated the usually easy process of frontier settlement. Colfax County, then, was in essence the scene of a fight between men who held an American or public domain concept of the frontier and an organization which insisted that the region, because of its Spanish-Mexican origins, was private property. Once again the difficulty of governing and settling a region where different land laws and approaches to government existed were dramatically evident. Even so, the Colfax War lost the center of the stage for a time after 1878, for a new war had broken out in Lincoln County.

SUGGESTED READINGS

William A. Keleher, *Maxwell Land Grant: A New Mexico Item* (Santa Fe 1942);
Jim B. Pearson, *The Maxwell Land Grant* (Norman 1961);
Herbert O. Brayer, *William Blackmore: The Spanish-Mexican Land Grants of New Mexico and Colorado, 1863–1878* (Denver 1949);
Arie W. Poldervaart, *Black Robed Justice* (Albuquerque 1965);
Victor Westphall, *The Public Domain in New Mexico* (Albuquerque 1965);
Howard H. Lamar, "Edmund G. Ross as Governor of New Mexico Territory: A Reappraisal," *New Mexico Historical Review*, vol. XXXVI (July 1961);
Ira G. Clark, *Then Came the Railroads: The Century from Steam to Diesel in the Southwest* (Norman 1958).

14
The Lincoln County War

Like many frontier regions New Mexico Territory was plagued by lawlessness and violence, and territorial institutions appeared unable to deal with such threats to stability and order. The most famous breakdown of law and order occurred in Lincoln County between 1876 and 1878 when economic rivalry, cattle rustling, an argument over an insurance policy, and, undoubtedly, personality differences led to open warfare between two large factions. The unprecedented wave of violence left several of the principals dead and brought a presidential declaration that a state of insurrection existed. It caused a federal investigation and the removal of Governor Samuel B. Axtell and was the subject of diplomatic discussions between the United States and Great Britain because of the murder of John Tunstall, an English national. The Lincoln County War has also attracted attention because of the participation of Billy the Kid.

William Keleher, a lawyer, has diligently searched the records for material on the conflict, and his book, *Violence in Lincoln County*, has been described as "the most reliable history yet published" on the subject. In this chapter Keleher describes the showdown in Lincoln in which Alexander McSween, a leader of one of the factions, was killed.

That a crisis was approaching was apparent from a letter written by John S. Chisum from Bosque Redondo on July 1, 1878, to Irwin, Allen & Co., which was published in the Kansas City *Commercial Indicator* and other papers. The Pecos River country, according to Chisum, was being cleared of cattle. Chisum's letter, in part:

Hunter & Evans have up to this date, started from Col. Hunter's range on the Pecos river, to Kansas, 8,068 head of mixed cattle, and has now

> about 4,000 more ready for the road. In about another month they will start another herd of 4,000. I think I may say one half of those cattle will be put on the market, and the remainder will be kept on their range. No other cattle will be driven from the Pecos to any market. There are but few cattle on this river except R. D. Hunter's.

The *Gazette* of July 20, 1878, reported the progress of events:

> About July 1, a party of 12 or 13 men arrived on the Pecos from Seven Rivers. They were accompanied by T. B. Powell, deputy sheriff, who had warrants for the parties charged with the murder of Major Brady. Alex. McSween, with a party of 14 to 18 men, was at the ranch of John S. Chisum. About the 4th Powell and his friends invested the Chisum ranch and continued the attack all day and all night. Not succeeding in reducing the camp, the siege was raised and Powell's party left. Then McSween's party also started up the Pecos. Powell had been reinforced by Marion Turner and some 12 or 14 men, making about 35 in all; Turner was also deputized to make arrests. The two parties combined pursued the fugitives. They found a break up the river was a blind, as the McSween crowd had left the river and struck off by the Capitan in the direction of Lincoln. Turner, Powell and their friends pursued, and word was given out that they were between Lincoln and Capitan on the morning of July 10th. At that time McSween's forces were at San Patricio with 40 men. The danger of a severe battle is imminent. Before the parties went down the Pecos, three fights occurred in San Patricio in one day; one man was severely wounded and several horses were killed.

Sheriff George Peppin, seeking support from any and every available source, had the benefit of the advice and counsel of James J. Dolan. Peppin sent riders to all parts of the county with an urgent plea for help, promising a deputy sheriff's commission to all who would volunteer to fight on his side. Dolan had taken the precaution to engage the services of John Kinney, and some fifteen hired gunfighters from Doña Ana and Grant counties. Kinney and his men rode into Lincoln from the Rio Grande at a critical time and placed themselves at Peppin's disposal. Peppin gained the support of Henry Beckwith, and his two sons, John and Robert, from the Seven Rivers country, after he had sent word to them that he was desperately in need of their help in a fight against their common enemy, John S. Chisum.

The battle of July 19 was inevitable, and could not have been avoided except through cowardice on one side or the other. Leadership in the crisis, by the logic of events, had been thrust upon Lawyer McSween. Hounded and harassed by citations and writs issued out of Judge Bristol's court, the result in part of District Attorney Rynerson's maneuvering, poor Mr. McSween gave every evidence, in the last days of June and early days of July, 1878, of being in a state of resigned confusion. He recognized the hopelessness of trying to remain in the Lincoln country, and attempting to carry on the fight against the combined power of Bristol and Rynerson. Hopeful of finding a way out of his difficulties, McSween had traveled horseback to South Spring Ranch, and sought the advice of John S. Chisum. After talking to Chisum, McSween reached his decision. He began the return journey to Lincoln, convinced that he had no alternative but to stand his ground and fight. Some of John Chisum's most trusted cowboys, acting as a bodyguard, accompanied McSween on the return trip. As he rode north along the Pecos River, and turned in the direction of San Patricio and Lincoln, McSween was encouraged from time to time to note that men began to ride along with him, some from the Pecos, others from the Feliz, the Peñasco, the Hondo, the Bonito, still others from far off mountain tops and remote valleys of the upper country. Some of the men who joined McSween were ordinary farmers and ranchers, none hankering for a fight; others were well-known gunfighters. McSween would have been the first man to admit that he was not a fighting man, and that he had no stomach at all for the panoply of war.

Riding from the South Spring Ranch toward Lincoln, McSween's thoughts in all probability revolved around his own lack of ability for leadership in the enterprise in which he found himself unwillingly and fatefully committed, an enterprise demanding an inherent love of combat, a native, instinctive, animal-like knowledge of how to attack and when to go in for the kill. McSween realized that affairs in Lincoln County had now reached a point where no man's life or property could be said to be safe or secure, either day or night; that no prudent man dared venture in the open, even at high noon, without a gun in hand.

There was no doubt but that McSween and his supporters were standing at the crossroads. As he neared Lincoln, McSween undoubtedly realized that he was a marked man, and that for him death lurked in every turn of the road. But there was no turning back now, no way by which he might honorably avoid the ordeal confronting him. By the time he reached Lincoln, about sundown on July 15, McSween found himself the fateful captain of an army of forty-one men. Some rode along in high spirits, as if bent on a crusade of righteousness, fearless and anxious for a showdown fight; others were silent and apprehensive of things to come. Upon reaching the outskirts of the town, McSween deployed his forces. He took ten men to his own home; others were billeted in the Ellis and Montano homes; some made camp on the banks of the Bonito and in the hills beyond, north of town.

Sheriff Peppin had not been idle during the two days it had taken McSween and his followers to ride from Chisum's ranch to Lincoln. Peppin had commandeered and recruited about forty men, and true to his promise, had commissioned each and every one a deputy sheriff. Among leaders ready to fight on Peppin's side were: Joseph Nash, Henry, Robert and John Beckwith, Robert and Wallace Olinger, Andrew Boyle, John Hurley, J. B. Matthews, James J. Dolan, "Buck" Waters, "Buck" Powell, John Chambers, John Kinney, Tom Jones, Jesse Evans, Pantaleon Gallegos, Marion Turner, John Long, Jose Chaves y Baca, Sam Perry, James Reese. Peppin placed his men at strategic points in and about Lincoln. The Peppin forces were called the "Sheriff's Party," and their opponents were known as the "McSween Crowd." If Peppin's forces included Jesse Evans, one of Tunstall's alleged slayers, there was no denying that McSween's forces had the assistance of several notorious characters, among them William H. Bonney, one of the alleged slayers of Sheriff Brady and Deputy Hindman.

During all hours of the day and night of July 16, 17 and 18, it was not safe for man, woman or child to be on the streets of Lincoln. Bullets occasionally whizzed and whined through the air, but whether from poor marksmanship or otherwise, surprisingly few casualties resulted. Unfortunately for McSween's crowd, a stray bullet on July 16 hit and slightly wounded Benjamin Robinson, a soldier from Fort Stanton. Robinson claimed that while walking along the main street of Lincoln, peacefully and unarmed, four shots had been fired at him from the vicinity of McSween's house, and that he had narrowly escaped being killed.

As of daylight on July 19, the battle between the McSween and anti-McSween forces had reached a stalemate. Neither the Sheriff nor any of his deputies had succeeded in arresting, or serving warrants on any of the men barricaded in McSween's house. There was every indication that the military, nine miles away at Fort Stanton, would maintain neutrality. On July 7, 1878, R. C. Drum, Assistant Adjutant General in Washington, had issued General Orders No. 49, directing the attention of all army officers to the provisions of an Act of Congress approved June 18, 1878. These orders forbade the use of federal troops in assisting civil authorities as a posse comitatus, or in executing the laws, except in conformity with the provisions of the Constitution of the United States, or pursuant to an Act of Congress. In a word, federal troops could not be used in civil matters in the Territory, without the express permission of the President, obtained through military channels. (Text of order in LVG, August 17, 1878.)

Notwithstanding Drum's General Orders, Sheriff Peppin asked for help from Commanding Officer Dudley at Fort Stanton, writing him a politely worded letter on July 16:

> GENERAL: I have the honor to respectfully state that mostly all the men for whom I have United States warrants are in town, and are being protected by A. A. McSween and a large party of his followers. They are in the houses of A. A. McSween, Ellis Sons, J. B. Patron and Jose Montano. They are resisting, and it is impossible for me to serve the warrants. If it

is in your power to loan me one of your howitzers, I am of the opinion the parties for whom I have said warrants would surrender without a shot being fired. Should it be in your power to do this, in favor of the law, you would confer a great favor on the majority of the people of this county, who are being persecuted by a lawless mob.

Acknowledging Peppin's note, Dudley promptly expressed regret because of his inability to furnish the howitzer as requested without instructions from Washington. Sheriff Peppin at once wrote another note to Dudley:

GENERAL: I have the honor to acknowledge the receipt of your very kind favor of date; am very sorry I cant get the assistance I asked for, but I will do the best I can. The McSween party fired on your soldier when coming into town. My men on seeing him tried to cover him, but of no use. The soldier will explain the circumstances to you. I take this opportunity of thanking you for your kindness in the name of all my people.

Peppin's second letter disclosing the fact that one of Dudley's soldiers had been fired on, gave him a reason to interfere. Calling a meeting of his staff officers to consider the situation, he told them of Sheriff Peppin's communications, and read to them a letter from Saturnino Baca of Lincoln, urgently requesting that enough soldiers be sent to Lincoln to protect women and children. Dudley's staff promptly agreed unanimously that troops be sent to Lincoln for the sole and only purpose, as Dudley later expressed it, of protecting "helpless woman and children." The parade of Lieutenant Colonel Dudley and his troops into Lincoln on July 19, proved an impressive spectacle: sixty cavalrymen, one lieutenant colonel, three captains, several lieutenants, one Gatling gun, one howitzer, and an ample supply of arms and ammunition. The arrival of the military, as subsequent events demonstrated, marked the beginning of the end for the McSween side. In a matter of hours, the tide of battle began to veer toward the Sheriff's party.

Soon after reaching Lincoln, Dudley's staff officers convinced a reluctant justice of the peace, John B. Wilson, that he would be justified in issuing warrants for arrest of Alex. A. McSween and others on a charge of assault with intent to kill upon the person of Benjamin Robinson. With Judge Wilson's warrants in hand, Peppin and his deputies lost no time in making plans to arrest the men against whom they had been issued, knowing that they would be protected under the law for any killing done in event of resistance.

About dusk on July 19, McSween's house was set on fire. Deputies Marion Turner and Robert Beckwith called upon the inmates to surrender, but they refused. In the shooting that followed, Vicente Romero, Harvey Morris, Francisco Zamora and Alex. McSween, of the McSween forces, were killed, and Robert Beckwith was killed on the Peppin side. William Bonney ran from McSween's house in a desperate attempt to reach Tunstall's store. Soldiers fired at him, compelling him to swerve in his course. Running toward the Bonito River, Bonney escaped in the gathering darkness.

A coroner's jury, made up of Felipe Miranda, Jose Garcia, Marciamiano Chavez, Octaviano Salas, Felipe Maes, and Jose Serna, held an inquest on July 20 over the bodies of the five dead men. Viewing the remains, the jury noted the number and location of the bullet wounds: McSween, five; Romero, three in the body and leg; Harvey Morris, and Zamora, one each; Beckwith, two in the head and one in the wrist. The jury returned a verdict finding that McSween, Romero, Morris and Zamora "came to their deaths by rifle shots fired from the hands of the Sheriff's posse, while they, the above named persons were resisting the posse with force and arms"; and that Beckwith "came to his death by two rifle shots from the hands of the above named McSween, Morris, Zamora and others, and while they were resisting the Sheriff's posse, and while Beckwith was a deputy sheriff, acting in the discharge of his duties, trying to arrest the parties for whom he had warrants."

The Grant County *Herald,* of August 3, 1878, published one version of the encounter between McSween and Beckwith:

> We learn McSween said after a hard fight that they would surrender. Beckwith said as he was a deputy sheriff he would go to the door; that they could surrender to him and he would protect them. As Beckwith approached the door, McSween and party jumped to the door and fired; it appeared that they expected more were coming and that they would kill all that were with him. Bob's gun failed to work; he received a ball in the corner of the left eye and fell dead. With a cry of "Revenge Bob Beckwith," no time was lost by the Sheriff's posse in firing with effect. McSween said: "Oh, my God! and dropped dead. . . . Mrs. McSween never went to see McSween after he was killed and did not attend the funeral. Beckwith was buried with honors at Fort Stanton.

Justice of the Peace John B. Wilson wrote an eyewitness account of the happenings of July 19, 1878, at the request of Gov. Lew. Wallace:

> I was ordered by Col. Dudley, Commanding Fort Stanton in New Mexico, on or about the 19th of July, 1878, to take the affidavits of Col. Purington, Capt. Blair and Dr. Appel accusing A. A. McSween and others that were in his house on July 16th, 1878, of having committed an assault on the person of one Benj. Robinson, a soldier of Ft. Stanton by having shot 4 or more shots at him with intent to kill as they had been informed and believed. I told Col. Dudley that I was not certain whether it was lawful for me to issue such an order or not and I thought it was the duty

> of a United States Commissioner to issue it, as there was a soldier concerned in it. He got very angry at me for refusing to issue it on that ground. He told me if I did not take the affidavit and issue the warrant forthwith that he would report me to the governor. He called me a coward and said many other bad words to me. I then went to my office and took the affidavits of the named officers and after they signed and swore to them I issued the warrant to the Sheriff of Lincoln county for the arrest of A. A. McSween and others that were in the house on the 16th day of July, 1878, as per the affidavits and gave it to George W. Peppin to serve returnable forthwith. The warrant has not been returned into my office up to this date by Peppin or any one for him. I did not issue the warrant by my own will but by peremptory order of Col. Dudley.

Isaac Ellis, a Lincoln merchant, in an unsigned statement corroborated Judge Wilson's recollections:

> On or about the 17th of July 1878 Sheriff Peppin and posse attacked the town of Lincoln and kept up firing from the neighboring hills until the morning of the 19th when Lieut. Col. N. A. M. Dudley, with Capt. George A. Purington, Capt. Blair, Lieut. Goodwin and Dr. Appel of Fort Stanton with a company of soldiers and 2 pieces of artillery arrived here and went into camp about the center of town and sent for me. When I arrived at the camp Dudley seemed to be greatly excited. When I was informed by Col. Dudley that if a gun was fired out of mine or any house in town he would immediately tear it to the ground regardless of women and children. While at the camp of Col. Dudley the so called Sheriff George W. Peppin came riding into camp with 3 soldiers, I think Peppin was riding a government horse. After talking a short time with Dudley, Dudley ordered the soldiers to go back with Sheriff Peppin. I then returned to my house. Dudley set one piece of artillery about 200 feet from and pointing towards my house. In a short time Peppin together with about nine men came from the direction of the camp of Dudley and came in my house and ordered me to give them coal oil for which they stated they intended to use in setting fire to the house of A. A. McSween. They further stated that they had him in the house and intended to burn him out. They took the coal oil with them and went back. When opposite the camp, Dudley came out and they, Dudley and Peppin talked for some time. They then went on towards the house of A. A. McSween and in a little while firing commenced around McSween's house and we saw some smoke arise from the house and firing was kept up until about nine o'clock at night. The following morning McSween with two others were found dead in the yard riddled with bullets and the house and contents were totally destroyed by fire. The same morning the store of John H. Tunstall, dec'd was broke open and robbed of about six thousand dollars worth of goods. After the store was robbed Col. Dudley broke up camp and returned to Fort Stanton.

SUGGESTED READINGS

Frederick W. Nolan, *The Life and Death of John Henry Tunstall* (Albuquerque 1965);

Maurice Garland Fulton, *History of the Lincoln County War* edited by Robert N. Mullin (Tucson 1968);

Ramon F. Adams, *A Fitting Death for Billy the Kid* (Norman 1960);

Philip J. Rasch, "Exit Axtell: Enter Wallace," *New Mexico Historical Review*, vol. XXXI (July 1957);

Rasch, "The Horrell War," *New Mexico Historical Review*, vol. XXX (July 1956).

15
The Penitentes

From a very early date visitors to New Mexico have been fascinated by the Penitentes, and the number of newspaper and magazine accounts of them in the nineteenth and twentieth centuries is remarkable. Scholars, too, have devoted considerable attention to this religious organization although they do not agree on its origins. As Professor Warren A. Beck indicates, some scholars believe that the Penitentes are indigenous to New Mexico, while others trace them back to the Middle Ages. Beck believes that they are "a true representation of Spanish religious thought and Spanish culture" but that they are also unique because they borrowed heavily from others and then preserved their culture in remote villages in northern New Mexico.

Although the shroud of secrecy surrounding the Penitentes has stimulated the interest of scholars and many observers have been attracted by the practice of flagellation and the ceremonies of Holy Week, the Penitentes also fulfill political and social functions. In this essay Professor Beck calls attention to their cultural contributions.

Los Hermanos Penitentes or Los Hermanos de Sangre de Cristo is a religious brotherhood found among the Spanish American citizens in New Mexico, in Southern Colorado, and in contiguous territory across the border of Mexico. They practice flagellation and the actual dramatization of the Biblical story of the Passion. Their rites during the Lenten season have attracted much attention from many observers, usually Protestants who found these ceremonies quite different from what their church practiced. In addition to their religious function, which is of primary importance, the Penitentes have exercised a charitable role among their members, have been directly involved in politics, have even played a judicial role in

---

Warren A. Beck, "The Cultural Contributions of the Penitentes," paper read at the Western History Association, October 1968. By permission of the author.

some communities, and have provided the primary social outlet for their members.

What were the origins of the Penitentes? Some have attributed the movement to Indian influence. Others have claimed that it represented a degeneration of the lay Third Order of St. Francis. Still others have traced its beginnings back to the practices of the Flagellants of the Middle Ages, while a few authorities see the Penitentes as an outgrowth of the confraternities of Spain. Some even contend that it is indigenous to New Mexico, originating along the Rio Grande between 1777 and 1833 and deny that the Penitentes have any Spanish origin at all.

However, in the opinion of this observer, to claim that the Penitentes are a product of New Mexico alone is to blind oneself to practices similar to theirs throughout the Spanish-speaking world, for flagellation, as well as simulated crucifixion, are basic religious rites of the Penitentes practiced in many parts of Mexico and South America as well as in the Philippines and even in Puerto Rico. In addition, such practices have been common in Spain herself. While in Mexico City this past spring a Mexican friend and fellow historian helped locate an extensive documentary collection on Penitentes, especially in the state of Michoacan. When I have had an opportunity to fully examine this material I am sure we will find that this religious sect was far more prevalent in old Mexico than has hitherto been believed. But it is not the objective of this paper to settle the historical question of the exact origin of the Penitentes. Regardless of their exact origins, it is the opinion of this observer that the Penitentes of New Mexico are a true representation of Spanish religious thought and Spanish culture in general. Furthermore, they have been able to preserve the artistic and musical heritage of old Spain in a frontier area.

To fully understand this claim that the Penitentes are truly representative of Spanish culture, an extensive examination of Hispanic character would be in order. Such a task is beyond the scope of this paper. Yet, it is necessary to at least examine the distinctive features of the Roman Catholic Church in Spain. For this Church is different from Catholicism in the rest of the world.

First of all, Christianity in Spain has always had a decided Old Testament flavor. As Unamuno has noted, "Christianity sprang from two great spiritual streams—the Judaic and Hellenic." In the Spaniard's emphasis upon the Old Testament, Hebraic and Moorish influences are evident. How these two streams helped mold Hispanic religious thought has been interpreted by one authority in these words: "The God of the Old Testament and the God of Islam are rather like artists who could never set their work free as finished and perfect. The man created in Genesis faltered time and again, and had to be made over and saved by the Christian God. Islamic man and everything that exists for him are a continual endeavor in which the fingers of his creator are never still. His being and his truth cannot be fulfilled save at the moment of becoming one again in his point of origin when man returns from the temporal to the eternal." In other words, the religion of the Moors and the Jews was an unfulfilled one. It was built upon the expectation of the future coming of a Messiah, and the long period of coexistence fostered such a concept in Hispanic religious thought.

Thus, we can say that to the Spaniard his religion is also unfulfilled. He is waiting for something else. The deeply religious Spaniard is, in the words of Madariaga, "in a state of expectation, awaiting some providential event which is going to alter his life fundamentally, and of course for the better. There is a phrase, typically Spanish in its mixture of piety and irreverence, which describes this state of mind; 'esperar el santo advenimiento,' to hope for the holy event. . . . for the present we may link up with it the Spanish attachment to lotteries." Among orthodox Moslems, Mohammed was of course to be the last prophet inspired by God. Nevertheless, Moslem thought still nurtures the hopeful dream of a Messiah. Recognizing also the actual presence of Hispanic Jews, as well as Jewish converts to Christianity in all classes of society, one can better understand the Messianic character of Hispanic religion. Unamuno expresses this idea in another way when he says, "the true Christian makes himself another Christ. St. Paul knew this well: he experienced Christ being born, being in agony, and dying within himself." The Messianic attitude is also reflected in the Spanish emphasis on the infant Jesus, on the Virgin Mary, and on the suffering and death of Christ, with little emphasis on the redemptive character of Christ's suffering and death on the cross. An obvious question in contemplating this Messianic concept is: is not the Penitente in his quest for communion with God through his rites being the man of the Old Testament who is still seeking for something? Is the Penitente who is being hung from the cross anticipating that he might be the new Messiah?

The most significant feature of Spanish religion is its emphasis on death. In fact, one might even say that Christ has become the center of a cult of death. John Mackay, in *The Other Spanish Christ,* discusses this infatuation with the death of Christ in these words: "The contemplation of His Passion produces a sort of catharsis, as Aristotle would say, in the soul of the worshipper. Just as in the bullfight, an analogous creation of the Spanish spirit, the Spaniard sees and feels death in all its dread reality in the fate of a victim. The total sensation intensifies his sense of the reality and terribleness of death; it increases his passion for life, and, in the religious realm, makes him cling desperately and tragically to the dead victim that died to give him immortality."

Havelock Ellis contends that the Spaniards find pleasure in the sight of the sufferings of Christ. It is certain that the Spanish artist has sought to portray the most agonized images of the suffering of Christ, and Spanish worshippers have surrounded themselves with such art. This Spanish interest in blood, and in the satisfaction of shedding it, has even intruded itself not only into art but also, as Ganivet suggests, into medicine. Easily the most notable contribution of Spain in the field of medicine was the discovery of the circulation of blood by Servetus.

In its preoccupation with death, the Spanish-speaking world is far more realistic than the Anglo world which has sought to banish death. Octavio Paz, in his *El laberinto de la soledad* analyzes the attitude of the Mexican toward death which is perhaps typical of the Hispanic world:

> Death also lacks meaning for the modern Mexican. It is no longer a transition, an access to another life more alive than our own. But although we do not view death as a transcendence, we have not eliminated it from our daily lives. The word death is not pronounced in New York, in Paris, in London, because it burns the lips. The Mexican, in contrast, is familiar with death, jokes about it, caresses it, sleeps with it, celebrates it; it is one of his favorite toys and his most steadfast love.

It is this preoccupation with death which is the most distinguishing feature of the Penitentes. The high point of their worship is the re-creation of Christ's passion on the cross. It is widely believed, although not totally authenticated, that initially the man playing the role of the Christ was nailed to the cross. As a result, it was reported that death frequently resulted. But the family who lost a member in such a manner took pride in their contribution. If a man who had acted this role lived, it was assumed that he was cleansed of all sin. After the coming of the Americans and the embarrassment of legal investigations over reported deaths, the man on the cross was tied on with horsehide ropes that were still dangerous because they curtailed the circulation. The emphasis on death is represented in the decoration of the chapter houses, the *moradas* of the Penitentes. The emphasis upon death is carried out in all of the decorations, including the cart of death.

Another important characteristic of the Spaniard's attitude toward religion is his love of formalism, ritual, and ceremony. To the Anglo-Saxon, ceremonial functions are for the most part an unreal and uncongenial convention which he carries through to the best of his ability, sometimes with awkward solemnity. To the Spaniard, ceremonialism is so real that in his hands it becomes gracious, simple, and natural. Much has been written about the Spaniard's love of ceremony in his everyday life, but this is not the occasion for a further exposition on it. Unfortunately, when rigid formalism is applied to a religion, it frequently results in a people possessing religion without the religion possessing them.

Many contemporary critics of Spanish religion claim that the Spanish practice religion, but they do not live it. They go to church through habit. They participate in the sacraments, and some of them put on the appearance of Christian piety. But, this emphasis on formalism and ceremony does not carry with it any real understanding of religious faith. In the last few years church leaders have finally admitted that most individuals have an inadequate knowledge of what the sacraments are supposed to mean. Havelock Ellis remarked that the Spanish emphasis upon ritual in religion "involved a faith in exteriority which is almost fetishism." Unamuno tells the story of the bandit, who when about to die, requests of his executioner to not cut off his head until he had said the creed as far as the words "I believe in the resurrection of the body." There is much of this kind of formalism in the religious rites of the Penitentes, a formalism which displays a great deal of emphasis upon practice and little upon total meaning.

Combined with a strong emphasis upon formality in religion, the Spaniard has a strong commitment to asceticism and mysticism. Of course, the mystic was the most complete of the ascetics. He sought to attain spiritual communion with God, a oneness with God by means of a state of contemplation which rejected the world around him until the individual soul was brought into union with the divine. The escape of the mystic from reality was one of the most complete ever accomplished. In his search for God, the mystic was claimed from the real world in which he found himself; and many leaders such as Santa Teresa, St. John of the Cross, and Friar Luis de Leon had trouble with the Inquisition because if mysticism were carried to its logical conclusion it could destroy the church. There is no question that Spanish mysticism represented the mingling of neo-Platonic thought as it was modified by the Moors. In fact, to really understand Spanish mysticism, one must examine the Moorish heritage, for it springs from 900 years of Christian-Islamic interrelationships, as previously noted. One might also mention in passing that many mystics, like Santa Teresa, were of Jewish heritage. The structure of the Moslem faith helped to create an atmosphere wherein the individual was brought into a closer relationship to his God that was both more immediate and more casual than that of the Christians. In the Moslem's case, the elements of the relationship were the believer, the sacred book, and God. The religious bond was established through ritual prayer, the pilgrimage to Mecca, fasting, and giving alms. A visible church as such did not exist, nor were there sacraments such as penance and communion to bind the faithful together in a spiritual community.

On the other hand, the path between the Christian and his God was mapped out and guarded by the spiritual and political authority of the Church. This was made manifest in a hierarchy which closely followed the government of the Roman Empire. To be a Christian consisted first of all in recognizing this hierarchy made up of God's ministers. They were the only persons authorized to administer the sacraments and perform the rites of the Church. In other words, there was a wide area of external regulation for the Christian. In Islam, on the other hand, there were no priests nor really any religious hierarchy. Their places were taken by men learned in Koranic law, and they were the ones who directed prayer in the mosques. The believers had a direct relationship with God and with his prophet through prayer and spiritual works, and this brought with it a more personal and a more casual attitude than that possible for the average Christian. The close communion between the Spaniard and the Moslem meant that many of these attitudes were transferred to the Christian faith. Angel Ganivet observed that "Spain was the nation which created a form of Christianity most personal."

One of the primary sources of Moorish mysticism was the sect, Sufism. The members of the sect attributed reality to God alone. Man participated only so far as he attained identification with the divinity. It was greatly influenced by Christian mysticism and Gnosticism, and its basic principle was the cultivation of religious experience. The stress on a religious experience which originated in the heart of the believer alone tended to denigrate the importance of the organized structure of the church. Purification and sanctification are prerequisites before the soul can come into fellowship with God. To accomplish this, it was first necessary for man to cleanse himself of himself. Only then was he ready to see God face to face, and in seeing him become one with him. Such a process tended to "blur the boundaries between man and God."

Sufism greatly influenced Spanish Christianity just as it, in turn, had been greatly influenced by the Christian faith itself. Thus, there was much in the Moslem faith that Christians could readily accept such as the desire to enter into a mystical communion with God. In my opinion, what the Christian could not accept is the idea of the negation, annihilation, or complete obliteration of the human personality in its seeking of oneness with God, or, as stated earlier, in blurring the line between God and man. Of course, the Penitentes' approach to this divine union is different, and it involves a mortification of the flesh borrowed from the Flagellants. But in seeking to emulate Christ's crucifixion, they are certainly attempting to imitate Christ.

Thus, it can be seen that regardless of their exact origin, the Penitentes of New Mexico are true representatives of the fusion of Moorish and Judaic traditions into Hispanic civilization. Their practices can only be understood within this framework. What Americo Castro has said of the religious processions in Seville during Holy Week would be equally applicable to the rites of the Penitentes: "What is important is that the man includes himself in a halo, in something that is 'his' but which, being his, transcends him. He lives trusting something that is located outside him and operates outside what he himself does." In going through his religious rites, the Penitente believes that he is cleansing himself of the sins that he has committed during the year. By these actions, he is just as certain that he is brought into a close relationship with God as were the mystics. Like the mystic, the Penitente is also using his religious observances as a means of fleeing from the reality of the harsh life he is forced to lead. If the Penitente is a true believer, and most are, he feels radiant and transfigured after his religious observances, and merges his own small soul with God. Like St. John of the Cross, he feels that God is a deathless spring, hidden by night; and therefore he goes into the darkness to drink of him.

The Penitentes of New Mexico were able to retain their traditions while similar organizations in other parts of the Spanish world were induced to give up theirs. This was true because of their isolation from authority in the mountain vastness of the northern part of the state. Then too, the growth of the Penitentes of New Mexico was a result of historical factors unrelated to the Church. Beginning with the ousting of Spain from Mexico in 1821, the territory went through a long period of transition wherein the simple social mores of the natives were constantly subject to change. First, their priests were largely driven out by the Mexicans (as they were Spanish nationals), creating a spiritual vacuum which the Penitente order attempted to fill. Officials of the groups soon performed many of the functions of priests. Frequently the Hermano Mayor was also the local alcalde. And as the old way of life was consistently threatened with change, the Penitentes became "an organization of the common man against his masters—a brotherhood with temporal benefits and a pure solidarity and secretness." Although its religious basis remained predominant, the absence of qualified clerical supervision led to a perversion of its teachings and practices, which the Catholic Church was to later have much difficulty in controlling. In fact, when Bishop Lamy arrived in the mid-nineteenth century, the reforms which he tried to put into operation were bitterly opposed by the few native priests in New Mexico whose concept of Christianity was vastly different from that of their French supervisor.

Not only did the Penitentes preserve their Spanish religious heritage, they also quite effectively preserved their cultural heritage, especially in terms of music and art. The earliest Spanish missionaries to the New World quickly discovered the importance of music as a means by which the Indians could be induced to accept Christianity. Both vocal and instrumental music were used effectively, and it is probable that music was taught more extensively to the natives than any other subject. The enthusiasm with which the Indians could be taught their catechism with music led to a stress upon its use. The first European music teacher to come into New Mexico was Percival de Quinanes, who came to Mexico between

1598 and 1604. He even brought an organ with him to the remote colonies.

Music played a key role in the religious rites of the Penitentes. Apparently the only universal musical instrument used by them was the pito. This reedlike flute has been used down through the ages to imitate the reactions of people to tragedy. The music produced by the pito had a wailing sound that echoed and re-echoed through the countryside and could be heard for great distances. Indispensable during the processionals during Holy Week, it was also used when the Penitentes observed their wakes (*velorios*) or at the religious rites they held on Saints' days. The matraca was the only other instrument extensively employed in the Penitente rites. The latter was a type of wooden rattle composed of a stiff stick slipping over a notched wheel which made a large clacking sound. However, some Penitente chapters also used the drum.

Most of the singing of the Penitentes was *a cappella.* Hymns were collected in copybooks in most chapters. However, as few people could read, the usual pattern was for the children to learn their hymns early in life and pass them on to the succeeding generation. The New Mexican alabado is a hymn which begins with the words *alabada sea* ("praise be in honor of the blessed sacrament"). Through the passage of time, the word came to suggest any religious hymn so the technical explanation is no longer applicable in New Mexico. Many of the hymns are simply the Penitential psalms. Because of the lack of a written tradition, the same hymns may be sung to different music in different communities and even have different words.

Some of the hymns have an untold number of verses which reflect local improvisation. Some were undoubtedly even written by the natives, but most were brought in from the outside. There were regular Catholic hymns that the Penitentes or their ancestors may have learned from the priests. Many alabados originated in fifteenth or sixteenth century Spain. The music for these hymns is reminiscent of the Gregorian chants, "but often with a wilder, more primitive strain, particularly in the case of songs sung by an individual Penitent, which suddenly startle the listener with the piercing note of the *saeta,* 'arrow song' of Seville—undoubtedly of Moorish origin." Friar Chavez concurs in this origin. "Their hymns and alabados are also Sevillan, both in metric form and in their minor-key cadences, as well as in their uninhibited manner of delivery. It is the *Cante Jondo,* a deep singing brought up from the very depths of being, a cry wrenched from the soul as in a fit of paroxysm, and trailing off in unexpected tones and half-tones." Another observer comments that while traveling through the villages of old Castille, he was frequently surprised to find that a New Mexican tune which he had learned in childhood was almost identical to one still used in Castille. Some of the songs of the Penitentes undoubtedly saw their origin in Jewish canticles. The theological content of the hymns was decidedly limited, and the brief verses were intended to be sung repeatedly during the lengthy ceremonies, especially during the passion season.

Of one collection of eighty-nine New Mexican alabados, thirty-eight are concerned with the Passion. These hymns reflect the familiarity the Spaniard feels for his God. Christ's wounds are minutely described with much emphasis being placed upon the shedding of blood. He is depicted in the processional, while suffering on the cross, as the broken, bloody body that is given to Mary, and in the sepulchre. Nine hymns are in praise of the Lord and only four are for Holy Communion. Twenty-two are in praise of the Virgin or ask her intercession. The remainder are of a miscellaneous nature, but they also stress the petitions of the helpless sinner. The music was so simple that the tunes could be sung by the Penitente families in their daily devotions or even as they labored in the fields. However, not all of the music was of a reverent nature. The Pentitentes sang corridos as did other Spaniards; even during the sombre processional of Passion Week, a flippant tune was heard.

However, as important as music was, visual art was the most significant cultural expression of the Penitentes. As Unamuno contends: "The highest artistic expression of . . . Spanish Catholicism is in the art that is most material, tangible, and permanent . . . , in sculpture and painting, in the quest of Velasquez, that Christ who is ever dying, yet never finishes dying, in order that he may give us life." And the sacred art of the Penitentes of northern New Mexico ably portrays the depth of human religious feeling of simple people. As one observer has commented: "It embodies not only the mood of Medievalism, but the asceticism of El Greco, the grief imbued in the Gothic, and the Miserere of Rouault, as well as the stark simplicity of the frescos in the catacombs beneath Rome, that were tantamount to prayers and offerings for the salvation of the deceased." The tradition of Spanish folk religion is ably expressed in the artistic creations of the simple Penitente in his quest for oneness with God. Penitente art may be favorably compared to the Russian icon wherein the simple peasant was able to reveal his inner religious feelings, the nobility of his soul, and the depth of his thought on religious matters. In their artistic creations the Penitentes expressed their love of God and the feelings they had for His suffering son. In doing so, they were also revealing their own fears: their fears of the harsh life they were forced to undergo on earth and the fears they had of hell. Their art reflects the depth of religious feeling so ably expressed in their enactment of the crucifixion: a rite wherein they vicariously suffered with their Lord.

Charles Lummis has referred to New Mexico as the land of *poco tiempo,* or literally, "the land where time has stood still." This cultural isolation is the only thing that accounts for the preservation of the religious folk art of the region. As a recent article remarks, "religious art in the Rio Grande Valley was tucked away in a time capsule—nicely insulated against foreign influences, in a sort of cultural hypnosis. Even church authority was missing, thanks to the ecclesiastical squabble with civil administration, ending in the desecularization of the clergy. Outmoded concepts sometimes continued in fashion, oblivious to officialdom; the Holy Trinity represented as three identical personages—a Byzantine concept—had been banned by Pope Benedict XIV in 1745. The news failed to impress the New Mexican faithful where this heretical version flourished throughout the nineteenth century." Of course, the purpose of such art amongst a predominantly illiterate people was reflected in the words of St. Augustine when he spoke of sacred pictures as the "books of the simple."

The full flowering of Penitente art was not reflected in architecture. Their church, the morada, was the ultimate in simplicity. It was usually located wherever convenient and sometimes in the midst of the local cemetery. It was usually long, low, and very close to the earth, perhaps reflecting the way in which the people themselves were always close to that earth which was waiting to claim them. Its massive walls of adobe were seldom, if ever, broken by windows. But such simplicity could be deceptive. One authority suggests that "here in the dark recesses of the Morada a basic people have fathomed the mystery of basic faith, the genesis of Christian philosophy." The decoration, except for a small cross, was saved for the interior; that is, except for the doors. Through the passage of time man's quest for beauty was reflected in the artistic work that went into the doors of the moradas. When one considers that all of the work was done by hand, and usually without iron tools, the accomplishment is the more marvelous. On most of them St. Andrew's cross is the prominent feature. But sometimes the cross is rendered in the molding on the doorway so that it's barely discernable. The doors themselves were frequently painted blue, perhaps because of the identification of that color with the Franciscan fathers who came from Zacatecas.

The lack of decoration of the exterior of the morada was more than compensated for by the artistic expression displayed within. As one authority has put it:

> In the decoration of the hamlet churches and in equipping them for use, one of the most interesting art styles to be found anywhere in the world developed. It has been very appropriately called *Santero* Art after its saint-maker artists who were the *Santeros* (saint makers) for the village chapels and homes. They produced the statues of the saints, the altar paintings, and the general interior decoration for the chapels. They executed their art on skins, on plaques of wood, in carved wooden figures, and the like—from materials at hand as their Indian predecessors had

> done. *Santero* Art is an indigenous religious expression of a native Spanish-speaking peasantry born in the little hamlets hidden away in New Mexico's mountain solitudes. Its like can be seen nowhere else in the world for it comes out of the very soul of native New Mexico. Only in New Mexico occurred the unique combination of circumstances which brought it forth —Franciscanism, Spanish-Roman Catholicism, Pueblo Indian Animism, Los Hermanos Penitentes, New Mexican isolation.

The making of santos undoubtedly went back to the early period of Franciscan missionary activity in New Mexico. The use of religious statues and paintings of religious themes had long been significant as a means of instructing the natives. As New Mexico was remote from the usual centers of trade and supply, the clergy taught the people to produce their own religious art. And when the clergy were no longer available, the people themselves continued such production. Santeros, or those who produced the santos, could be the individuals who simply produced them for the home or the santero craftsman who spent the winter making his statues and paintings, and then set out in the late spring to sell his wares to the people. Religious art became of greater importance as the clergy decreased in numbers and the people were virtually responsible for their own religious welfare. This unique religious folk art of New Mexico began to decline after the American occupation. Traders soon flooded the previously isolated area with lithographed images which had greater appeal to the people than did their own crude productions. Even Currier and Ives entered the market. Then too, the French missionaries who arrived in the 1850s discouraged the worship of the santos. Factory-produced, plaster statuary began to adorn New Mexico's churches and homes.

The santos were of two types: the retablos, which were simply pictures painted upon wood, and the bultos, which were carved statues. The retablos were sometimes as large as twenty inches square, but the usual size was eight by ten inches. Initially, the paint was applied directly to the wood, but it was soon learned that it would crack and peel off. A more durable finish and a better surface for painting was attained by covering the panel with a native material known as yeso. Sometimes this gypsum-like material was used for molding the figures into bas-relief. The subjects were those one would expect: the saints, led by St. Francis who is important in New Mexico for obvious reasons; the Virgin; and, of course, numerous portrayals of Christ. Little attention was paid to physical proportion in these presentations; they reflect the Byzantine influence which the Moors had brought to Spain and show no knowledge of the great artistic changes brought about during the Quattrocento in Italy. The crucified Christ was depicted in untutored realism, with the five wounds gushing blood and a crown of thorns imparting human suffering. "They were wrought in agony of spirit which was dramatized in their human experiences in Penitente crucifixions." A people living a more natural life were also not afraid to depict the figures as stark naked, necessitating the addition of clothes in a later period.

One of the more unique santos is colored in part with blood. White roses, cut from paper, are pasted on it. It represents the drawing of a crucifixion, perhaps the leading theme of Penitente art. The bultos were usually carved from cottonwood, which was easily shaped with the poor tools the santero had to use. It was formed in several pieces and later assembled using glue and wooden dowels. They too, were covered with yeso before painting. Some of the larger statuary was constructed so that limbs could move. Some even had human hair. Clothing was usually portrayed by putting yeso over a frame of cloth. Madariaga has observed that "color is the predominant character of Spanish art." The New Mexico santeros certainly carried out this tradition in their lavish use of bright colors such as red, blue, and yellow which not even time has completely dulled. Their paint was made from indigo, clay, the juice of cactus, and the dye of leaves and bark and was usually applied as watercolor or mixed with oil. As mentioned previously, human blood was probably used on occasion.

Not all of the art of the santos can be attributed to the Penitentes, but as the Penitentes were a quasi-secret organization, it was not always possible to differentiate between the art produced by their members, and that of others. Those that were obviously Penitente depicted Christ in all his suffering, sometimes showing the whip of flagellation and the cross. Then too, Penitente art is more starkly realistic, intending to shock the viewer. The beard may be soiled with blood and the body show the proverbial five wounds. Some of the Cristos were man-sized and were intended to be carried in the processional, or even affixed to the cross in some Penitente chapters. When this was true, the legs and arms were pliable at the knees and shoulder joints so as to make it possible to fasten it to the cross.

Another common Penitente art form was *El Santo Entierro*. This is simply the Cristo resting in the coffin. As one expert describes it: "The colors of the figure are a reddish-yellow for the flesh tints, and red for the blood is freely used, especially on the shoulders and on the back. The ribs are outlined with pale blue, the loincloth is dark green and gray-brown with narrow red stripes in between. Hair and beard are black."

Perhaps most representative of Penitente art forms was the *carreta de la muerte*. This was the cart that was pulled in the Penitente Passion processional. It symbolizes the triumph of death and epitomizes the true artistic expression of the Penitente. Such an attitude was common during the Middle Ages, and its retention is indicative of the Medieval attitude that had continued in Spain and which was retained in New Mexico. One figure of death was described in the following words: "It is remarkable in that the shoulders, stomach muscles, and hips are beautifully carved in semblance of the living flesh, but with the ribs carved *outside* the chest; and the whole painted white. The hips end in a square block to which the movable legs are fastened with wooden pegs; and the head, above the accurate realism of the body, is a very much simplified death mask, with inset mother-of-pearl eyes." The terrifying effect of such a figure is enhanced by the bow and arrow representing death in its hands.

Thus, we have seen the Penitentes of New Mexico, although having many similarities to Flagellants in different parts of the Hispanic world at different periods in history, are nevertheless unique for they have been able to synthesize the religious beliefs of Medieval Catholicism, borrow heavily from Islam, and perhaps even borrow some practices from the Indians, and then preserve their culture in the mountain vastnesses remote from centers of population. The Roman Catholic Church was largely able to eliminate such religious sects in Mexico herself because of more extensive control. The lack of clergy in New Mexico led to an indigenous development that was unique. The Spaniard in Spain had retreated into the castle of his own person during the period of the Moorish occupation and resisted acculturation. In this, he was not totally successful as he was unquestionably influenced by his conqueror. Similarly the New Mexican, isolated in his mountain vastness, sought to preserve the Hispanic civilization that he had brought with him. In recent years, studies have shown that in the hill country of Appalachia in the United States there have been preserved songs, mannerisms of speech, and folkways that date back to seventeenth-century England. We have seen that in New Mexico there was created a citadel wherein the traditions of Spain had been similarly preserved. This is especially evident, as we have noted in music and art, which are the most concrete manifestations of the culture of the Penitentes.

SUGGESTED READINGS

Fray Angelico Chavez, "Penitentes of New Mexico," *New Mexico Historical Review*, vol. XXIX (April 1954);

Charles F. Lummis, *The Land of Poco Tiempo* (New York 1893 and Albuquerque 1952);

Bill Tate, *The Penitentes of the Sangre de Cristo* (Truchas, N.M. 1967);

Jack E. Holmes, *Politics in New Mexico* (Albuquerque 1967).

16
Populism in New Mexico

Scholarly interest in the Populist movement of the 1890s has centered on the Midwest and South and has largely ignored the Rocky Mountains and Southwest. Historians disagree greatly in their interpretations of Populism and have described the movement as both radical and conservative. Nor do they agree on the importance of the free silver issue. Robert Larson focuses his attention on the Populist movement in New Mexico and on the reasons for its development. He believes, for example, that the roots of New Mexico Populism are not to be found in the silver issue. The Populists and their predecessors, the Alliance, were opposed to cattle barons, land companies, and alien land ownership. In San Miguel County, citizens formed the White Caps to fight land encroachments and soon found an ally in the Knights of Labor. It is not surprising that the People's party formed there in 1888. In 1890 San Miguel County sent Populists to both houses of the legislature, and four years later the party held a territorial convention in Albuquerque. Larson's fresh appraisal of New Mexico Populism is especially valuable because he places it in the context of national developments.

In his highly acclaimed study, *The Age of Reform,* Richard Hofstadter wrote that the "free-silver Populism of the mountain-states variety was not agrarian Populism at all, but simply silverism." Populism in the Rocky Mountain area was, thus, effectively isolated by Hofstadter from the mainstream of the movement in the Midwest and South, for, by concluding that the Colorado or Wyoming Populist was almost solely interested in the "free and unlimited coinage" of silver, he was discouraging badly needed research into other possible causes of discontent in the mountain West, such as fear of monopoly or heavy mortgage indebtedness.

Robert W. Larson, "Roots of New Mexico Populism." Paper read at the Western History Association, October 1970. By permission of the author.

A study of New Mexico Populism has revealed that there were other important causes of reform agitation to rival the undeniably sharp concern over the price of silver and the continuance of a government market for the white metal. Indeed, the roots of the movement in the Territory of New Mexico can be found in the very traditional concerns of agrarian Populists. In massive Lincoln County in the southeastern corner of the territory, for instance, a newspaper acting as the official organ for the county's Farmers' Alliance was bitterly assailing a so-called cattle monopoly as early as 1888. The strong bias against bigness of *The Nogal Nugget,* as the journal was called, was not only characteristic of the radical agrarianism that preceded the organization of a national People's party elsewhere, but its expression in this mountain territory occurred several years before silver became a serious local issue and almost eight years before the cry for free coinage became the trumpet call of the mountain West.

The Lincoln Alliance was a chapter of the powerful Southern Alliance and was operating in a primarily stock-grazing county, although the territorial Bureau of Immigration, admittedly a biased source, described the county several years later as being "dotted with thrifty farms." Beans, alfalfa, and truck crops were raised by some of the members, but most of them were little stockmen, struggling for existence against the big cattlemen of the county. The *Nugget,* edited by a ranch manager named J. E. Sligh, was vigorous in its attack on those who threatened its readers and was especially critical of New Mexico Republicans, who, it contended, were in league with the cattle kings. The territorial Republican party had obediently passed laws to protect the "Cattle Association monopoly" when it was in power, showing practically no concern for the little settler. It consistently protected the railroads from taxation and ignored the "just demands" of the people for lower freight rates. Even though very partial to the Democratic party, the *Nugget* attacked Democratic Governor Edmund G. Ross, who, along with most of the territorial legislators, supported a quarantine law to keep cattle carrying Texas Fever out of New Mexico. The law was not a legitimate measure to protect cattle against the disease, but merely a blind to allow the members of the cattle association to retain their "*monopoly of the public domain.*" The measure, in actuality, would keep out "small farmers," as they cannot afford to leave their stock behind and come to New Mexico. "Thus the Cattle Baron is 'protected' from the man with the hoe and the plow."

To the north in Colfax County, which stretched all across the northeastern corner of the vast territory, big stock companies comprised another cattle monopoly, with such outfits as the Scottish-controlled Prairie Cattle Company and the Illinois Live Stock and Palo Blanco Cattle companies dominating acres of fine range land. But an even greater threat to the small homesteaders in the big county was a land company, the famous

Maxwell Land Grant and Railroad Company, which claimed almost 2,000,000 acres. Originally a Mexican land grant made by Governor Manuel Armijo in 1841, the Maxwell acreage had passed from the hands of the original Mexican families to American speculators, then to English owners, and finally to a group of Dutch bankers. A sensational example of alien landownership, the small stockmen and farmers of Colfax resisted the sweeping claims of the Maxwell Company, and squatter's clubs and anti-Grant groups were organized in Cimarron and Raton. One member of the active Farmer's Alliance operating in Colfax County commiserated with those Alliance "brethren" on the grant, who were "being oppressed by foreign capital. Every true American should do the same." Even the Republican *Las Vegas Daily Optic* was alarmed at the "land companies and trusts whose purpose is not honest and whose every method is crooked." By such motivation and tactics "large strips of land that would in a European country be sufficient for several kingdoms if not empires" were being acquired. The seeds of agitation against wealthy aliens owning American land, a major Populist concern, were rapidly germinating in Colfax County.

Although there were other problems of serious concern among the small operators in the county, such as the disturbing drop in the assessed value of cattle and the high territorial interest rate, which was 10.05 in 1890, it was the land and cattle monopolies which posed the greatest immediate threat. Because of the power of the immense enterprises moving into New Mexico during the eighties, organizing and politicking became essential. Chapters of the Colfax County Farmers' Alliance were located in Cimarron, Ute Park, Raton, and Elizabethtown or E'town. Newspapers friendly to the cause of the small stockmen and farmers waged an active campaign against the land and stock combines. The *Wagon Mound Settler* was for a time the official voice of the county Alliance, but there were also sympathetic newspapers such as the *Raton Weekly Independent* and the *Clayton Enterprise*. The struggle waged by these determined Alliancemen was, to use an expression coined by Robert G. Athearn, much like "bucking big business out on the plains."

"Land grabbing" was a common accusation in the Territory of New Mexico at this time. Numerous grants dating back to the Spanish and Mexican periods had provided irresistible temptations to acquisitive Anglos, many of whom employed their legal knowledge to acquire a share of ownership by defending the rights of original grantees in court. Stephen B. Elkins, who later acquired national fame, was one of them. Thomas B. Catron, who became one of the largest landowners in the nation, was another. Both Catron and Elkins were organizers of the powerful Santa Fe Ring, more descriptively called the Land Grant Ring, which manipulated the business and political activities of the territory for many years.

One example of "land grabbing" that led directly to the formation of the first genuine People's party in New Mexico occurred in San Miguel County. A communal holding known as the Las Vegas Grant was involved and the "grabbers" in this instance were Anglo ranchers, who bought tracts of land from some of the original landowners and fenced them, contrary to the purpose of a community grant. In 1888, a secret, masked group of angry Hispanos, called the White Caps or *Gorras Blancas,* began to terrorize these new intruders by conducting violent night raids, in which fences were cut and barns were burned. The Las Vegas Land Grant Association was formed to fight all outside encroachments on the community grant, and sympathetic members of the local Knights of Labor organization gave their whole-hearted support. The alliance between the Knights and the White Caps that grew from this common effort to save the Las Vegas Grant for the people was to have a major impact. Juan Jose Herrera, organizer of the White Caps, and his brother Pablo joined the Knights. The *Gorras* took an active interest in labor matters. Teams hauling railroad ties, for instance, were frequently stopped and, if it was discovered that the drivers were not charging the contractors enough, the White Caps would chop up the ties or burn them. The *Optic* reported on July 23, 1890 that the Atchison, Topeka and Santa Fe Railroad was so disturbed by this practice, that it announced it would discontinue its purchase of railroad ties in the Las Vegas area, a decision which would purportedly cost the local economy $100,000 a year.

An opportunistic newspaperman, F. A. Blake, editor of the Las Vegas *News,* saw the political advantage of capitalizing on the controversy over the Las Vegas Grant and on the increasing discontent with the dominant county Republican organization. With a few members of the Knights of Labor he founded a "peoples party" in 1888. Polling only 140 votes, the new political organization grew in numbers as anger over the intrusions on the community grant mounted. In 1890, the new party triumphed over its Republican and Democratic rivals, and Theodore B. Mills, a prominent businessman and mining expert, was elected as the only Populist to the territorial Council, while a solid delegation of Populists was elected to the House, including among its members Pablo Herrera, the White Cap leader. The Knights thrived on this new political activity and on their identification with the White Caps, many of whom had infiltrated the local lodges of their organization. Starting with three lodges in East Las Vegas, West Las Vegas, and Tecolote before the White Cap agitation, the Knights grew to fifty lodges by 1890. Their new found strength was symbolized by an impressive thousand-man parade during the Fourth of July celebration of that year.

In the months following the victory of the territory's first Populist party in San Miguel County in 1890, a sharp decline in the controversial White

Cap organization took place. A reaction to its terror tactics was one cause for the downward course; one critic compared the *Gorras* to the Molly Maguires of the Pennsylvania coal fields. The decrease of outside encroachments on the Las Vegas Grant and removal of the hated fences were other reasons. With the gradual recession of White Cap strength, the influence of the Knights of Labor, following the national pattern, also declined. In the meantime a powerful county Democrat, Felix Martinez, who made an insincere conversion to Populism in 1890, assumed domination of the San Miguel County People's party and, by 1892, was so preeminent in its operations, he was able to almost handpick its nominees for the election of that year. Blake and some of the Knights who organized the original party left during the nominating convention, and, after the election, the People's party gradually disintegrated, many of the genuine Populists following Blake's example and departing.

In 1894, there was a revival of Populism in New Mexico, with the center for third-party activity shifting to Bernalillo County. A territorial-wide Populist convention was held in Albuquerque on the twelfth and thirteenth of September. Mills, who had moved to Bernalillo County to prospect for mineral wealth near Cochiti, was nominated as candidate for Territorial Delegate, defeating M. P. Stamm, an idealistic merchant from Albuquerque. The national Populist platform adopted in Omaha in 1892 was enthusiastically endorsed, and ten resolutions of special concern were approved by the Albuquerque delegates. Some of the special resolves had already been accepted by the Omaha delegates two years previous and were repeated; others were early declarations made by angry predecessors of Populism. The abolition of the national banks and creation of postal savings banks were demanded; the direct election of senators was advocated, along with such a vote for the President, Vice President, and local officials; pensions to Union veterans plus their dependents were endorsed. The plight of urban labor was not forgotten as the delegates, responding to the Pullman Strike, condemned interference by the military into civil affairs during time of peace. Local considerations were not neglected either, as the assembled Populists called for the admission of New Mexico to statehood, demanded a popular referendum for all laws passed by the legislature before they were implemented, and forcefully urged that public arid land be turned over to states and territories for irrigating purposes to be sold to "actual settlers only."

Although statements in the original Omaha platform had been reiterated in several of the ten resolutions, the allegedly dominant concern for the free and unlimited coinage of silver had not been given such expression. The Republican *Las Vegas Daily Optic* noted this omission two days later. The Populist convention had "not one word to say about free coinage of silver, the most important principle the pops[.] of Colorado have to work on. Dodging the silver question," it warned Mills, the Populist candidate, "will not aid you among the miners and laboring classes." Whether this lack of interest in the silver issue, impugned by the *Optic*, caused Mills' decisive defeat in November is an intriguing question, but a far more important one would be whether there really was a lukewarm attitude toward the coinage question by territorial Populists.

By 1894, it was obvious that silver was of vital concern to all political parties in New Mexico; the Populists were no exception. The failure of the Populists of Albuquerque to draft a special resolution demanding the free coinage of silver does clearly show, however, that silver was not the raison d'être of the People's movement in New Mexico. The coinage issue had been seized by the Democrats in the territory as early as 1890 and had been more enthusiastically advanced by the party of Jackson ever since, a situation similar to the one in Wyoming where Democrats also took the lead.

Silver was a non-partisan issue supported by practically every politico in the mountain West, until the national Republican party forced its western adherents to make the difficult choice between McKinley and gold and party insurgency in 1896. In the arid West the Populists appear to be the most multi-issue oriented of all the active parties. They seemed most responsive to the needs of the small farmer or stockmen or miner. The price of silver, it is true, was important, exceedingly important, to the economies of many of the mountainous western states and territories. But there were other serious problems. By 1890, for instance, Colorado was the second highest state in mortgage indebtedness in the nation. In 1892, the dispatch of a mercenary army by big cattlemen in Wyoming during the Johnson County War not only prompted a resolution of condemnation in the national Populist platform, but gave local Populists their best political issue. In New Mexico the roots of Populism were found in issues other than Silverism. Anti-monopoly movements against cattle combines and land-hungry companies or mogals reflected the major concern. In some cases Democrats were able to absorb this protest fervor, but the Populists won their share of converts by capitalizing on the fears and insecurities of threatened stockmen and farmers in the frontier territory.

SUGGESTED READINGS

Robert W. Larson, *New Mexico's Quest for Statehood, 1846–1912* (Albuquerque 1968);

Miguel A. Otero, *My Life on the Frontier*, 2 vols. (New York 1935–39);

Howard R. Lamar, *The Far Southwest* (New Haven 1966);

Richard Hofstadter, *The Age of Reform: From Bryan to F. D. R.* (New York 1955)

17
Statehood

New Mexico has the dubious distinction of having remained a territory longer than any other state in the continental United States, and as a result statehood was an important issue in New Mexico politics for over sixty years. The reasons for repeated failure are many; and, while occasionally New Mexicans themselves were responsible for the defeat of statehood bills, congressional rejection can best be explained by national attitudes and issues.

The defeat of New Mexico statehood in the 1850s because of the slavery issue indicated that statehood could not be divorced from national politics. In the 1890s when New Mexico supported free silver, the territory was out of step with the national mood, and a few years later in the Progressive Era, New Mexico appeared conservative and allied to big business. Other issues, however, also delayed statehood. Eastern interests feared the growing political influence of the West, while much of the nation reflected a spirit of Anglo-Saxon superiority and criticized New Mexico as the home of illiterate "half-breeds, 'greasers,' 'outlaws' " who comprised "the tag end of all that is objectionable in an imperfect civilization." New Mexicans also weakened their cause by internal dissension and by periodically losing interest in statehood. As a result the people watched their statehood bills meet defeat while other newer and less populous territories achieved it.

The concluding years of the long quest for statehood are described by Robert Larson. Striding across the stage in leading roles are Thomas B. Catron and Albert Fall of New Mexico and national figures such as President William Howard Taft, Senator Albert Beveridge of Indiana and Senator Robert Owen of Oklahoma. Larson describes the role of these and other men and provides a fine summary of the issues which delayed statehood until 1912.

New Mexicans considered their conservative constitution a likely candidate for approval despite a national Democratic victory in the 1910 congressional election. At the time thc constitution was completed, a "lame duck" Republican Congress was still in session, and a President known to be cautious and scrupulously legal was in the White House.

But in 1910 it was not Santa Fe or Washington that halted the march toward statehood, it was Phoenix. There on December 9, Arizona Territory completed its constitution. Long, liberal, and very unlike New Mexico's, it contained measures for initiative, referendum, and recall, and a child labor provision. In every phase of legislation, Arizona's constitution reflected a liberal mood, astounding those who had been sure Arizona was a corporation-controlled baliwick. President Taft may have understood the situation a little better. He had visited the territory in 1909 and observed that strong labor forces under the guidance of a prominent businessman, George W. P. Hunt, had gained control of the Twenty-fifth Territorial Legislature. Taft had subtly warned the territory at that time to refrain from radical provisions in its constitution. The Progressivism spreading throughout America at this time could not, however, have been checked by President Taft or any one else. In Arizona, where workers, farmers, and small businessmen had long been under the yoke of big business, Progressivism grew as dissatisfaction with the status quo mounted. The election for constitutional convention delegates showed the strength of the workers by giving 41 out of 52 seats to Democrats, and Democrats triumphed again when Hunt, who had travelled to Oregon and California to study Progressive laws and constitutions, was elected president of the convention. After nearly two months of debate and maneuver, Progressivism prevailed and a constitution considered almost radical for its time was adopted.

The recall provision in the new document was thought to be most dangerous. Prior to Arizona's adoption of the measure, only Oregon had incorporated such a provision into her constitution. Although California was to follow shortly thereafter, the newness of this instrument of direct legislation caused lifted eyebrows. The inclusion of judges in the provision only made it more unacceptable. According to the Arizona recall, any elective officer, having been in office six months or more, was subject to a recall election upon the petition of 25 per cent of the voters who participated in the last election. Other provisions for direct legislation included an initiative in which 10 per cent of the voters could propose a law and, if a majority approved it at the next election, the law would be final. A referendum was also provided whereby 5 per cent of the vote could, by petition, order the submission to the people of any enactment of the legislature, except for those acts immediately necessary to preserve "public peace, health or safety."

Before Arizonans voted approval or disapproval of their constitution, the press across the nation had much to say on the subject. The *El Paso Herald*, three days before the February 9 election to ratify the new instrument, recommended that if Arizona really wanted a constitution, the smartest thing that she could do would be to reject the instrument adopted by the Phoenix convention. The President would never approve the document and this would cause unnecessary delay. If the people rejected the constitution, they would have a chance to vote on it again in a few weeks without the objectionable recall provision. The New York *Evening Post*, although sharing the dislike for recall—especially recall of judges—felt the threat was exaggerated. ". . . The Union will survive even if Arizona does her worst; nor need the judges of the Supreme Court at Washington tremble for what may be done at Phoenix . . . ." Perhaps this was sagacious advice, because Arizonans ratified the constitution by a vote of 12,187 to 3,302.

Prominent individuals had their opinions about the new constitution too. Catron adamantly opposed the provisions for direct legislation. "I do not believe in either the initiative, referendum, or recall; they are heresies and constitute the first movement in the direction of anarchy in this government of ours; that is, we will all be nihilists in a few years or in a nihilist government if those radicals who are starting such a movement are allowed to get control." However, a much more potent figure, former President Roosevelt, gave the new document his wholehearted support and alienated his more conservative following a year later by coming out for the recall of judicial decision by popular vote.

New Mexicans little realized that the controversy over Arizona's constitution would affect them. They were having their own problems, for the territorial vote which had ratified the constitution was being challenged. Local prohibitionists, including three ministers from Albuquerque, had aroused the national W.C.T.U. and Anti-Saloon League with accusations of "fraud, bribery, violence, and intimidation." Letters and telegrams poured into the House of Representatives and Senate asking for a congressional investigation of the January 21 election. A former senator from New Hampshire, Henry W. Blair, was leader of the attack in Washington. Acting as attorney for protesting New Mexicans he produced a letter from a Republican leader in New Mexico to the members of the Republican central committee with the admonition: "Be sure if you can . . . [to] see that no ballots against the constitution are printed." The House Committee on the Territories felt compelled to draft four resolutions, three of which endorsed the constitution and relieved the committee of responsibility for investigating the matter. The fourth resolution, which required action, stated that the committee desired further information "upon the question of the validity of the election for the ratification or rejection of the Constitution."

Andrews, sensing the seriousness of the situation, wired officers and citizens of the territory for affidavits testifying as to the fairness of the election. These were presented to the House committee along with a copy of the governor's proclamation of January 20, 1911, requesting peace officers and district attorneys to inquire into all complaints of fraud or intimidation and "vigorously prosecute" them. The affidavits showed that ballots were printed and distributed in every county and precinct of the Territory of New Mexico, that saloons were closed all day on January 21 and in many places did not open until the following morning, and that order and peace prevailed throughout the territory on an election day free from "intimidation, bribery or corruption."

The affidavit from Santa Fe County was an especially forceful one, signed by such prominent residents as Catron, Nathan Jaffa, secretary of the territory, and Benjamin M. Read, a prominent prohibitionist. It contended that the charges made regarding the election were "wicked and malicious slanders on our good people." It denied that the registration lists were fraudulent, and that saloonkeepers gave voters liquor and forced them to vote for the constitution. Every saloon in Santa Fe was closed from midnight of January 20 to midnight of January 22, the day after election being Sunday. It also swore that an equal number of ballots for and against the constitution had been delivered to opposition workers as well as Republicans in every precinct of the county.

The territory's problems with prohibitionists were largely resolved by President Taft, who on February 24, 1911, formally approved the constitution and sent it to Congress with a recommendation that approval be given. The House quickly acceded to the President's wishes. Four days after receiving Taft's recommendation, the Committee on Territories accepted the constitution, and on March 1, 1911, the House gave its approval. The measure, called House Joint Resolution No. 295, was then sent to the upper house, where Andrews seemed encouraged about favorable action. "We have a lot of good friends in the senate," he wrote Catron, but admitted that Senator Beveridge was the key to success or failure. Although the Indianan had been defeated for re-election, he was still chairman of the Senate territorial committee until the 61st Congress adjourned. "The President said he would make him report it off the bat and if so, why it will require no debate in the senate." Apparently Andrews was right, for three days later the Beveridge committee reported the resolution.

Senator Robert Owen from Oklahoma shattered the prevailing confidence when he objected during the last hours of the 61st Congress to passing the resolution until it included approval of the controversial Arizona constitution. He threatened to prevent passage of the sundry civil conference report, a post office bill, and a post roads bill, and launched into a filibuster which tied up legislation for hours. Adjournment being imminent, the senator's action was regarded as a serious threat to the legislative program. Finally, the President and members of the upper house took action to end the filibuster. The Senate agreed to vote on House Joint Resolution No. 295, as amended by Owen to include the Arizona constitution. The result was an adverse vote of 45 to 39 and a defeat for the statehood aspirations of both territories. But to get action, Taft had to assure Owen that an extraordinary session would be called immediately after the close of the 61st Congress to deal with the Canadian reciprocity treaty, at which time the statehood question could again be considered. This message, sent through Vice President James S. Sherman, apparently was satisfactory as the Oklahoman agreed to end his filibuster, enabling the 61st Congress to complete its legislation and adjourn.

Owen's filibuster caused bitterness in New Mexico despite the fact that the territory would have another chance during the extra session convening on April 4. Catron vented his anger by writing: "Its too bad that we failed; but when things get to the point where one louzy [sic] whelp can make trouble and do harm you will always find the individual who is equal to the occasion." The fact that Owen came from Oklahoma, a state which had labored with New Mexico for many years to achieve statehood, particularly irked Catron. "One would have thought that Owen was the last man who would have obstructed us. . . . This is ingratitude of the basest kind and one that our people will never forget." Fall saw partisan politics in Owen's action. "Naturally, the Democrats want Arizona admitted along with New Mexico, as the latter will probably send two Republican senators and the former two Democrats."

The *El Paso Times* saw another motive in the filibuster. It declared that the *New York Tribune* had information proving that Owen was not devoted to Arizona's liberal constitution, but rather hoped that by filibustering he could prevent another bill from coming up which would have questioned the deals which had brought him possession of many acres of rich land belonging to the Indians, "to which race the senator himself belongs." According to the story, for two years the sundry civil bill had carried an appropriation of $50,000 "to give the law department the means to get after this defendant, and others in the attempt to restore the lands in question to the defrauded Indians."

Senator Owen had his own explanation for the much publicized filibuster. "My fight against the New Mexico bill was made primarily to bring the issue of the initiative and referendum squarely before the American people." The senator vowed to oppose the admission of New Mexico not because he wished to keep the territory out of the Union, but because he felt Arizona was equally entitled to admission. He also had aroused the ire of many New Mexico papers by supporting the prohibitionists and threatening to investigate the election that had resulted in the adoption of the constitution.

About three weeks before the opening of the special session, Andrews confidently wrote Catron that if no action were taken during the extra session, he had been assured by the Attorney General, George W. Wickersham, that he would rule that New Mexico had complied with the terms of the enabling act and should be brought into the Union at the end of the first regular session of the 62d Congress, providing she was not disapproved by Congress or the President in the meantime. In another exchange between the two men, the delegate spoke bitterly of Beveridge's last-ditch obstructionism in reporting House Joint Resolution No. 295. ". . . Beveridge refused to do anything with it and at 12:00 midnight Friday, March 3d, it took the combined efforts of four Senators and Postmaster General Hitchcock to make Beveridge give up and allow Dillingham to report it . . . ."

The correspondence between the pair revealed the amazing power that Catron wielded after long years in New Mexico's rough and tumble political scene. On March 11, Andrews felt compelled to deny reports reaching the Santa Fean that he and Fall had made a deal regarding the two senatorships the territory would receive. Through Catron's pressure, Andrews took great pains to make sure that a certain appointment would not be made on the commission authorized by congressional action to relocate the old Clark boundary line north of El Paso between Texas and New Mexico.

The first day of the extra congressional session brought to the floor Representative Henry D. Flood, a Democrat from Virginia, who had taken Hamilton's position as chairman of the Committee on the Territories in the new Democratic House. He introduced a joint resolution calling for the admission of Arizona and New Mexico on the basis of their submitted constitutions. Andrews also introduced a joint resolution which provided for the admission of New Mexico singly, while Delegate Smith of Arizona did the same for his territory. These early maneuvers were followed by a series of committee hearings conducted by Flood on his proposal, House Joint Resolution No. 14, which extended from the middle to the latter part of April. If the hearings accomplished nothing else, they forced New Mexicans to air their dirty linen before a national audience. Hostile Democrats like Fergusson, J. D. Hand, and Andrieus A. Jones were there to castigate the new constitution, and insurgent Republicans such as Hagerman and Richard H. Hanna of Santa Fe were there to help them. Jones, who had chaired the Democratic meeting that issued the thirteen objections to the Santa Fe constitution, attacked the awkward amending procedure of the document, declaring that a majority of members at the convention had been pledged to an initiative and referendum but had failed to fulfill their commitment. He decried the apportionment and corporation articles and denounced the language qualification. Fergusson and Hand requested that the Flood committee adjourn for a week to enable them to prepare a better-documented case against the constitution. Critics of New Mexico were aided by former Senator Blair who testified that the election to ratify the constitution was crooked.

Defenders of the new document also fought to be heard. Fall gave what Andrews described as "a bully good talk" defending the provisions of the constitution; the convention had only done what he had heard Taft recommend several times—adopt a "safe and sane" constitution. Curry, who with Andrews and Clancy gave testimony, provided the only important break in the defense. He indicated that he was not personally opposed to any move that would make the constitution easier to amend. The majority of people had heretofore opposed tampering with the amendment clause because they felt it would delay admission.

The press was in an uproar after hearing the testimony of the Democratic leaders. Republican papers in the territory were downright bitter. If the people of New Mexico wanted to experiment with recall, they might wait a hundred years before finding a more opportune time than the present for using it on J. D. Hand, A. A. Jones, and H. B. Fergusson, "self styled leaders who are now engaged in fighting statehood." New Mexico's position was pictured as greatly injured by the testimony of these three. So constant were the attacks of the Republican papers that the *El Paso Times* remarked: "It was no crime for the machine bosses to hogtie the free men of that territory in the proposed constitution in such a manner as would serve to perpetuate Republican rule for at least a quarter of [a] century. The crime lies in the effort that is being made to break up the unholy combination." Watching sympathetically from the sidelines, the *Boston Herald* provided the only comedy relief during the stormy controversy by suggesting that the territory change its name to Jefferson "to win friends and hold them strongly."

Although they resented the attacks on their constitution, many Republican leaders began to see the handwriting on the wall. The *New Mexican*, always a good barometer of Republican sentiment, expressed the belief that a greater part of the people of New Mexico would not mind having a clause put into the constitution to make it more easily amendable, if that would bring statehood. The paper did hope, however, that the protection given the Spanish-speaking people would not be tampered with, for native New Mexicans had a right "to protest against being put in the same status as the negro in Mississippi." Jones predicted accurately what action the committee would eventually take. Writing to a friend in Albuquerque, he stated that a substitute for the amendment article would be voted upon by New Mexicans at the first state election. "This substitute provides for the submission of amendments by a majority thereon." Arizona, too, would have to vote upon a substitute for her recall article. This, in substance, was the final form of House Joint Resolution No. 14, better known as the Flood resolution, which was reported by the Committee on the Territories on May 12, 1911, about two weeks after the hearings ended, and which the House passed by a *viva voce* vote on May 23.

Once the resolution reached the Senate, the usual delay was encountered. Republican Senator William Alden Smith of Michigan, the new chairman of the Senate Committee on Territories, was absent from Washington and was not expected back until about the middle of June. Senator Owen had been called to Oklahoma to mend his "political fences." Consequently, the bill was bottled up in committee for a month and a half. Fergusson, one of the New Mexicans most responsible for the Flood amendment, became impatient. Writing to Owen, he insisted that there were enough Democratic and progressive Republican votes in the Senate to pass the resolution.

> The scheme of the corruptionists in New Mexico and of the old standpat element in Washington and in the Senate,—more and more made plain with each passing day, is to prevent the admission of Arizona altogether, and to delay the admission of New Mexico, by preventing a vote on the Flood resolution in the Senate, until after the end of the next regular session of Congress to convene next December, when by operation of the law of the enabling act of June 20th, 1911 [1910], New Mexico will be in the Union under its drastic special interest constitution as made by the gang: Arizona remaining a Territory.

Senate action was not the only concern; Taft's position was a constant source of worry. One report had the President promising Curry and Flood that although he would not use his influence to push statehood under the Flood resolution, he would sign the resolution if the Senate approved. Taft denied this. Notwithstanding his approval of the New Mexico constitution, he declined to commit himself on the resolution.

The Senate territorial committee took action on the measure after conducting hearings on June 16, 17, and 23. The resolution was favorably reported to the Senate, but three days later, on July 13, Senator Nelson of the committee offered an alternative. The clause in the Arizona constitution providing for recall of judges would have to be eliminated as a "fundamental condition" of admission. The Flood resolution had provided for a referendum on the recall clause, the territory to be admitted regardless of the vote, but under the substitute the people must veto the recall provision. Regarding New Mexico's constitution, Nelson would not require the people to vote on an easier amending procedure as specified in the original resolution.

With two such proposals in abeyance, the conservative and liberal camps in the Senate each had a measure to champion. Although recall was an important feature of the progressive program, its application to judges caused real alarm. Even Senator William E. Borah of Idaho, who usually voted as a progressive Republican, expressed his concern. "Without a free and independent judiciary popular government would be tantamount to a tormenting delusion." The senator was opposed to the recall because he believed judges would be dissuaded from their convictions and legal guidance by the will of the majority, and this would undermine the stability of legal protection now afforded to American citizens. Senator Elihu Root of New York, usually a calm, analytical speaker, was emotionally roused by the subject too, and stated that while judges were supposed to decide cases by evidence, the judges themselves would now be judged by newspaper accounts of the case, "necessarily brief and partial." Newspapers were looking for the sensational features of a trial, and people form their opinion largely from these accounts.

Despite these strong opinions held by powerful men, the Nelson amendment was voted down on August 8 by a vote of 43 to 26, while the Flood resolution was approved, 53 to 18. Evidently a majority felt, as Republican Senator Miles Poindexter of Washington did, that it would be "a travesty on self government" to try to compel the people of Arizona to adopt a resolution, which they themselves did not want, but which the people of other states thought they should have.

What would President Taft do now that both houses of Congress had approved the Flood resolution? It was well known that the President disliked recall as heartily as Root and Borah. But Congressman Flood felt confident that Taft would not veto his resolution in view of the record vote given it in the Senate, where a more than two-thirds majority was achieved. Some felt that the President would allow the bill to become law without his signature, while others predicted a veto. The latter speculation seemed most valid, as the New York *World* reported that the President on August 8 had informed opponents of recall in the Senate that he would never stand for the provision. Also, on the day after the vote, he announced to a visiting delegation of New Mexico Democrats led by Fergusson, Jones, and Hand his intention to veto the Flood resolution, even though he "heartily" endorsed New Mexico's constitution. Privately, Taft was greatly irked. "What a lot of cowards they are in the Senate! There is not a handful of men there, either Democrats or Republicans, who believe in the Recall of the Judiciary, and yet they send me the Constitution of Arizona with this provision in it."

True to his word, President Taft vetoed the Flood resolution in a message kept a carefully guarded secret until the day it was read in Congress, August 15, 1911. Referring to the controversial recall, the President declared: "This provision of the Arizona constitution, in its application to county and State judges, seems to me so pernicious in its effect, so destructive of independence in the judiciary, so likely to subject the rights of the individual to the possible tyranny of a popular majority, and, therefore, to be so injurious to the cause of free government, that I must disapprove a constitution containing it." The rejection was explosive. Conservatives were delighted and, when the message was read to the House, a burst of applause rose from the Republican side while Democrats remained silent. Leading newspapers like the *Chicago Tribune* and the New York *World* supported the action. The *World* hailed Taft's veto as a measure that would halt the drift of unenlightened opinion being exploited by demagogic leaders. Because New Mexico was included in the Flood resolution, her statehood hopes were smashed, too. This provoked stinging criticism of Taft by much of the territorial press. The *Roosevelt County Herald* labeled the veto an "act of wanton, without reason, without justification and without precedent." This was the first time in America's history that a President had refused to approve a properly presented constitution. The *Pecos Valley News* was especially bitter. "It seems to us that Mr. Taft has assumed, first, that the people of the southwest are not possessed of sufficient judgment and ability to form a state constitution and again, that communities are not capable of self government."

The President was quite sensitive to public reaction. Responding to a telegram sent by a group of Las Vegas citizens, he stated: "The spirit with which you bear the disappointment of delayed Statehood reassures me and strengthens my conviction with respect to the performance of an unpleasant duty." A look at the Taft correspondence following his veto reveals that the President was grateful for all the support he could get.

There was talk in Congress of overriding the presidential veto. One Democratic representative from the House territorial committee was especially critical and insisted upon overriding the veto by pushing the Flood resolution through Congress. Other Democrats insisted that if an acceptable compromise could not be worked out the veto should be made a national issue. But cooler heads won out. Senator Smith, on the day the veto message was read, introduced Senate Joint Resolution No. 55, which would amend the Flood measure by requiring that the recall clause be eliminated from the Arizona constitution—such action to be voted upon by the people of the territory. New Mexico would still vote on an easier amendment clause, although the vote would have no bearing on her admission. A joint committee from both houses met to consider the plan. Because two Democratic moderates were willing to vote with the Republicans from the House side, the Smith proposal was accepted. Smith, in behalf of the Senate territorial committee, reported the resolution, known as Senate Joint Resolution No. 57, to the floor of the Senate on August 17. A vote taken the following day approved the compromise resolution by 53 to 9, and on August 19 the House passed it without a roll call.

Democratic fears that Republican New Mexico might enter the Union alone under the terms of her enabling act doubtless facilitated action on the resolution.

Anticipating presidential approval, a gleeful Andrews telegraphed Catron: "I will have accomplished what the people of New Mexico sent me to Congress for." At 3:08 P.M., August 21, 1911, President Taft signed the new compromise resolution promising statehood to New Mexico and Arizona if the terms of the resolution were met. "Well, gentlemen, it's done," remarked Taft to the delegation on hand to witness the ceremony. The President used three pens for the occasion. One he gave to Delegate Ralph Cameron of Arizona, another to Senator Smith, and a third to Andrews. Overjoyed New Mexicans held statehood meetings throughout the territory—"the people being anxious to express their satisfaction at the successful termination of the half century fight for statehood." Andrews quickly registered at the Navy Department to have the next new dreadnaught battleship being constructed named after the new state. ". . . You will soon see our name on the high seas."

On August 22, 1911, the extraordinary session of the 62d Congress adjourned and President Taft went to his home at Beverly, Massachusetts, for a rest. The territories now acted according to the specifications in the compromise. Governor Mills issued a proclamation calling for the first state election on November 7, 1911. Among the officials to be chosen were the governor, two representatives to Congress, members of the first state legislature, and a host of county and state officers. Aside from this, New Mexicans were to vote on a proposal to make the constitution easier to amend. A change could be proposed by a simple majority of all members in each legislative house, and this action could be ratified by a majority at the "next election after adjournment," or in a special election held in not less than six months after adjournment. The amendment ballots would be separate, and "printed on paper of the blue tint, so that they might be readily distinguishable from the white ballots provided the election of county and state officers. . . ." Because of the color specification, this amendment became known as the "Blue Ballot" amendment.

The governor's proclamation, coming as it did so soon after Taft's approval, found Fergusson in real distress. Writing to William Jennings Bryan, he complained: "The enabling act provided for the election not less than sixty nor more than ninety days after the governor's call. As a willing tool of corruptionists long in control here, the governor called the election for November 7, the shortest time possible. They know their machine is all ready with abundance of money,—that we are without money or effective organization." This cry of distress was followed by a warning. ". . . You know how the local bosses and corrupt corporations make political contributions as investments certain to bring big returns.

As a state, the inducements to put up money are many times multiplied. Outside, the prospect of two corrupt or stand-pat senators and one member of the House; within, the rich picking for the local gang, with the alternative of the penitentiary for many of them if they lose." The letter concluded with an urgent plea for money. ". . . Democrats have no special interests to draw upon for money . . . [but with] one dollar we can get [more] than our opponents can do with ten."

Fergusson's belief that money could do the trick was not without substantial basis. Republicans were sharply divided, and events of the next few months were to show how severe the split was. Marked dissension was revealed at their convention in Las Vegas on September 28. Bursum's selection as gubernatorial candidate met with bitter opposition, while the choice of Curry as candidate for one of the two seats allowed the new state in the House made many delegates unhappy. Colorful Elfego Baca of Socorro County, the other choice, endorsed the stand taken by the convention against the Blue Ballot, but Curry told convention members that the condemnation of the Blue Ballot was a mistake. ". . . I could not ask the people of New Mexico for their support and at the same time tell them they were incapable of amending their own constitution."

Disharmony at the Las Vegas gathering was augmented by developments at the Democratic meeting in Santa Fe on October 2. Here it was announced that a group of "Independent Republicans" headed by former Governor Hagerman and Hanna would join the Democrats in forming a fusion ticket. They were given two spots on the ticket while top jobs went to leading Democrats. William C. McDonald of Lincoln County, chairman of the Democratic central committee, was nominated for governor, and Fergusson and Paz Valverde were selected as candidates for the national House of Representatives. Moreover, it was announced that Hagerman and Hanna under the banner of "Progressive Republicans" would conduct a separate campaign chiefly against the candidacy of Holm Bursum.

This combination was so strong that Bursum was defeated by McDonald, and a resurgent Democratic organization elected Fergusson and gained control of about half the state offices. Curry was elected because he refused to campaign against the Blue Ballot. In the legislative elections, the apportionment provision of the new constitution saved the day for Republicans, who elected 15 of the 24 state senators and 32 of the 49 representatives. The Blue Ballot amendment carried by a vote of 34,897 to 22,831.

Curry interpreted the election results as a victory for the Democrats and declared that Republican opposition to an easier amendment process was the chief cause. He was willing to admit that there were other reasons, such as overconfidence of Republican leaders, opposition of Independent

Republicans, and revival of charges against Bursum's conduct as prison superintendent. He might also have added the opposition of prohibitionists. But the crusade against the Blue Ballot was the costliest blunder; only 7 of the 26 counties of the territory polled majorities against the proposal for a workable amending clause. "The fact is that rigid provisions in the constitution, making amendment almost impossible, had been written into it by powerful corporate interests for entirely selfish ends. The people knew this and resented it. The Democrats took full advantage of this popular feeling in the ensuing campaign.

The first state election did not complete the slate of officials who would govern the new commonwealth. New Mexico's first two senators were to be chosen by the newly elected legislature which was scheduled to convene in the spring. These two posts were regarded as rightful prizes by some of the territory's more vigorous fighters for statehood. Catron, Andrews, Fall, and Governor Mills were all top contenders whose various supporters were busy as early as September, securing all the backing they could.

Andrews seemed by all odds certain to be one of the first senators. As delegate to Congress when the enabling act was passed, he had increased his popularity with the people of New Mexico. His determination, skill as a lobbyist, and national political connections with men like the late Matthew Quay, still remembered in New Mexico for his support of the Knox bill, were other advantages. Senator Boise Penrose, heir to Quay as a political boss of Pennsylvania, had assured Taft in the presence of Andrews that he would support the delegate's political aspirations. Penrose was quite popular among many New Mexicans because of his support of statehood. Early in May, 1911, the *Ft. Sumner Review* remarked: "If New Mexico receives statehood from the special session of Congress . . . it will not be because of the lack of his friendship and his active support . . . ."

Andrews' early start gave him further advantage. As early as August 16, 1910, he felt compelled to deny in a speech that he and Catron had formed a coalition to assure their election to the United States Senate. "Statehood for New Mexico is bigger than any personal ambition of mine or Mr. Catron['s]. . . ." In September, 1911, he came out for a direct primary in the election of senators. Apparently sensing a lack of support for his candidacy among Republican leaders of the territory, he declared: "No Republican could object to going before the people of his party and letting them make the choice at the polls." In November, 1911, following the first state election, a more direct bid for support was attempted. "I am a candidate for United States Senator, I would be obliged if you will see your members of the Legislature in my behalf, some of the corporation managers are against me and I need your help . . . ."

But Andrews, despite political support and backing from Eastern financial interests, was doomed to failure. His competition was too shrewd, too well entrenched. Although Mills was not an active candidate, Fall and Catron were, and two more formidable opponents could not be found. Bronson Cutting, a transplanted New Yorker and new leader of the Progressive Republicans in New Mexico, called Catron the "most unscrupulous man in the Southwest" and easily the "ablest of the bunch." Fall was also regarded with trepidation—the "most dangerous man of the bunch."

The actual account of how Catron and Fall won the new state's two Senate seats is a confused one. One report states that Andrews nobly withdrew his candidacy during a secret meeting attended by Luna, Bursum, Catron, and other party leaders. According to this version, Andrews, Fall, Catron, and Mills were high men when the new state legislature met in the spring of 1912, but the balloting went on for days and days without the legislature being able to narrow the choice to two men. Fall clearly had the advantage as Luna, the national committeeman, was championing the cause of Fall and Catron, while Bursum, the former state chairman, was supporting Fall and Andrews. At the secret meeting, called one night in Andrews' home in Santa Fe, the former delegate withdrew his name for the "sake of party harmony."

This version fails to account for Andrews' bitterness following the selection of Catron and Fall on March 28. He, along with Governor McDonald and the *Albuquerque Journal-Democrat*, questioned the legality of Fall's election. Apparently, seventeen members of the House joined the Senate in a little pre-election maneuver and decided upon Fall, the legislature in joint assembly merely ratifying the action the following day. This procedure caused such an uproar that Fall wrote: "Their continual yawping and talk about the illegality of my election and that I could not be re-elected by this legislature etc., simply aggravates me to the point of stubbornness." In stubbornness Fall continued a public career which was in all respects sensational.

Even more damaging was an account of four Spanish-speaking legislators, all supporters of Andrews, being lured into the old Palace Hotel in Santa Fe by Elfego Baca, where they were arrested for allegedly trying to sell their votes. The four were forced to resign their offices and were jailed for two nights and a greater part of two days. A request by the sergeant-at-arms that they be released was ignored for eighteen hours. Upon their release, they were exonerated of the charges preferred against them and declared entitled to their seats. The conclusion of the report was that the whole incident was a frame-up initiated by Baca, Apolonio Sena of the state mounted police, Spiess, Springer, Major Llewellyn, and Bursum to advance the candidacy of Fall, who would be assured of victory if the four were removed. It was obvious that steamroller tactics had won for Fall, despite Andrews' skill and experience in political manipulation.

Statehood had, however, been safely achieved before the election of Catron and Fall. Arizona had complied with the wishes of the President and a majority in Congress by eliminating the recall provision, at least until a state government was formed. Although the two new congressmen, Curry and Fergusson, were told by the President on January 3, 1912, that he would sign the proclamation the following day, on January 5 the last of a long series of delays occurred. Crowds gathered in Santa Fe to hear the eagerly awaited news, but suddenly, in Washington, Andrews received a message from the White House to the effect that the Department of Justice wanted the signing of the statehood proclamation delayed until it could take final action in the old timber cases. The Alamogordo Lumber Company was one of the concerns involved, and the Department of Justice wanted to issue a writ of error to transfer the case from the dying Territorial Supreme Court to federal jurisdiction so that the interest of the federal government in certain public lands could be protected. Taft was displeased and anxious that there be no additional delay, and his irritation brought results. The Department wired its representatives in New Mexico to take immediate action so that statehood could be proclaimed. Although quickly solved, this last difficulty was symbolic of New Mexico's entire, frustrating statehood fight.

Very frequently over the years, the territory's political inclinations were in direct opposition to the prevalent mood in the nation's capital, resulting in indifference, and often hostility, to New Mexico's statehood aspirations. As early as 1850, the territory's fate was affected by national issues. The bitter slavery debate was finally, momentarily, calmed by the Compromise of 1850 which gave to New Mexico the territorial status in which she would remain for more than sixty years. Although the Civil War and difficult Reconstruction years disrupted any systematic admission policy for the territories, Nevada, despite a tiny population, was admitted because her three electoral votes would aid Lincoln's re-election and help gain approval of the Thirteenth Amendment. Unfortunately, when Colorado was admitted in 1876, her three electoral votes went to Hayes in the "Stolen Election," causing Democrats to balk at the admission of any more Western states. In 1889, however, the Springer omnibus bill did bring statehood to the Dakotas, Washington, and Montana, despite failure of Democratic efforts to include New Mexico in the bill. In the turbulent decade of the nineties, New Mexico allied herself with Free Silver and Populism, thus losing the support of conservatives and "goldbugs" in Washington who viewed these causes as Western radicalism. In the first years of the twentieth century, New Mexico shifted to conservatism but by this time most of the country was caught up in the reform spirit of the Progressive Era. But for once New Mexico's long and continual association with Arizona was fortunate, because the conservative constitution written by the territory's leaders in 1910 was balanced by the liberal constitution Arizonans had written. Taft, a man torn by the political currents of the day, was pleased with the New Mexico document and in 1912 would personally help end the long quest for statehood.

New Mexico's conservative leanings and connections with big business interests, especially those in Pennsylvania, made Albert Beveridge the territory's most implacable and powerful enemy over the years. To one of the leading progressives of his day, the special economic interests supporting both the New Mexico and Arizona statehood movements simply could not be allowed to bring about statehood for their own financial benefit. Beveridge also embodied some of the common and widespread prejudices of Easterners toward the *Hispano,* Catholic population of New Mexico. The general feeling of Anglo-Saxon superiority was certainly present in Beveridge, a leading spokesman for the new American imperialism. The Indianan remained suspicious of the territory to the very end, and when the final enabling act was being prepared, it was he who attached provisions and safeguards which he ardently hoped would prevent any corrupt "ring" of politicians from controlling the new state.

Outside forces cannot be totally blamed for New Mexico's long wait to join the Union. Internal dissension and periodic loss of interest were major problems. The early bid in 1850 was crippled by the feud between Weightman's statehood group and Houghton's territorial group. In 1866, a statehood convention dissolved, having accomplished nothing because the group was so lacking in interest and enthusiasm that it failed to obtain a quorum. The territory certainly did not appear eager to receive statehood when it failed to approve the fairly progressive constitution of 1872. Again, in 1889, a constitution was defeated at the polls by partisanship, opposition to secular schools, and a belief by many citizens that primarily "land grabbers" wanted statehood. Although a dedicated campaign by Governor Otero and Delegate Rodey significantly weakened opposition to statehood, subsequent opposition to jointure alienated not only Otero but also Tom Catron from the statehood movement, at least temporarily. Even after the prized enabling act had been passed, New Mexicans quarreled over the conservative constitution and its lack of provisions for direct legislation.

From the time the Treaty of Guadalupe Hidalgo was signed, there were New Mexicans who for varying reasons honestly preferred territorial status to statehood. Some feared increased taxation under a state government, and it was frequently charged that federal officials in the territory objected to a change that would jeopardize their jobs. Some Anglos and *Hispanos* feared that statehood would result in a domination of one group by the other, with ensuing complications in Church-state relations. Nevertheless, there were throughout the years numerous important champions of statehood.

The early self-promoting efforts for admission by Weightman were followed by the rather half-hearted actions of a few governors, such as Connelly and Giddings, who tried to instill in New Mexicans a desire for statehood. An effective and unswerving advocate was Bradford Prince, whose zeal for the cause was matched by such fighters as Bernard "Statehood" Rodey and the forceful Stephen Elkins. Tom Catron and Edmund Ross both fought for admission, although increased value for his vast land holdings appears to have been a prime motivation for Catron, not to mention Prince and Elkins, while Ross's concern was that statehood be granted only when a good public school system was established and corrupt "land grabbers" were under control. Delegate Andrews desired statehood as much as he desired to be one of the new state's first senators, although this ambition proved to be futile.

Why was New Mexico so long denied statehood despite increasing numbers of inhabitants determined to rise above the second-class citizenship of territorial status? Examination reveals that the principal arguments openly used by Easterners and others opposing New Mexico statehood applied with equal veracity to the other Western territories. Small populations and the fear that Westerners would hold a disproportionate amount of power in the Senate did not prevent Idaho and Wyoming from receiving statehood at a time when each had a smaller population than New Mexico. Certainly they were overrepresented in the upper house. These territories were also slow to develop economically, a favorite argument against New Mexico, and much of their land was arid, a fact which was used to refute the hope of natural development when applied to New Mexico, but which did not prevent these two territories from becoming states more than two decades before the Southwestern territory.

Factional strife and political discord do not fully account for the fact that New Mexico was never considered in the same light as the other territories. The unique population of New Mexico profoundly separated the territory from most of the remainder of the West where Anglo pioneers had slowly filled the frontiers with a fairly homogeneous population of Western European stock. In the long years between 1846 and 1912, frequent newspaper articles and speeches by congressmen indicated a strong prejudice toward the Spanish-speaking, Roman Catholic people of New Mexico. Nativism in America, sometimes concealed and at other times brought out into the open, was thus the major obstruction to the territory's statehood aspirations. Some remarks concerning the widespread use of Spanish in the schools, courts, and businesses of the territory had merit, but many reflected a most unfair bias against a people labeled by one congressman "a race speaking an alien language" and not representing the "best blood on the American continent." The actions of the territory's Catholic hierarchy, especially its determined opposition to the constitution of 1889 because of a secular school provision, only aggravated the prejudice and dislike of a predominantly Protestant nation. Thus, an unfortunate but instinctive distrust of New Mexico's essentially foreign culture was the last and most durable brick added to the strong wall of opposition that prevented the territory from joining the Union until 1912.

But now the last barrier was removed, and on January 6, 1912, a delegation including Andrews and the two congressmen-elect from New Mexico gathered at the White House and proudly witnessed the making of their new state at exactly 1:35 P.M. After affixing his signature to the proclamation, Taft turned and smilingly said: "Well, it is all over. I am glad to give you life. I hope you will be healthy." Arizona, so long associated with New Mexico in the long fight, was proclaimed a state on February 14, 1912. Consequently, almost sixty-four years after the signing of the Treaty of Guadalupe Hidalgo, the sister territories of the Southwest were brought into the Union.

SUGGESTED READINGS

Robert W. Larson, "Taft, Roosevelt, and New Mexico Statehood," *Mid-America,* vol. VL (April 1963);
Howard R. Lamar, "The Reluctant Admission: The Struggle to Admit Arizona and New Mexico to the Union," in *The American West: An Appraisal,* edited by Robert G. Ferris (Santa Fe 1963);
Lamar, *The Far Southwest* (New Haven 1966);
Miguel A. Otero, *My Nine Years as Governor of the Territory of New Mexico* (Albuquerque 1940);
Marion Dargan, "New Mexico's Fight for Statehood, 1895–1912," *New Mexico Historical Review,* vol. XIV (January and April 1939), vol. XV (April 1940), vol. XVI (January and October 1941), vol. XVIII (January and April 1943).

18
Albert B. Fall

Albert Fall was surrounded by controversy and often by conflict throughout most of his adult life. As the leader of the Democratic machine in southern New Mexico in the latter part of the nineteenth century, he was a figure to be reckoned with. He had considerable success as a lawyer and rarely lost a case, for he was a master of frontier legal practices. His successful defense of his friend, Oliver Lee, against the charge of the murder of Republican leader Albert Jennings Fountain attests to that. In 1929, however, Fall was the defendant in a federal case which resulted in his conviction and imprisonment and which destroyed his career.

Fall began his political career as a Democrat, but as Professor David Stratton points out, he eventually switched to the Republican Party. He served as an important force in the New Mexico Constitutional Convention of 1910 and was elected to the United States Senate in 1912 by the first state legislature. Nine years later he became Secretary of the Interior, the highest position in the United States government ever attained by a New Mexican, but within a few years Fall also became the first American cabinet officer to be convicted and imprisoned for a felony while in office. Fall was convicted of receiving a bribe to lease the Teapot Dome and Elk Hills oil reserves to Harry F. Sinclair and Edward L. Doheny, and the names Teapot Dome and Albert Fall became synonymous with political corruption.

Professor Stratton argues that Fall, who was convicted of receiving a bribe while Sinclair and Doheny were cleared of the charge of giving one, was a typical Westerner, especially in his attitude toward the conservation of natural resources. Fall believed that resources should be exploited to the fullest, and thus it is not out of character that he leased the naval oil reserves to his friends. Fall would have done this, Stratton believes, even without a bribe.

Reprinted by permission of the publisher from David H. Stratton, "New Mexican Machiavellian? The Story of Albert B. Fall," *Montana, The Magazine of Western History*, pp. 2–14.

ORPHAN HOLD
DO NOT SHIP

H1 – 000000000636

ISBN 9780826302151

New Mexico, Past and Present : A Historical Reader

CLIENT	Alternate Sourcing
STATION	TPP Receiving Station 01
HELD	2026 – 10 – 12 13:40

SHELF

If its order arrives, scan this label at a receiving station.

As innumerable booming headlines of the 1920's revealed, Albert B. Fall's chief claim to renown was his leasing of the Teapot Dome Naval Oil Reserve in Wyoming and a similar reservc at Elk Hills, California, to two oil magnates, Harry F. Sinclair and Edward L. Doheny. This occurred while he was Secretary of the Interior in the Cabinet of President Warren G. Harding. Prior to this, Fall had served periodically, but never inconspicuously, as a public office holder in territorial New Mexico, and had spent nine tempestuous years in the United States Senate as "The Gentleman from New Mexico" before his fellow senator and close friend, President-elect Harding, named him for the Cabinet in 1921. But it was the naval oil controversy which put Fall's name in the index of every general account of American history.

The more intimate aspects of Fall's negotiations with the two oil millionaires were exposed when a Senate investigating committee under the leadership of stern, determined, Thomas J. Walsh, Senator from Montana, disclosed first in 1924, and later in 1928, that Secretary Fall had also received personally at least $404,000 and assorted livestock from the two oilmen, Sinclair and Doheny. This inquiry placed Fall in an extremely disadvantageous position, especially because the Teapot Dome revelations erupted just in time to become a major issue in the presidential election of 1924. Calvin Coolidge and the Republicans desperately needed a scapegoat for their oil sins; Albert B. Fall, who had been the main target of the Teapot Dome investigators, was the most likely prospect. The Democrats, on the other hand, saw the so-called Teapot Dome scandal as a choice campaign issue, and they nourished it through the elections of 1924 and 1928 in particular, giving it so much notoriety as a corruption label for their opponents that it became a permanent part of their campaign repertoire, and is now a symbol of corruption in American political folklore.

In the decade of civil and criminal litigation which followed the Teapot Dome investigation Fall again turned up as the scapegoat. He was the only defendant convicted in the original cases resulting directly from the Senate probe of 1923–24. All the transgressions associated with the oil scandal, and to a certain extent all the iniquity of the besmirched Harding administration, were imputed to him. Old and ill, the former Secretary of the Interior, riding in an ambulance, went to prison in 1931 for accepting a bribe, and became the first American Cabinet officer ever convicted and imprisoned for a felony committed while in office. The two oil millionaires went free. Fall was broken in health, reputation, and finances, and died in 1944 in near poverty. Although in the eyes of the public as a whole he had been an unfaithful public servant, he insisted to the end that his personal acquisitions from Sinclair and Doheny were legitimate loans and normal business transactions having no bearing on the official leasing policy for the naval oil reserves.

Until the Teapot Dome affair tainted his reputation, however, the most marked impression Albert B. Fall had left on the public mind during the years of his public service was that of an epitomized Westerner. And he did not discourage this popular conception.

Fall had not always lived in the West, but he spent his entire adult life there after leaving Kentucky, where he had been born in the first year of the Civil War. He grew up in the Reconstruction South. With some experience as a school teacher coupled with a short spell of "reading law" in Blackstone's *Commentaries* in his spare time, young Fall left Kentucky in 1881 for Clarksville on the Red River in Texas, having been in that area briefly two years before for the twin purposes of a prospecting expedition and the regaining of his health. Although for a time his one ambition was the amassing of a fortune large enough to buy a Kentucky farm, Fall was never again in his native state for an extended period.

The work of a bookkeeper in Clarksville did not help the young man's fragile health; so he turned to the life of a cowboy, hoping that an outdoor life and hard exercise would be strengthening. While working with cattle outfits in Texas, he performed the regular tasks of a cowhand and also had a try at the most celebrated calling of a cow camp, chuck wagon "bossing," or cooking. Years later he wrote of this experience:

> I soon learned . . . as no ranch cook could be employed, that my [next] occupation was to be the driving of the chuck wagon and purveying to the appetites of about eighteen to twenty-five cow punchers. I knew how to cook plain food and to make good bread and coffee. Of course, I could drive a team and I rather enjoyed the privileges of a cook around camp. The boys, needless to say, liked to stand in with the cook and it was well understood, that if one of them objected too seriously to the food prepared for him and would get rid of the cook by any method, which might appear to him, he was likely [to] fall heir to the cook's job and at the same time incur a certain degree of unpopularity.

Fall's cooking must have been at least palatable because his health, which was always uncertain, evidently improved enough to allow him to return for a short time to a more sedentary life at Clarksville. Again, in a desultory manner, he "read law." He dabbled in real estate and insurance, ran a grocery store, and, in 1883, married Emma Garland Morgan, whose father had been a representative from Texas to the Confederate Congress.

The ideal of owning a Kentucky farm was now gone, and Fall looked around for other possibilities of fame and fortune. The mines of Mexico seemed promising; so he left Clarksville for a prospecting trip south of the border. He rode on horseback through eight states of that republic, finally locating at Nieves in the state of Zacatecas. There he worked as a practical miner, as a timberman, mucker, and mining foreman. While serving his apprenticeship, he became skilled in the operation of the hoist and the pump. He sorted ore, constructed roads, and sharpened drills. Besides learning much about mining operations, and making some investments of his own, he began to acquire a speaking knowledge of Spanish, a faculty which afterwards served him well in the political arena of bilingual New Mexico. And, years later, Fall returned to Mexico as the manager and general counsel for Colonel William C. Greene, sometimes called the "Copper King" of Mexico, and made a fortune for himself in the gold and silver mines, timber, and railroads of Chihuahua and Sonora.

Fall came back to the United States in May, 1884, on the Mexican Central Railroad's first through train from Mexico City to El Paso, Texas. But after another several months in the Clarksville area he was again engaged in mining activities. This time, along with his brother-in-law, Joe Morgan, he went prospecting in the mountains of southern New Mexico, and landed finally in the booming and brawling mining camp of Kingston in the Black Range. His experiences at Kingston are among the most significant and fabled of his life, mainly because it was here that he met a fellow miner, Edward L. Doheny, who later struck it rich in oil and in the naval oil episode sent Fall a little black bag filled with $100,000.

Kingston was one of those legendary mining camps of the West where the rich finds of silver and other ore helped to precipitate the tidal wave of mining activity which swept through the Western states and territories during that period. It presented to the prospector all the "get-rich-quick" possibilities fostered by Sutter's Mill, the Comstock Lode, Virginia City, Montana, and Central City, Colorado. Although overdrawn as to the actual opportunities for quick wealth, this description sets the scene:

> It was at Kingston that the prospector sallied forth a poor man in the morning, returning a millionaire in the afternoon for he had "struck it rich." Here fortunes grew in a single day to vanish as quickly by games of chance, under the shadow of the pines, at night. The clinking of glasses, in drinking to the health and good luck of a "pard" and the dizzy whirl in the dance hall under the flaring and flickering flames of pine knots and tallow candles, were vivid scenes of the stirring times in the "good old days" of the early eighties.

When Fall and Morgan arrived at Kingston, they were armed with rifles and six-shooters, which prospectors there considered as necessary as a pick. The Apache Indians under Victorio, Nane, and Geronimo had terrorized southwestern New Mexico for years. Between 1879 and 1886 at least 140 casualties were suffered by the whites in Grant, Sierra (in which Kingston is located), and Socorro counties alone. Not until 1886, with the capture of Geronimo, did the fear of these Indian depredations diminish.

Completely out of money when he reached Kingston, Fall capitalized on his previous mining experience and had no trouble getting a job underground in the Grey Eagle Mine on South Percha Creek, about six miles from the town. This was tough, dirty work, the sweat and toil of practical mining with all the limitations of equipment and technique of a frontier locale. The newcomer from Texas worked "on the hammer" and performed the other tedious tasks of the hard rock miner at a wage of $3.50 per day. While working at the Grey Eagle, he lived in an earthen dugout a short distance away.

Fall decided to give up mining for the time being and to move to Las Cruces, when he concluded after several months in the Kingston area that other pursuits would provide a larger income for his growing family. His wife, whose poor health might benefit from the dry, sunny climate of southern New Mexico, and his two young children were still in Texas.

Las Cruces, on the banks of the Rio Grande River in Dona Ana County, was the largest town in the irrigated Mesilla Valley. It was in the heart of a rich agricultural, mining, and stock-raising section. Nourished by the ancient Mexican *acequias*, or irrigation canals, which siphoned off the muddy water of the Rio Grande, the arid lands of the Mesilla Valley blossomed with orchards, vineyards and alfalfa fields.

But the principal activity of Las Cruces and Dona Ana County was neither mining nor agriculture; it was politics. The citizens of that section, of whom the majority were Spanish-Americans, had a religious zeal for politics, and almost every community affair had some political significance. Through an aggressive group of leaders of both parties Dona Ana always tried to dominate every political convention and contest in the Territory of New Mexico, no matter what party was involved. Much of the time they were successful. The county was renowned for its political battles, which often resulted in mass demonstrations and bloodshed, and bitter personal feuds stemming from election quarrels dragged on for years, sometimes punctuated by six-shooter duels in the streets or public places, or by murders in ambush in more secluded locales.

Some more sensitive souls were completely repulsed by the operation of American democracy in Dona Ana County. A sophisticated Englishwoman, in New Mexico to regain her health, commented in horror:

> Small-beer politics [is] the curse of this fair land. . . . One method of securing the votes of our enlightened fellow-citizens is worthy of mention. On the evening before election-day, the henchmen of one political party rounded up forty or fifty Mexicans well primed in advance with whiskey, and, putting them into a corral as if they were a bunch of steers, kept them under guard all night for the purpose of ensuring their "straight" vote on the morrow. This incident is only one of the anomalies of a country whose freedom is not only in perpetual danger of degenerating

> into license, but which does constantly degenerate into some of the worst forms of slavery. . . .

The editor of a local newspaper, who, of course, had often seen such perversions of democracy and could confirm this foreigner's observations, wrote following an election:

> The money spent for whiskey and votes by the politicians of Las Cruces in the late election would have built an adequate system of water works for the town, put the streets in decent condition and planted rows of trees along every important street.

An opposing journal blamed the constant "state of ferment" about who would fill the county offices and the overpowering interest of the populace in this "absorbing theme" for the retarded financial development of the community. In every election old political wounds were torn open, heated personal quarrels ensued, and the prominent citizens who were most needed to promote progress were rendered incapable of uniting.

It was in this tumultuous setting that A. B. Fall (he was not Albert B. Fall until he became a United States Senator) served his political apprenticeship. He was no reformer, and there is little indication that conditions improved because of his presence. In fact, according to the opposition newspaper, he only stirred up more "strife and array," and, continued this partisan observer, "When the blessed Redeemer uttered that great humanitarian doctrine, 'Blessed are the peace makers,' he evidently did not refer to A. B. Fall." Fall did not cleanse Dona Ana politics, but he did master all its Machiavellian techniques and maneuvers. He became the political power of southern New Mexico.

There was little question about which party Fall would choose. In many respects he was still a Kentuckian, and for a Southerner there was no other party but Democrat. This raised a difficulty. Territorial New Mexico was veneered with Republicanism because most of the influential public offices were filled by appointment as the national administration in Washington saw fit. And because Republican presidents occupied the White House most of the time for fifty years after the Civil War, this made it hard for Fall to obtain the important political positions and recognition which his ambition demanded. A well-entrenched Republican machine, feeding on the beneficence of Washington, controlled New Mexico, including Dona Ana County. At the head of this territorial organization was Thomas B. Catron and his so-called "Santa Fe Ring." These Republican leaders, with influential ties in Washington, did their best to maintain a ruthless dominance over federal patronage and the favors emanating from the territorial capital at Santa Fe. Frontier politics, reminiscent of the

Jacksonian period, resulted, and often the practices of Dona Ana County spread all over New Mexico.

A. B. Fall, only a short time ago a mucker in the Grey Eagle Mine at Kingston, decided to "fight the devil with fire." He challenged the Dona Ana Republican machine, which meant also, of course, that he would be pitted against Thomas B. Catron and the "Santa Fe Ring." As one of his closest friends has written of Fall:

> His nature was not one of those ordinary individuals, who drop into the life of a community without ripple or disturbance, and remain submerged a part of the general scheme of affairs, filling an unnoticed niche and creating no disturbance . . . [in] existing conditions or no change of usual surroundings. It was inevitable that his presence should be noticed, his activities observed, his ambitions sounded and possibilities analyzed.

He became a master of sulphurous phrases and political vitriol. Whenever an opportunity presented itself (or he created one), whether in a public meeting, in court, or in private conversation, he harangued and castigated the Republicans. He cultivated the friendship and support of the Spanish-American element, and they seldom forgot their "amigo" on election day. He purchased a struggling weekly newspaper, the *Mesilla Valley Democrat,* which had all but failed in its Republican surroundings because of the bias signified by its name. His father and brother ostensibly ran the journal, whose name was changed to the *Independent Democrat,* but there was no doubt about who directed its editorial policy. Fall learned to resort to more forceful methods than the power of the press, however, when it was a matter of assembling a cavalry of armed cowboys furnished by a rancher friend, Oliver Lee, to disperse an opposing force of armed Republicans who were "guarding" the ballot boxes, or when conditions necessitated more individual combat.

As the Democrats gained power under Fall's leadership, political rivalry became even more heated. Both factions were constantly armed and ready for trouble. By tacit agreement Main Street was a dividing line, the east side with the Palmilla Club (one of the better saloons) and the town's leading barber shop was reserved for the Democrats. The west side, where the principal general store, the Masonic Temple, and numerous saloons of lesser grandeur were located, was set aside for the Republicans.

Fall claimed his life had been threatened and he was seldom seen on the streets without one or the other of his unofficial bodyguards, his brother-in-law, Joe Morgan, or his rancher friend, Oliver Lee. One September night in 1895 the tense situation was suddenly punctuated with gunfire. As Fall, his law partner, R. L. ("Deacon") Young, and Joe Morgan stood talking in the shadows outside the law partner's office on the east (Democratic) side of Main Street, a member of the opposition, Ben

Williams, who had the reputation of a gunman, came walking down the same side of the street. Perhaps it was because the Republicans had hired Williams to kill Fall, or, perhaps, it was for other reasons, doubtless political in some part, that either Morgan or Williams, who had an old grudge, started shooting. At any rate, Morgan fired the first shot to take effect. It grazed Williams' head, badly powder-burning his face. Another shot, perhaps fired by Fall, passed through Williams' hat. A third shot, from Morgan's six-shooter at close range, shattered Williams' left elbow, passed out at the shoulder, and knocked him to the ground. Soon after this Williams, who had been returning the fire, got across to the Republican side of the street, shooting as he went, backed into a saloon, shot out the lights, and was quickly cared for by his friends. Fall was not injured, but his brother-in-law had a flesh wound in the upper arm.

One report had it that Williams was "out to get" Fall and had stumbled into the saloon after the shooting saying he had done the job. The Republicans denied this. They said Williams had been the victim of a premeditated and unprovoked attack. Fall maintained that he did no shooting in the episode. And when the grand jury, composed of sixteen Democrats and five Republicans, convened, it refused to find indictments against Fall and Morgan, but instead issued two separate nuisance indictments concerning matters apart from the shooting against Williams and Colonel Albert J. Fountain, the county's leading Republican. These last two charges were dismissed a short time later, and the Democratic-Republican rivalry continued along other paths. By now the fiery Democratic chieftain was no longer a novice in the political affairs of territorial New Mexico.

Although he had practiced law in some capacity earlier, Fall was formally admitted to practice before the territorial supreme court and the lesser courts of New Mexico in 1891, about four years after arriving in Las Cruces. This was the culmination of a long process of "reading law" intermittently since his youth in Kentucky. Within a few years he was recognized as one of most competent attorneys in that part of the Southwest. Much of his practice concerned both United States and Mexican law, especially in cases regarding land titles, water and mineral rights, and the legality of Mexican marriages under United States law, because of the proximity of Dona Ana County to Mexico, and because it was formerly Mexican territory. Cattle rustling cases also took much of his time. He afterward declared that he had defended some 500 persons accused of rustling and could not recall having lost one such case. Moreover, he was employed by livestock associations in the prosecution of rustlers and maintained that he had never lost one of these cases either. Murder cases, too, constituted a great part of his practice. Perhaps fifty of these involved first degree murder, only one of them resulting in conviction, according to Fall.

Three of the most famous murder cases in which Fall acted as a defense attorney received wide notoriety. One was the shooting in El Paso of John Wesley Hardin, the infamous Texas killer, by John Selman in 1895. The celebrated Fountain case of 1896–99, in which Fall's right-hand man Oliver Lee and others were charged with murder in the disappearance on the White Sands of the Dona Ana Republican leader, Colonel Albert J. Fountain, and his nine-year-old son, drew the anxious attention of the entire Southwest and threatened to result in a bloody range war with the sides divided according to political alignments. Fall headed the defense again in the 1908 trial of Wayne Brazel, the accused assassin of Pat F. Garrett, the Lincoln County sheriff who had disposed of Billy the Kid. All of these trials ended in acquittal. In the events preceding and accompanying the Fountain trial Fall was closely associated with Eugene Manlove Rhodes, afterwards recognized as the bard-chronicler of the Cattle Kingdom, and the two remained lifelong friends. In fact Rhodes used Fall as a character in some of his stories.

A. B. Fall was a familiar figure in the courts of southern New Mexico, and his law practice became most profitable. Intermittently for many years he was connected with W. A. Hawkins and other attorneys-in-law partnerships in Las Cruces, El Paso, and Clifton, Arizona. He represented irrigation and development enterprises, mining companies, lumber concerns, railroads, and other industrial interests.

But still he had time for politics. He served in both houses of the territorial legislature, having been elected to the lower house first in 1890, as an associate justice of the New Mexico supreme court from 1893 to 1895 by appointment from Democratic President Grover Cleveland, and briefly as territorial attorney general twice, once in 1897 and again in 1907. In his early public career, as later, he often acted independently, sometimes refusing to attend Democratic caucuses, and he was always surrounded by controversy. Once, during a heated debate on the floor of the legislature, he impulsively stepped over from the Democratic side to slap the face of Charles A. Spiess, one of the territory's most prominent Republicans. Spiess did not reciprocate.

When the Spanish-American War erupted, Fall readily took time off from his political and legal activities to lead the local company of militia, but the war was too short for Captain Fall to cover himself with the military glory which so enhanced the political fortunes of many New Mexicans who served with Theodore Roosevelt and the Rough Rider Regiment. The closest he ever got to the fighting was the peanut fields of Georgia, where he and his troops underwent training at Camp Churchman.

Following this brief army experience, Fall returned to Las Cruces and his law office. He expanded his practice, increased his mine holdings in New Mexico, in which he had been interested since his early days in the territory, acquired bank stocks, and made additional investments in Mexican mining. These interests were the foundation of his fortune, but the cornerstone came through his association with that colorful Western capitalist, Colonel William C. Greene.

As manager, organizer, and general counsel for the colonel's vast mining, timber, and railroad enterprises principally in Chihuahua and Sonora, Mexico, Fall had a key role in a multi-million dollar operation. This was his big opportunity, and he was equal to it. With a staff of lawyers and thousands of Mexican laborers under his supervision, he maintained offices in El Paso, New York, and at Concheno, Chihuahua, and at other points in Mexico. This undertaking provided an intimate knowledge of Mexican law, government, and society, besides affording an acquaintance with many influential Mexicans, including the old dictator, Porfirio Diaz. Later, when Mexico was convulsed in revolution and American property and lives were lost, Fall was in the Senate and became the outstanding advocate in that body for United States' intervention south of the border.

While directing Greene's operations, Fall had an opportunity to make investments of his own in those enterprises and elsewhere in Mexico. Then he closed out a large portion of his friend's interests, when Greene faced bankruptcy in the early 1900's, and, by advancing money of his own to meet certain of the Colonel's obligations, he secured titles to a remnant of the Greene properties, some of which he still held during the revolutionary period.

With the profits from his Mexican interests A. B. Fall acquired a historic ranch near Tularosa, New Mexico, from Patrick Coghlan, who was reputed to have been a friend of Billy the Kid and the entrepreneur of a cattle rustling gang of which the Kid was the titular leader. The ranch was located at the edge of the Tularosa Basin (where the first atomic bomb was exploded in July, 1945) in the rough hill country at the foot of the Sierra Blanca Mountain. It controlled most of the lower part of the Tres Ritos (more correctly "Tres Rios,") or Three Rivers Valley, just to the north of the great mountain.

In 1904 Fall moved his home to the Three Rivers ranch, whose headquarters ranchhouse, shaded by giant cottonwoods, had walls of adobe three feet thick. Ownership of this rugged ranch gave him tremendous satisfaction, and although he could never be there as much as he wished, he was able to devote more time to its supervision when his Mexican investments declined, and he spent his fortune expanding and developing it until eventually it encompassed about 650,000 acres. In fact the ranch brought about his downfall. Most of the $404,000 he obtained from Sinclair and Doheny was used for the addition of more land, the construction of a hydroelectric plant, the laying of several miles of concrete irrigation ditches, and other improvements at Three Rivers. This show of affluence was the first thing to raise questions in the Teapot Dome investigation about his financial affairs.

Mexican operations had taken most of his time for a few years, but Fall could not stay away from New Mexico politics. He astounded everyone in the territory by switching to the Republican Party, and voting that way in the 1906 election. It was not uncommon in New Mexico for top political leaders to change parties; however, no other switch was as surprising as Fall's, for he had been "one of the most uncompromising of democratic partisans ever identified with the political history of the State. . . . ," or, even worse, "the most rabid and intense Democrat in the whole Southwest. . . ." But his affiliation with the Republican Party was quickly accepted, and soon he was blasting the Democrats just as energetically as he had the Republicans. This did represent nevertheless, a significant point of transition in Fall's life. With his switch from the Democrats to the Republicans, Fall lost the last important vestige of identification with the South. When he was willing to turn his back on the South's traditional party, he was no longer a Southerner. He was now a Westerner.

Toward the end of his life, when asked about this change of party allegiance, Fall simply smiled and replied, "I know when to change horses." And this probably explains his political metamorphosis as well as anything else. Some day New Mexico was going to become a state, which in all probability would mean the election of two Republicans to the United States Senate. By this time Fall's aspirations demanded more prominence than local politics could bestow; he wanted to be one of the newly-admitted state's first Senators. After that, who could tell what would come next? A. B. Fall's driving ambition had taken him a long way since the days when he had served up sourdough biscuits, coffee, sow belly bacon, and other delicacies to Texas cowhands from his chuck wagon.

In 1910 he was a delegate to the convention which produced a constitution for New Mexico's statehood. Then, in 1912, the first legislature of the forty-seventh state elected him and his old Republican enemy of Las Cruces days, Thomas B. Catron, as the first United States Senators. After nine years in the Senate, Fall was elevated to the Cabinet by his friend President Harding. Two years later, in March, 1923, he resigned as Secretary of the Interior, and within a year the Teapot Dome investigation had unleashed the revelations which ruined him politically and financially.

The time to view Fall as an epitomized Westerner, then, is not at the end of his life, but in 1923, just as he retired from the Department of the Interior, and before his reputation crumpled. This was when his prestige was at its height, and the public still seemed to regard him as a "typical," highly successful Westerner.

Why had he left this impression during the years of his public office holding, and how well did he measure up to the popular conception? To begin with, Fall was a self-made man, a feat always dear to the promoters of the Western tradition. He had only a few years of formal schooling; this was all the education he ever got from other men. Also he loved horses, and for that matter, any kind of fine blooded stock. Every year he attended the Kentucky Derby, and a friend once declared, ". . . I think if he was in his grave and you mentioned a race horse he would jump right up and ask about it." A black, broad brimmed Stetson hat became his trademark, just as he was noted for his combative nature, his soft drawl, which, incidentally, was probably more Kentuckian than Western, and his bronzed complexion. The rumor got around that he always carried a gun and was not afraid to use it.

Fall had a special talent for being a crony and played poker with a passion that made him a natural chum in his Senate days of poker-loving Warren G. Harding. His erect posture indicated to many that he was a "man who had spent much time in the saddle." He was described as a "fighting man whose career, to some extent, is reminiscent of Buffalo Bill. . . ," and with "the sort of eyes that one learned to beware of in the early frontier days as indicating a man who could take care of himself in almost any sort of company."

A subordinate in the Interior Department said of him: Fall was certainly a man of ability. He was a fighter who gave and took hard blows. I think that, and party politics, was the major cause of opposition to him rather than any special jealousy. I was fond of him but to be fair we must remember that his code was that of the frontier and frontier politics.

Fall himself put it another way in a letter in which he had frankly assessed the capability of a local politician and had concluded by telling the man, "You will excuse the 'poker' terms which I have used, but the game of politics is so much like a game of poker that these, it strikes me, are most appropriate."

His enormous ranch became a legend, especially with Easterners, and someone enamored with the West was forever writing him about a job on it, or wanting to send an ailing or erring son, whichever the case might be, there for restitution. And sometimes in true Western hospitality Fall graciously favored these requests. One such Eastern boy, of the ailing variety, lived on the Three Rivers ranch for eleven months, at the end of which the father asserted that his experience would no doubt prove more valuable to his son than any two or three years in the boy's lifetime.

In the Harding Cabinet, as in the New Mexico territorial legislature, Albert B. Fall showed what some Easterners might consider the spirit of the "untamed" West. Actually, he was simply a rebel, or sometimes, as he afterwards characterized his position in the Cabinet, a "kicker."

> I became unintentionally the kicker of the Cabinet. It got so I was expected to make objections. Most of the rest of them were more reserved. I wish now that I had been, too. For every time I kicked about something I made an enemy, and in later years all these little disaffections piled up against me. As we say out west, I spoke too many times when I should have been listening.

Some of these qualities mentioned might appear in any man, Easterner as well as Westerner, but in his attitude toward the conservation of natural resources Fall was without doubt typically Western. He was by no means a conservationist in the popular conception of the term, as many of his speeches and actions while in the Senate and Interior Department reveal. Fall admired Theodore Roosevelt and nominated him for the Presidency in the 1916 Republican National Convention. Roosevelt once called Fall "the kind of public servant of whom all Americans should feel proud," and another time he stated, "For two or three years Senator Fall has been on the whole, with the possible exception of Senator Poindexter, the man with whom I have been able most cordially to co-operate among all of the people at Washington." This friendship was based, however, on a mutual disapproval of President Woodrow Wilson's "watchful waiting" policy in Mexico rather than on common ground in conservation views. In fact Fall was specifically repulsed by Roosevelt's conservation program as expressed in the 1912 Progressive Party platform.

Fall had been exploiting the natural resources in the Southwest and in Mexico as a rancher and in various mining ventures for nearly forty years when he became Secretary of the Interior, and he believed that the land, timber, and minerals of the Western states should be used for the immediate development of that section, just as they had been in the older states. Once when an official of the National Park Service challenged him on his wide-open attitude toward the public lands, asking what sort of heritage this would leave the next generation, Fall replied easily:

> I'm surprised at you. You've had a good education. You know something about history. Every generation from Adam and Eve down has lived better than the generation before. I don't know how . . . [the next generation will] do it—maybe they'll use the energy of the sun or the sea waves—but . . . [they] will live better than we do. I stand for opening up every resource.

Consequently it should not have been surprising that as Secretary of the Interior, after rather surreptitiously assuming control of the naval oil reserves, set aside for the Navy's use only in case of emergency, he negotiated leasing arrangements with Sinclair and Doheny for these reserves. The astonishing part came when it was discovered he had taken money from the two oilmen at about the same time the leases were being made. Fall went to prison for accepting a bribe, but it must be said in his behalf that with his typically Western attitude of unrestrained and immediate disposition of the natural resources, and for this reason alone, he no doubt would have turned over the reserves to Sinclair and Doheny, or to some other representatives of private enterprise.

In a peculiar manner the natural resources of the West made and broke Albert B. Fall. His life is "an American success story" with an unhappy ending!

SUGGESTED READINGS

David H. Stratton, "Behind Teapot Dome: Some Personal Insights," *Business History Review*, vol. XXXI (Winter 1957);

Stratton, editor, *The Memoirs of Albert B. Fall*, Monograph No. 15, Southwestern Studies (El Paso 1966);

William A. Keleher, *The Fabulous Frontier: Twelve New Mexico Items* (Santa Fe 1945);

Burl Noggle, *Teapot Dome: Oil and Politics in the 1920's* (Baton Rouge 1962);

A. M. Gibson, *The Life and Death of Colonel Albert Jennings Fountain* (Norman 1965);

Leonard J. Bates, "The Teapot Dome Scandal and the Election of 1924," *American Historical Review*, vol. LX (January 1955).

19
Bronson Cutting, Politician

Soon after his arrival in New Mexico in 1910 Bronson Cutting, a wealthy young Easterner, became involved in politics. He purchased the Santa Fe *New Mexican* and began to develop a power base in the Republican Party. A member of the Progressive wing of the party, Cutting was an inveterate foe of bossism and political corruption, and he waged a long battle with members of the Old Guard such as Thomas Catron and Albert Fall and Holm Bursum. Much of his early career was devoted to a campaign to reform state government.

Cutting was a political maverick and never permitted himself to be restrained by party loyalty. He refused to back some Republican candidates and occasionally associated with the Democratic Party, and his willingness to break with his party was undoubtedly the most distinctive characteristic of his political career. Although Cutting was often unable to work effectively with others, he was a skilled politician and quickly molded a strong political organization despite the fact that he was a newcomer to the state. In this selection Professor Seligman describes the development of this organization and Cutting's reliance upon the Spanish-Americans and the newly organized American Legion.

In the spring of 1910 Bronson Murray Cutting arrived in Santa Fe, New Mexico Territory. The young, wealthy Cutting suffered from tuberculosis which had recently taken his older brother's life. He came to the desert Southwest for its mild climate, and he stayed to become an outstanding political figure.

In 1912, Cutting purchased the Santa Fe *New Mexican* and began to establish himself as a formidable figure in the Progressive Republican

---

Paper by Gustav L. Seligman at the Western History Association, October 1968. Reprinted by permission of the author.

wing of New Mexico politics. During the period 1912–17 he generally supported the Republican Party nationally, but he frequently crossed party lines at the state and local level, particularly when he disagreed with the activities of the Republican Old Guard, led by Thomas Catron and Albert Bacon Fall. In 1917 he volunteered for military service, received a captain's commission and was posted to intelligence duty in the United States Embassy in London. In the 1918 election, the *New Mexican,* under the control of his sister Justine Ward, backed the Republican Octaviano Larrazolo in his successful governor's campaign.

In the years following the war, Cutting's political activities assumed a different emphasis. Previously he was interested primarily in reforming the state's government. His actions now shifted towards developing his own political organization. The two pillars of his organization were the Mexican-Americans and the veterans. An assessment of the bases of Cutting's power will provide a background to an understanding of Cutting's actions while he was a senator.

In developing his political power, Cutting used his large personal fortune to good advantage. As Eugene Manlove Rhodes said:

> Senator Cutting has given his money freely to nonpartisan, or more accurately, bipartisan societies—and to American Legion Posts, etc. Not cash to divide. A hall to meet in, a billiard table, a tennis court, a baseball diamond, expenses of delegates. Also legitimate travel and hotel expenses of candidates, committee men, etc., in actual campaigns. He has asked for nothing—and it seems has got a great deal. A thousand details to be told by moonlight alone—most of all—he has never high-hatted anybody—and that includes any Mexican. This is a conquered race—and a proud and sensitive race—when you take 'em where they were born and raised. They may forgive you for taking a shot or two at them—but *never* for high-hatting. Cutting has won more votes from this course alone than all the money he has spent.

Thus Cutting's political following of Mexican-Americans and veterans, and his own personality and wealth formed a commanding presence in New Mexico politics from 1918–35.

The first basis of his *support* was the Mexican-American. The reason for this does not lend itself to a simple analysis. Prior to statehood most of the Mexicans usually followed the lead of the *patrón,* Anglo or Mexican, but with the gradual end of the open range and the decrease in size of the large land holdings, this role vanished. Some Mexican-American politicians like Larrazolo stepped into the temporary vacuum, but Cutting eventually became the statewide political *patrón.* His methods are only partially discernible and can only partially be verified by the available evidence. Perhaps his greatest attribute was his attitude toward the Mexicans. He genuinely liked and respected them. He could read, write, and speak their language, it is true, but many of the politicians in the state could do that. His real secret was that:

> When Bronson Cutting was alive he seemed to enjoy sincerely the company of the poorest natives, and he attended their delight making festivals as well as their all-night wakes over the dead as one of them. In turn they thought nothing of calling him at his mansion for all manner of reasons, whether great or trivial; just as a friend might.

This kind of support is difficult to alienate. A further indication of the place of Cutting in the Mexican's feelings is shown by his nickname *El Viejo,* "the old one." Native society in New Mexico is strongly patriarchal: for a person as young as Cutting to be known by this term shows deep respect.

The other basis of Cutting's support came from the New Mexico veterans. Here Donald Blevins was very instrumental in solidifying support, but had Cutting not given generously of his time and his money it would never have materialized. New Mexico, as an agricultural state, did not enjoy the general prosperity of the twenties; its rural isolation produced a cultural deprivation and the discrimination of isolation. Thus, veterans who returned to these isolated areas soon got out of touch with the Veterans' Bureau and the various medical facilities and other benefits for which they might be eligible. The activities of the American Legion helped to keep them in touch with the outside world. This garnering of the veterans, many of whom were Mexican-Americans, meant that Cutting succeeded in gaining the support of those very elements in the native community he could not reach as a *patrón.* These veterans were often the only inhabitants of their village who had ventured outside the state boundaries and while they could have been, under different circumstances, disruptive factors in Cutting's control of the native votes they were also bound rather closely to him and his programs. Like that of the Mexican-Americans, he earned this backing of the veterans for himself and not because of party affiliation. When he shifted parties his followers shifted with him. This type of support is a two-edged sword; a leader must continually lead in a direction compatible with the wishes of his following. This meant that Cutting was also a captive of his supporters and could not go too far afield from their desires.

The American Legion was formed in March 1919 under the leadership of Theodore Roosevelt, Jr. At a later meeting held in St. Louis plans for a national convention and methods of forming local organization were discussed. Cutting was not only present at the initial meetings but he also prepared a list of potential leaders from the state of New Mexico. On the state scene, Cutting, working through intermediaries, induced Colonel Walter du Bremond to become temporary state leader. In April at the state caucus, du Bremond, Henry Dorman, Donald Blevins, Miguel Otero, Jr., and Cutting were among the state delegates chosen to attend the national meeting in St. Louis. At the St. Louis meeting Cutting and several other New Mexicans were put on the national committee. Soon du Bremond resigned because of ill health and left the Legion's organizational reins in the hands of Cutting, Dorman, Blevins, and the younger Otero.

With Blevins organizing and Cutting paying most of the expenses, a well-knit organization soon developed in the state. (The isolation of New Mexico communities worked in Cutting's favor—frequently Blevins would be the only stranger in months to visit an isolated community.) Blevins directed the disabled or ill veteran to the proper source of aid and intervened to help the needy find employment, thereby strengthening the veteran's attraction to Cutting. Cutting became closely connected with the group, not only through Blevins' activities, but through the prizes he offered for organizational activities. These prizes, ranging from fifty to one hundred dollars in cash, were offered in Cutting's name to the posts which showed the greatest expansion. As a result of this organizational effort thirty-one posts were established in the state by September 1919. At the October state convention Herman Baca was elected Department Commander and Cutting became a National Committeeman. Under Baca's leadership the number of posts in the state increased to fifty-one during the next year. It was to Cutting's long-term advantage that he devoted much of his time and energy to Legion activities in this crucial period which would probably have been impossible had Larrazolo not been the type of Governor that Cutting had wanted for several years.

Cutting supported programs that Larrazolo advocated, particularly the improvement of teacher's qualifications, child labor laws, women's suffrage, and bilingual instruction in the public schools. With a friend and ally in the State House Cutting had ample time for activities other than those of the Legion. He supported General Leonard Wood for the 1920 Republican Presidential nomination. From the days of the Rough Riders, their commander Wood had been a favorite in New Mexico. When Wood arrived there in August 1919 he received a warm welcome. While in Santa Fe, he was Cutting's house guest. Wood's speech of appreciation at a parade held in his honor, made in both Spanish and English, further increased his popularity. This popularity, quietly fanned by Cutting, manifested itself when the New Mexico Republicans chose their delegates to the national presidential convention. The New Mexico delegation was instructed for Wood although Senator Albert B. Fall worked very hard to have the delegation pledged to himself as a favorite son.

By late 1919 Cutting realized that the renomination of Larrazolo was not going to be an easy task for, "sooner or later, he [Larrazolo] will have to make a choice between the support of the decent element in the Republican Party (plus his native personal following) and the support of the Bursum-Hawkins crowd." Whether Larrazolo was ever given an opportunity to make this choice or not is difficult to determine but the choice was made. Following a convention which was about as vitriolic as any in the history of the state, the delegates finally selected a judge from Socorro, Merritt Mechem, as Republican candidate for governor. Once again Cutting bolted the party, and he and the Progressives supported the Democrats locally and statewide as in previous elections. However, the conservative Republicans soundly defeated the Democrats and the Progressives in New Mexico as Harding and Mechem easily carried the state. For the next two years Cutting had little to do except work with the Legion and attack the Republicans.

The Legion founders at the national level had constructed a nonpolitical organization. It soon changed character, and this change in tactics was probably necessary if the Legion was to flourish. In this new role as a nonfraternal organization, the Legionnaires pressed the claim that the veterans constituted a voting block capable of award or punishment at the polls. The fact that it became necessary to enter the political arena does not, of course, explain why the Legion should espouse "Americanism" of a variety quite incompatible with the New Mexico situation. The national leadership viewed the organization as a white, English-speaking organization, but these qualifications seriously hindered Cutting's efforts in New Mexico. The issue came to a head when the national leadership of the Legion proposed that English be the only legal language of public instruction. In a long letter to the chairman of the Legion's Americanization Committee, Cutting called such a measure unwise, impractical, and politically unfeasible insofar as it applied to New Mexico. The Assistant Director of the Committee replied to the effect that he could not see how Cutting could condone such a practice as teaching in Spanish and that the Legion policy would remain unchanged on this issue. Cutting chose to side with the interests of the state rather than the national organization on this issue and demonstrated, at least to the Mexican-Americans, where his heart lay.

In 1922 the Legion in New Mexico, headed by Cutting and his newspaper, campaigned for the election of a Democrat to the United States Senate, A. A. Jones. "Two hundred of the men who fought 'Over There,' some in uniform and wearing medals, a few on crutches, young men all, marched through the streets of Albuquerque with Senator Jones marching at their head." Cutting did not endorse the Democratic nominee for governor, James Hinkle, but his support of the Republican candidate was so negligible that many of the state's voters believed that he was supporting the entire Democratic ticket. The charges against the Republicans were the usual ones of corruption and scandal. For the corruption the Democrats pointed to the replacement of the president of the State Normal School with a political hack; for the scandal they pointed to the forced resignation of the superintendent of the penitentiary over an incident involving the killing of a convict during a food strike. Despite these issues, the *New Mexican* commented editorially that the campaign seemed "the dullest in 30 years." The result was a Democratic landslide. Not only did they capture the major offices on the ballot but they gained a three vote majority in the lower house, the first time since statehood that the Democrats had held a majority in either house.

With the election of Hinkle it appeared that Cutting would be able to give him his wholehearted support. Not only was the Democratic platform quite acceptable to Cutting but the new governor's record in his previous political positions was one of both an honest man and one interested in the welfare of the state and its people. In general Cutting approved of Hinkle's entire program with the exception of a property tax exemption for veterans which he felt hurt the nonproperty-owning veterans, a large group in New Mexico. The two finally split over that mundane but important issue of patronage. Hinkle, coming from Chavez County on the east side of the state, the anti-Mexican area of New Mexico, was not giving the native element what they and Cutting felt to be their fair share of the more prestigious positions. Here again Cutting publicly sided with the Mexican-American elements in the state.

In the summer of 1924 Cutting, now officially a Democrat, helped his followers gain control of the Democratic organization in Santa Fe County; they then elected a slate of delegates pledged to nominate him for Governor. Cutting's strength grew until he could claim 277 of the 600 convention voters. At this point Hinkle withdrew from the fight, and his withdrawal was followed almost immediately by Cutting's, which left the field open to Arthur T. Hannett of Gallup. Why Cutting did this is unclear, but the sequence of events indicates that he was probably prompted by a desire to stop Hinkle, coupled with the feeling that he could not beat Hannett.

As befitted a new member of the Democratic party Cutting supported the entire ticket and once again his candidates won office. One of Hannett's first appointments was to place Cutting on the Board of Commissioners of the State Penitentiary in the hope that he could complete the job of reform begun by Hinkle. Cutting began the task with considerable enthusiasm; he hoped to be able to effect some permanent reforms in the New Mexico penal system. But before any basic changes could be instituted Cutting and Hannett split.

There were several reasons for the split. Hannett claimed that the cleavage resulted from Cutting's demand for a Labor Commission and a Veterans' Bureau at the state level. Hannett felt the added departments would conflict with his economy pledges, and they would also build up Cutting's political following. H. O. Bursum, Miguel Otero, Jr., and M. L. Fox, an Albuquerque editor, asserted that the division developed over Hannett's attempts to use the beginnings of patronage to build a permanent machine. Both versions are probably true. The editorial pages of the *New Mexican* revealed the first hint of the break by the end of May 1925. The irrevocable split, however, came over a project both Cutting and Hannett were interested in: revision of the election code. Finally Hannett demanded Cutting's resignation on the general grounds of disloyalty. Cutting refused to step down immediately and took the rather unusual step of publishing the entire correspondence in the *New Mexican.*

It is an irony of politics that Cutting and Hannett should break completely over a reform which both considered so important. Hannett appointed a committee consisting of himself, two Democrats, two Republicans, and two state legislators of opposing parties to draw up a new election code for the state. Among other things the proposed law provided for personal re-registration every six years, uniform ballot boxes, no more than 300 voters per polling place, absentee voting, a uniform and simplified contest law, provisions forbidding the accompaniment of the non-handicapped voter into the voting booth and the elimination of the provision for straight ticket balloting by making a single mark. Cutting saw these changes, particularly the provision against aiding a voter to mark his ballot, as discrimination against the semiliterate or illiterate Mexican-American voter. The Republicans soon joined him in the controversy. In addition they opposed the provision against registration by mail and the provisions which made straight ticket voting more difficult. By election time Cutting agreed with the Republicans on the single most important issue of the campaign and gave his support to their nominee, Richard C. Dillon. The combination of regular Republicans, the Cutting faction, and the Mexican-American voters who believed that the Hannett Code discriminated against them insured victory.

Governor Dillon's first term could be called the "era of good feelings" in New Mexico politics. There were, of course, dissident voices, such as Hannett's newspaper column in the Albuquerque *Journal,* but by and large his administration ran very smoothly. His legislative message, the shortest ever delivered, called for an election code, effective prohibition, free text books, elimination of the road tax, an extended workingman's compensation law, and several other less important reforms. The Republican-dominated legislature went to work with a will and much of the governor's program was soon passed even including much of the Hannett Election Code. Dillon got along well with the legislature, and he got along so well with Cutting that when Senator A. A. Jones died in December 1927 Dillon appointed Cutting "because of the statewide endorsement of him by the people from all walks of life."

The story, however, is not this simple. The Dillon Papers contain a rather bulky file of letters dealing with this appointment and while the letters themselves say nothing that would disprove the statement, Cutting's name only appears once in this file—in a letter recommending another man as a better Republican than Cutting for the position. Moreover, according to a "number of men who were active in politics at the time." It was well known that Jones was very ill and that Hannett hoped to appoint himself to the interim position if he were reelected in 1926. If Jones' illness was known about the state it would appear possible that Cutting might have insisted on the Senate appointment as the price for his support. This argument is strengthened by the fact that Cutting ostensibly left the Democrats over the voting law changes yet he did not protest when the Republican legislature passed essentially the same legislation which Hannett had proposed earlier.

With this appointment to the United States Senate, Cutting began a new phase of his political career. Cutting had lived in the state for seventeen years and during this time created a large, loyal organization. The most "natural" element of this following was the political reformers, generally upper or middle class, and always the "respectable" elements of society. These people, the Hagermans, the Oteros, and others, saw in Cutting a Messiah whose money and newspaper could lead them into the promised land of reform and good government—a government which would keep the lower and less respectable social class content without giving them the reins of power. When Cutting began suggesting fundamental reforms in the body politic, he rapidly lost the support of this element. Yet the groups with which he had the least in common socially—the poor Mexican-Americans and the veterans—supported him until his untimely death in an airplane crash in 1935.

SUGGESTED READINGS

Robert W. Larson, "The Profile of a New Mexico Progressive," *New Mexico Historical Review,* vol. XLV (July 1970);

Patricia Armstrong, *A Portrait of Bronson Cutting Through His Papers, 1910–1927* (Albuquerque 1959);

Jack E. Holmes, *Politics in New Mexico* (Albuquerque 1967);

H. B. Hening, editor, *George Curry, 1861–1947: An Autobiography* (Albuquerque 1958);

Otis L. Graham, *An Encore for Reform: The Old Progressives and the New Deal* (New York 1967);

Gustav L. Seligman, "The Political Career of Senator Bronson M. Cutting" (Unpublished Ph.D. dissertation, University of Arizona, 1967).

20
The Atomic Bomb

The incredible burst of light that shattered the early morning darkness of the Tularosa Basin on July 16, 1945 marked the success of the Manhattan Project and signaled the beginning of the Atomic Age. The successful nuclear test at Trinity Site and the subsequent use of nuclear weapons at Hiroshima and Nagasaki not only shortened the war, but also had a long-term effect on international relations. New Mexico, as the site of the first nuclear test and as the home of the new, secret Los Alamos Scientific Laboratory, caught worldwide attention in the summer of 1945.

The Los Alamos Project, headed by Dr. J. Robert Oppenheimer, was just part of the organization which developed the atomic bomb, but its contribution was crucial. The finest equipment and the best scientific minds joined to form what has been described as perhaps the best-equipped physics research laboratory in the world; but no one knew for sure that the device would work or if it did what the explosive yield would be. Nor was it possible to accurately estimate radiation intensities, fallout, and other results. The decision, therefore, was made to test the device in New Mexico preparatory to using it against the enemy, and the dramatic hours preceding the test and the reactions of the scientists to their handiwork are related here.

Historians have debated the advisability of using the atomic bomb against Japan, and they have attempted to evaluate the role of atomic weapons in international diplomacy during the subsequent years; recently some authorities have become concerned with the peaceful application of nuclear energy and its possible impact upon the environment. One thing is certain, however. The test at Trinity Site signaled the entrance of New Mexico into a new era and marked the integration of the oldest settled portion of the United States with industrial and urban America, for the growth of industry and cities in New Mexico

---

Reprinted from *The Atom,* vol. II (July 16, 1965), pp. 24–31.

really began during World War II. New Mexico in the 1970s, relying heavily upon the defense industry and related enterprises, is a far cry from New Mexico of 1933 when the largest city had a population of less than 35,000 and when fewer than 3,000 people were employed in factories.

All through the night the spectators had been gathering to await the most spectacular dawn the world had ever seen.

They waited on high ground outside the control bunker. They waited at the observation posts at West and North 10,000. They waited in arroyos and in surrounding hills. A group of guards waited in slit trenches in Mockingbird Gap between Oscuro and Little Burro Peaks.

All had been instructed to lie face down on the ground with their feet toward the blast, to close their eyes and cover them as the countdown approached zero. As soon as they became aware of the flash they could turn over and watch through the darkened glass that had been supplied.

On Compagna Hill, 20 miles northwest of Ground Zero, a large contingent of scientists waited along with Laurence of the *Times*. They shivered in the cold and listened to instructions read by flashlight by David Dow, in charge of that observation post. They ate a picnic breakfast. Edward Teller warned about sunburn and somebody passed around some sunburn lotion in the pitch darkness.

Fred Reines, a former Los Alamos physicist, waited with Greisen and I. I. Rabi, a project consultant, and heard the "Voice of America" burst forth on the short wave radio with "Star Spangled Banner" as if anticipating a momentous event.

Al and Elizabeth Graves, a husband and wife scientific team, waited in a dingy Carrizozo motel with their recording instruments. Others, mostly military men, waited at spots as far away as 200 miles, their instruments ready to record the phenomena.

In San Antonio, Restaurant Proprietor Jose Miera was awakened by the soldiers stationed at his place with seismographs. "If you come out in front of your store now, you'll see something the world has never seen before," they told him.

Just south of San Antonio, a group of hardy Los Alamos souls, who had climbed into the saddle of Chupadero Peak the day before, waited drowsily in their sleeping bags.

In Los Alamos, most people slept but some knew and went out to watch from the porches of their Sundt apartments. Others drove into the mountains for a better view. Mr. and Mrs. Darol Froman and a group of friends waited in their car, gave up and were heading back down the mountain when 5:30 came.

A group of wives, whose husbands had been off in the desert for endless weeks, waited in the chill air of Sawyer's Hill. Months later one of them described the agonizing hours.

"Four o'clock. Nothing was happening. Perhaps something was amiss down there in the desert where one's husband stood with other men to midwife the birth of the monster. Four fifteen and nothing yet. Maybe it had failed. At least, then, the husbands were safe. . . . Four thirty. The gray dawn rising in the east, and still no sign that the labor and struggle of the past three years had meant anything at all. . . . It hardly seemed worthwhile to stand there, scanning the sky, cold and so afraid."

Elsewhere the world slept or fought its war and President Truman waited at Potsdam.

Back at Trinity, over the intercoms, the FM radios, the public address system, Sam Allison's voice went on, counting first at five-minute intervals then in interminable seconds.

"Aren't you nervous?" Rabi asked Greisen as they lay face down on the ground.

"Nope," replied Greisen.

"As we approached the final minute," Groves wrote, "the quiet grew more intense. I was on the ground (at Base Camp) between Bush and Conant. As I lay their in the final seconds, I thought only of what I would do if the countdown got to zero and nothing happened."

Conant said he never knew seconds could be so long.

At the control point, General Farrell wrote later, "The scene inside the shelter was dramatic beyond words. . . . It can be safely said that most everyone present was praying. Oppenheimer grew tenser as the seconds ticked off. He scarcely breathed. He held on to a post to steady himself."

The countdown went on. At minus 45 seconds Joe McKibben threw the switch that started the precise automatic timer. Now it was out of man's control, except for Hornig who watched at his post at the stop switch.

Minus 30 seconds, and Williams and Bainbridge joined the others outside the control dugout.

Minus 10 seconds. Cool-headed Greisen changed his mind. "Now I'm scared," he suddenly blurted to Rabi.

Then, as the world teetered on the brink of a new age, Sam Allison's voice cried, "Now!"

At that instant—5:29:45 a.m. Mountain War Time on July 16, 1945—came an incredible burst of light, bathing the surrounding mountains in an unearthly brilliance. Then came the shock wave that knocked over two men at S 10,000, then the thunderous roar. A vast multi-colored cloud surged and billowed upward. The steel tower that held the bomb vanished, the tower that held Jumbo, 800 feet away, lay crumpled and broken on the ground.

Wrote Enrico Fermi shortly after the test:

"My first impression of the explosion was the very intense flash of light, and a sensation of heat on the parts of my body that were exposed. Although I did not look directly towards the object, I had the impression that suddenly the countryside became brighter than in full daylight. I subsequently looked in the direction of the explosion through the dark glass and could see something that looked like a conglomeration of flames that promptly started rising. After a few seconds the rising flames lost their brightness and appeared as a huge pillar of smoke with an expanded head like a gigantic mushroom that rose rapidly beyond the clouds, probably to a height of the order of 30,000 feet. After reaching full height, the smoke stayed stationary for a while before the wind started dispersing it."

Fermi then went on to explain the simple experiment he took time to conduct that helped considerably in making the first early estimates of the bomb's success.

"About 40 seconds after the explosion the air blast reached me. I tried to estimate its strength by dropping from about six feet small pieces of paper before, during and after the passage of the blast wave. Since, at the time, there was no wind, I could observe very distinctly and actually measure the displacement of the pieces of paper that were in the process of falling while the blast was passing. The shift was about two and a half meters, which at the time, I estimated to correspond to the blast that would be produced by ten thousand tons of TNT."

Hans Bethe wrote that "it looked like a giant magnesium flare which kept on for what seemed a whole minute but was actually one or two seconds. The white ball grew and after a few seconds became clouded with dust whipped up by the explosion from the ground and rose and left behind a black trail of dust particles. The rise, though it seemed slow, took place at a velocity of 120 meters per second. After more than half a minute the flame died down and the ball, which had been a brilliant white became a dull purple. It continued to rise and spread at the same time, and finally broke through and rose above the clouds which were 15,000 feet above the ground. It could be distinguished from the clouds by its color and could be followed to a height of 40,000 feet above the ground."

Joe McKibben recalls that "we had a lot of flood lights on for taking movies of the control panel. When the bomb went off, the lights were drowned out by the big light coming in through the open door in the back."

"After I threw my last switch I ran out to take a look and realized the shock wave hadn't arrived yet. I ducked behind an earth mound. Even then I had the impression that this thing had gone really big. It was just terriffic."

"The shot was truly awe-inspiring," Bradbury has said. "Most experiences in life can be comprehended by prior experiences but the atom bomb did not fit into any preconception possessed by anybody. The most startling feature was the intense light."

Bainbridge has said that the light was the one place where theoretical calculations had been off by a big factor. "Much more light was produced than had been anticipated."

A military man is reported to have exclaimed, "The long-hairs have let it get away from them!"

While scientists were able to describe the technical aspects of the explosion, for others it was more difficult.

"Words are inadequate tools for acquainting those not present with the physical, mental and psychological effects. It had to be witnessed to be realized," wrote General Farrell two days later. Nonetheless, many tried to describe the historic moment.

Farrell himself wrote:

"The effects could well be called unprecedented, magnificent, beautiful, stupendous, and terrifying. No man-made phenomenon of such tremendous power had ever occurred before. The lighting effects beggared description. The whole country was lighted by a searing light with the intensity many times that of the midday sun. It was golden, purple, violet, gray and blue. It lighted every peak, crevasse and ridge of the nearby mountain range with a clarity and beauty that cannot be described but must be seen to be imagined. Seconds after the explosion came, first, the air blast pressing hard against the people, to be followed almost immediately by the strong, sustained awesome roar which warned of doomsday and made us feel we puny things were blasphemous to dare tamper with the forces heretofore reserved for the Almighty."

William L. Laurence, whose sole job was to write down the moment for history, wrote:

"It was like the grand finale of a mighty symphony of the elements, fascinating and terrifying, uplifting and crushing, ominous, devastating, full of great promise and great foreboding."

Another time he said, "On that moment hung eternity. Time stood still. Space contracted to a pinpoint. It was as though the earth had opened and the skies split. One felt as though he had been privileged to witness the Birth of the World—to be present at the moment of Creation when the Lord said: Let there be light."

Oppenheimer, on the other hand, has said he was reminded of the ancient Hindu quotation:

"I am become Death, the destroyer of worlds."

At the time, however, probably few actually thought of the consequences of their work, beyond ending the war. Bradbury said recently, "For that first 15 seconds the sight was so incredible that the spectators could only gape at it in dumb amazement. I don't believe at that moment anyone said to himself, 'What have we done to civilization?' Feelings of conscience may have come later."

Bainbridge reports that his reactions were mixed. "When the bomb first went off I had the same feelings that anyone else would have who had worked for months to prepare this test, a feeling of exhilaration that the thing had actually worked. This was followed by another quick reaction, a sort of feeling of relief that I would not have to go to the bomb and find out why the thing didn't work."

But later he told Oppenheimer, "Now we're all sons of bitches."

Ernest O. Lawrence is quoted as saying that from his vantage point on Compagna Hill, "the grand, indeed almost cataclysmic proportion of the explosion produced a kind of solemnity in everyone's behavior immediately afterwards. There was a restrained applause, but more a hushed murmuring bordering on reverence as the event was commented upon."

At the control point, Farrell wrote, "The tension in the room let up and all started congratulating each other. All the pent-up emotions were released in those few minutes and all seemed to sense immediately that the explosion had far exceeded the most optimistic expectations and wildest hopes of the scientists."

Kistiakowsky, who had bet a month's salary against $10 that the gadget would work, put his arms around the director's shoulder and said, "Oppie, you owe me $10."

Elsewhere the momentous event had not gone unnoticed. The flash of light was seen in Albuquerque, Santa Fe, Silver City, Gallup and El Paso. Windows rattled in Silver City and Gallup. So intense was the light that a blind girl riding in an automobile near Albuquerque asked, "What was that?"

A rancher between Alamogordo and the test site was awakened suddenly. "I thought a plane had crashed in the yard. It was like somebody turned on a light bulb right in my face."

Another man, 30 miles away in Carrizozo, recalls, "It sure rocked the ground. You'd have thought it went off right in your back yard."

A sleepless patient in the Los Alamos hospital reported seeing a strange light. The wife, waiting on Sawyer's Hill behind Los Alamos, saw it too, and wrote later:

"Then it came. The blinding light like no other light one had ever seen. The trees, illuminated, leaping out. The mountains flashing into life. Later, the long slow rumble. Something had happened, all right, for good or ill."

At the test site, as the spectators watched the huge cloud billow into the sky, the medical officers took over leadership of the three observation points, watching their counters and maintaining contact with Paul Aebersold's crew of monitors patrolling the roads within the test site. An Entry Permission Group, consisting of Bainbridge, Dr. Hemplemann and Aebersold kept track of the reports and made decisions on movement of personnel around the site.

At first there was no sign of danger. Then suddenly, the instruments at N 10,000 began clicking rapidly showing that radioactivity was on the rise. Dr. Henry Barnett, in charge of the shelter, gave the order to evacuate and soon the trucks and cars were roaring past W 10,000 and on to Base Camp. It later proved to be a false alarm. Film badges worn by the personnel at the observation point indicated that no radioactivity had reached the shelter.

Before long those without further duties were permitted to return to Base Camp and those with instruments in the forward areas moved in to pick them up.

As the sun came up, air currents were created which swept radioactivity trapped in the inversion layer into the valley. Geiger counters at S 10,000 began to go wild. The few men remaining there put on masks and watched anxiously as the radioactive air quickly moved away before the danger level was reached. Around 9:30 a.m. Bainbridge radioed the men in the slit trench at Mockingbird Gap to return to Base Camp.

Shortly afterward a lead-lined tank, driven by Sgt. Bill Smith and carrying Herbert Anderson and Enrico Fermi, moved in to Ground Zero to recover equipment and to study debris in hope of getting information on long range detection of atomic explosions. The tank was equipped with a trap door through which earth samples could be safely picked up in the crater.

Fermi later reported to his wife that he found "a depressed area 400 yards in radius glazed with green, glass-like substance where the sand had melted and solidified again."

Meanwhile, General Groves, who had planned to wait at Base Camp until all danger of fallout was passed, hoped to make good use of the hours by discussing with Los Alamos people a number of problems connected with the next job on the agenda, the bombing of Japan.

"These plans were utterly impracticable," he wrote later, "for no one who had witnessed the test was in a frame of mind to discuss anything. The success was simply too great. It was not only that we had achieved success with the bomb; but that everyone—scientists, military officers and engineers—realized we had been personal participants and eyewitnesses to a major milestone in the world's history."

But Groves had other problems to keep him busy anyway.

The explosion had generated considerable excitement around the state and as far away as El Paso. At Associated Press in Albuquerque, the queries coming in were becoming more difficult to handle. Intelligence Officer Lt. Phil Belcher, now the Laboratory's Documents Division leader, was stationed at Albuquerque to keep any alarming dispatches about the explosion from going out. About 11 a.m. the AP man told Belcher he could no longer hold back the story. If nothing is put out now by the Army, he told him, AP's own stories would have to go on the wire.

The Army was prepared for this kind of determination. Weeks before a special press release had been prepared and sent to the Alamogordo Bombing Range with Lt. W. A. Parish from Groves' office. With it, Parish also carried a letter to the commanding officer, Col. William Eareckson, instructing him to follow Lt. Parish's instructions, no questions asked.

About 11 Parish was instructed to make his release:

Alamogordo, July 16—The Commanding Officer of the Alamogordo Army Air Base made the following statement today:

"Several inquiries have been received concerning a heavy explosion which occurred on the Alamogordo Air Base reservation this morning.

"A remotely located ammunition magazine containing a considerable amount of high explosives and pyrotechnics exploded.

"There was no loss of life or injury to anyone, and the property damage outside of the explosives magazine itself was negligible.

"Weather conditions affecting the content of gas shells exploded by the blast may make it desirable for the Army to evacuate temporarily a few civilians from their homes."

The news ran in New Mexico papers and spread up and down the West Coast by radio. It didn't fool everyone. Some days later, Groves reports, he was dismayed when a scientist from the Hanford project said to him: "By the way, General, everybody at DuPont sends their congratulations."

"What for?" the general asked innocently.

"This is the first time we've ever heard of the Army's storing high explosives, pyrotechnics and chemicals in one magazine," he replied.

Colonel Eareckson has since been nominated by sympathetic historians as one of the unsung heroes of World War II. Not only was he forced to take the blame for this gross mishandling of explosives, but he had to take his orders that day from a mere lieutenant.

By late afternoon it was clear there would be no difficulty with fallout. Bainbridge finally left the control center about 3 p.m. to return to the Base Camp for food and rest. General Groves, Conant and Bush left for Albuquerque to begin the trip back to Washington.

Groves' secretary, Mrs. Nora O'Leary, who had been standing by in Washington since early morning for word of the test, received a coded message from her boss and at 7:30 p.m. sent the following message to Secretary of War Stimson at Potsdam:

"Operated on this morning. Diagnosis not yet complete but results seem satisfactory and already exceed expectations. Local press release necessary as interest extends a great distance. Dr. Groves pleased. He returns tomorrow. I will keep you posted."

Although it would be weeks before the measurement could be correlated and interpreted it was immediately apparent that the implosion weapon was a technical success. The fire ball, Fermi's calculations with bits of paper and other data available immediately indicated the yield had been greater than the most optimistic predictions. It was therefore possible for Groves to follow up his first message to Potsdam with another optimistic one the next day:

"Doctor has just returned most enthusiastic and confident that the little boy is as husky as his big brother. The light in his eyes discernible from here to Highhold and I could hear his screams from here to my farm."

The message was clear. The power to crush Japan had taken on a new dimension. The device had worked beyond expectations, its flash seen for 250 miles, its thunder heard for 50, and Groves was sure the plutonium bomb was as potent as the uranium gun.

Through the day of July 16, cars of weary, excited men headed back toward Los Alamos. There was still a great deal of work to be done and for those who were going overseas, the test had simply been a rehearsal.

A new Fat Man was scheduled to be delivered August 6.

When they stopped for meals in Belen the men talked of inconsequential things and listened to mystified citizens discussing the strange sort of thunder they had heard that morning and the way "the sun came up and went right back down again." Occupants of one car did not recognize the occupants of the other. Security was as tight as ever. It was not until they reached the guarded gates of Los Alamos that the flood of talk burst loose.

Mrs. Fermi recalls the men returning late that evening. "They looked dried out, shrunken. They had baked in the roasting heat of the southern desert and they were dead tired. Enrico was so sleepy he went right to bed without a word. On the following morning all he had to say to the family was that for the first time in his life on coming back from Trinity he had felt it was not safe for him to drive."

"I heard no more about Trinity. The men resumed their work at the usual fast pace," she concluded.

But during the day, rumors of the brilliant light so many had watched for and seen spread through the town. Although few people knew officially what had happened, most were able to sense or guess that the project to which each had contributed his part during the long hectic months had been accomplished.

When he returned to the Hill that night, Fred Reines found the town jumping. One of the janitors Reines knew spotted the returning scientist, grinned proudly and said, "We did it, didn't we?"

"We sure did," Reines told him.

SUGGESTED READINGS

Stephane Groueff, *Manhattan Project: The Untold Story of the Making of the Atomic Bomb* (Boston 1967);

Leslie R. Groves, *Now it Can be Told: The Story of the Manhattan Project* (New York 1962);
Lansing Lamont, *Day of Trinity* (New York 1965);
George F. Meeter, *The Holloman Story* (Albuquerque 1967);
"Los Alamos—Boom Town Under Control," *New Mexico Business*, vol. VI (May 1953).

2.1 Spanish-American Activism

The best known Spanish-American organization in New Mexico is unquestionably the Alianza (*Alianza Federal de Mercedes* later renamed the *Alianza de los Pueblos Libres*) of Reies Lopez Tijerina. The dramatic confrontation at the courthouse at Tierra Amarilla in 1967 and the resulting manhunt which involved the use of the National Guard, tanks, airplanes, and a host of law enforcement agencies called attention to the fact that a large segment of New Mexico's Spanish-American population had grievances and that some had organized to express their discontent. The Alianza, however, is just one of these organizations.

Anthropologist Nancie L. González, who is of Spanish-American descent, has written the first general survey of Spanish-Americans in New Mexico in many years. She describes and evaluates Spanish-American organizations such as LULAC (League of United Latin American Citizens), UMAS (United Mexican-American Students), the Brown Berets, and *Los Comancheros del Norte* and mentions the activities of the underground Chicano press. However, she concentrates on the Alianza, the origins of which she discusses in an earlier chapter of her book. The Alianza is described as a "nativistic, revivalistic cult movement" which has recently become more of a true civil rights movement, and the history of the organization from 1967 is recounted here. Elsewhere in her book, which is anthropological in tone, Dr. González discusses the effects of urbanization, economic change, and migration of members of the Spanish-American community.

Activism itself is not particularly new in New Mexico or anywhere else, if one means by this the attempts of some members of a depressed or underprivileged sector (or their sympathizers) to improve their status. Romano (1968) has emphasized this fact in a highly critical essay on works by Anglos on Spanish-American culture. Some of the older activist organizations in New Mexico among Spanish-Americans include *La Mano Negra, Las Gorras Blancas,* LULAC (League of United Latin American Citizens), the G. I. Forum, the American Legion, Veterans of Foreign Wars, and others mentioned in the preceding chapters. The first four of these organizations were founded specifically by Spanish-Americans in order to fight for better conditions for their group. The first two used extra-legal means, while the others worked within established channels. As previously discussed, the veterans' organizations in New Mexico also worked actively for similar causes, and have been said by some (Holmes 1967) to have been instrumental in illustrating the political power of the Hispanos as a group. Aside from these there have always been activists within the various church groups and even within the structure of welfare, as seen in the Life With Pride organization described in Chapter V.

The list could be extended considerably, but today when activism is mentioned it is not generally groups such as these which are meant. Indeed, all those mentioned, with the exception of *La Mano Negra* and *Las Gorras Blancas,* would most likely be considered by the newer activists as being hopelessly embroiled in and controlled by the Establishment and therefore incapable of improving the lot of those they claim to serve. Others might argue that these same groups in fact are out of touch with the lower-class elements of their particular minority or ethnic group and are for these reasons unable to accomplish the goal of improving the lot of those lowest on the social scale.

The Alianza

In tracing the development of the more militant activist organizations in New Mexico at the present time, one must once again return to a consideration of the Alianza described in Chapter V. It may truly be said that this organization was the first movement with civil rights implications to attract attention within the state of New Mexico. Before this there had been other groups such as the Mexican-American Political Association (MAPA) and others which had managed to make a small dent in areas such as Colorado, Texas, and California but which went largely unnoticed here. The plight of the migrant workers—particularly the grape pickers under Cesar Chavez—was considered to have only local (Californian) implications, and the kinship of their *Causa* with that of the Spanish-speaking in New Mexico was apparently not at first appreciated by most New Mexicans. The 1966 Delano Proclamation and its cry of *"huelga"* (strike) found sympathizers here, but there was no immediate action linking this with conditions in New Mexico.

After the incidents in June 1967 at Tierra Amarilla, the Alianza attracted the attention of the whole country. The national news media such as *Newsweek* carried stories of this "wild west show," as it was often presented, and an incredulous public was made to realize the fact that the poor farmers of Spanish descent in northern New Mexico had serious problems and needed to be heard.

However, the initial reaction, largely stimulated by the sensational aspects of the events which were highly dramatized in the press, was that law and order had broken down in New Mexico (if indeed they had ever existed) and that New Mexicans were witnessing a return to the simpler but more brutal code of the frontier. In a sense, there was an element of this involved; however, contrary to what most people thought, the Alianza saw itself as a citizens' group called upon to correct an injustice which the regularly constituted law enforcement bodies could not handle, in part because they themselves were involved in bringing about the infringement of rights. Some members of the Alianza had been arrested and imprisoned for unlawful assembly after they had been forbidden by the state's attorney to gather. Their brethren then attempted to free them and at the same time make a citizen's arrest of the responsible party. The rest is history, but it is important to repeat that a jury found Reies Tijerina, the leader, not guilty of the state's three most serious charges stemming from this incident.

At first there seems to have been no direct connection between the Alianza and other activist organizations in existence outside the state of New Mexico. However, after Tierra Amarilla many of these groups made offers of assistance in order to bring the Alianza into the ranks of the Spanish-American and other radical civil rights movements.

Many of the people deeply involved in the Alianza took part in the Poor People's March on Washington in 1967, and here again national publicity was achieved. By this time many persons from outside the state had come to work with the Alianza and it appears that there were some attempts at reorganization or restructuring of the group at this time. There seem to have been efforts to model it after more radical civil rights movements elsewhere, but these efforts did not have complete success.

In addition to the Alianza, several other new activist-type organizations have appeared only recently on the New Mexican scene; they will be described very briefly, including what seem to this author to be the interrelationships among them and offering an interpretation of the relationships between this new activism and the rest of the New Mexican sociocultural system. Among the groups which will be considered are the Alianza itself, the Brown Berets, the United-Mexican American Students (UMAS), and two youth groups called *Los Caballeros de Nueva España* and *Los Co-*

mancheros del Norte. Finally, the development of an underground Chicano press, represented by eighteen newspapers which have recently popped up all over the Southwest, will be examined.

In the analysis of the Alianza as a nativistic, revivalistic cult movement presented in Chapter V, the author noted that many of the demands of the group were unrealistic and impractical and that survival might depend upon the group's willingness to modify some of its claims and doctrine and, at the same time, align itself more closely with other civil rights movements in the nation. As Frances Swadesh (1968) and Joseph Love (1969) have shown recently, the Alianza to an increasing extent has taken on many of the characteristics of true civil rights movements. Along with Love, but contrary to Swadesh, the author feels that the Alianza is still better understood as a nativistic cult than as a civil rights movement, in spite of the fact that it has tended to move in the latter direction over the past two years.

Tijerina, the leader of the Alianza, remains a charismatic figure and has become a symbol of the plight of the underdog Spanish-American in New Mexico. Yet he steadfastly refuses to modify many elements in his doctrine and his behavior which might bring his cult more fully in line with the broader New Left movements. He has been strongly criticized by non-Hispano spokesmen of the radical New Left, precisely on the basis of the charismatic and cultlike flavor of the movement (Kennedy 1968). As such, the Alianza remains something unique within New Mexico and among the Spanish-speaking everywhere. It is still largely rural in its membership; it is still almost exclusively dependent upon its leader for guidance and formation of doctrine; and it frequently comes into philosophical collision with representatives of other American minority groups such as Blacks, Jews, and White radicals. It is noteworthy that Cesar Chavez and his grape pickers union have not been particularly brotherly. Relations are cordial but not overly close between the two leaders. Chavez heads a union and a civil rights movement, not a revivalistic or nativistic cult.

It is perhaps significant to note the differences in the terminology used by the Alianza and the Californian and Texas activist movements. The Alianza stresses the mestizo blood of its members and places great value on being brown, a result of having sprung from a union between Indian and Spanish. In this respect, the activist movements share the ideology of the Mexican-American who also prides himself on being a mestizo. However, the term Mexican-American, which is so broadly accepted outside the state of New Mexico, is still not used by the Alianza itself. The Alianza prefers the term "*Indo-Hispano,*" and although the members frequently refer to themselves as *Mexicanos,* there is still no real identification with the term "Mexican-American."

The insistence upon use of *Indo-Hispano* has the effect of clouding the issue of Spanish theft of land belonging to the American Indians. This issue is one of the really weak spots in the peculiar logic of the Alianza. When Indians question the right of the Hispano to the lands as granted by the King of Spain, the answer, usually considered inadequate by Indian observers, is that the Alianza represents the interests of both Indians and the descendants of the early Hispano settlers. In fact, it is true that they represent the mixed-blood descendants of the Hispanicized Indians, but hardly of the Indians who have retained their ethnic identity and purity of race.

In the fall of 1968 the Alianza made its first venture into organized politics in the state of New Mexico. Tijerina ran for governor as a candidate of the Peoples Constitutionalist Party (the Alianza party) until his name was removed from the ballot at a very late point in the campaign on the grounds that he had been convicted of several charges in regard to the 1966 sit-in in the Echo Amphitheater incident. Since his case had been appealed before the District Circuit Court it was decided, after some dispute, that he really was not eligible to run for office. Therefore, the man chosen to run as his lieutenant governor (interestingly enough, an Indian, Jose Alfredo Maestas) ran in his stead. Only 1,540 votes were secured for the positions of governor and lieutenant governor.

The voting record probably reflects several related facts—first, the generally short campaign period, since the Alianza determined to run candidates at a fairly late date; second, the possibility that some votes were improperly counted (this possibility always exists in New Mexico, and there were many rumors to this effect in the fall of 1968); third, the probable decline in organization membership (recognized by Tijerina himself, who felt that by running he might be able to reawaken fervor among some of his former adherents); fourth, the very real and certain fact that Tijerina is a charismatic leader whose followers are not all likely to vote for a substitute even though endorsed by the leader himself. Other candidates of the Peoples Constitutionalist Party had varying success in gathering votes, although none won an office. Those who obtained the highest number of votes were well-known names in the community, often for reasons other than their association with the Alianza.

In assessing the present position of the Alianza the author would predict that it will continue to make itself heard and may have some success in stimulating social change. The fact that it is already having some impact is shown by the bombings of the Alianza headquarters and of the homes and property of its officers. There have been at the time of this writing four such bombings, the latest occurring on March 15, 1969. So far no one has been injured, and the bombings have been, in a sense, tokens of the resentment and fear that the Alianza awakens among some sectors of the New Mexican population. Another kind of evidence that the Alianza may be having some effect is the recent suggestion by Representative Gonzales from Texas that Congress investigate the land claims issue.

The Brown Berets

This group, modeled after the black berets of the Black Panther movement, has only recently appeared in New Mexico. It seems likely that the local organization sprang from contacts made by some New Mexicans in Washington for the Poor People's March. The Brown Beret idea apparently originated in California, and now there are local chapters in many southwestern cities. Unlike the Alianza, it is not only urban-based but has a much broader coverage. It includes primarily young people, which also sets it apart from the Alianza in which older persons predominate.

In Albuquerque the Brown Berets first burst upon the scene with demands for police reform following the killing of a young Spanish-speaking man by a police officer in the summer of 1968. It is reported that at the present time the organization has reached fifteen of the lower-class Spanish-American *barrios* in Albuquerque and that each of these is represented by three individuals whose names are kept secret for their personal protection. One of their spokesmen, whose name has been frequently in the local news in relation to Mexican-American civil rights, has also been associated with the Alianza, even though he has never been a member. During the recent school board election this spokesman ran as a candidate of the Peoples Constitutionalist Party. He and his running partner lost, although another person of Spanish surname garnered more votes than any other candidate in history.

The Brown Berets reject individuals such as the latter who cooperate with the Establishment. This includes persons who work for the Office of Economic Opportunity, Model Cities, and other governmental or governmentally funded agencies. Such persons are referred to as *vendidos* (sellouts), *Tio Tomases, Espanglos, Lulacks,* and, most recently, "Oreo Cookies" (brown on the outside and white on the inside).

This terminology reflects the increasing polarization among persons of Spanish heritage in New Mexico, as well as elsewhere. The group seems to be dividing along the politically defined lines of extreme Right on the one hand and extreme Left on the other. These differences are certainly linked to increasing radicalism in a broader political sense in the United States as a whole. There are clear linkages on the Right with the John Birch Society and other such groups. Similarly, there are linkages on the Left with non-Hispano groups such as the Students for a Democratic Society (SDS), the Third World Liberation Front, and others. The increasing differences between the poles is also symbolized by the terms Chicano and Hispano. Neither is a new term, but their more subtle meanings have changed.

Chicano has always had a bit of defiance in it and has also been used, at least in New Mexico, to indicate a clever person, one with the ability to outwit the unsuspecting Anglo. There has also been a certain amount of derogation in its usage, even by the Spanish themselves. However, it has only been recently that it has also come to include a sense of militancy. Today the youthful Spanish-Americans are using Chicano more and more, and as it becomes more fashionable it also becomes less derogatory.

On the other hand, the term Hispano is still preferred by many, especially the older persons and the less militant. In view of these linguistic distinctions, in the succeeding pages the term Chicano will be used when referring to the newer activist movements or ideology, and Hispano will be retained for the older type of activity, including what may be referred to as the Establishment "activism."

However, at this point some note should be made of the increasing usage of the term "Mexican-American" in New Mexico. Although, as has been pointed out several times, this term has for many years been resented by the local Spanish-speaking community, in the past two years there has been an increasing pride in making this self-identification—again largely among the more youthful militant activists. The author attributes this new usage to the greater linkages between local and Texan and Californian groups. It should be emphasized, however, that those who use the term "Mexican-American" are still probably a minority in New Mexico, and most of the persons preferring this term live in or south of Albuquerque.

There is some evidence that this newer terminology is becoming fashionable even among some middle-class Hispanos. One informant told of a recent incident at a LULAC meeting where the members were asking each other what term they preferred to use for themselves. The informant stated that most of the people replied "Mexican-American." This would hardly have been the case two years ago and would still not likely be true in the northern areas. Bodine (1968) has made this point in reference to Taos where he recently did field work.

The newer activism is found among youth ranging from high school through college and among the younger elements who are not necessarily highly educated at all. Thus, there is a group known as *Los Caballeros de Nueva España* (The Gentlemen of New Spain) which was formed in Albuquerque in the fall of 1968. They welcome members between the ages of 10 and 24, but most of them appear to be high school students or dropouts. The group claims to have about 150 members, and they are primarily interested in furthering educational policies which will be more beneficial for children of Spanish heritage.

Other Groups

Another group of youth, but with a rural rather than an urban base, is called *Los Comancheros del Norte*. This group appears to be centered in Tierra Amarilla, with members from the entire northern New Mexican area. It is important to note that both the Comancheros and the Caballeros have stated principles and goals which support the Alianza. In referring to themselves they use, at least in print, the term Indo-Hispano which is a self-conscious term used only by the Alianza.

In addition to an interest in improving the educational system, both of these youth groups emphasize the return of the land-grants and specifically mention the Alianza in this regard. Neither group expresses the militancy of the Brown Berets, although it is possible that they might become more militant in the future. One young Chicano was quoted in the newspaper, *El Grito del Norte* (January 11, 1969), as follows:

> Let's not fight among ourselves. Let's get organized and fight the gringo who controls everything. Let's not fight in the bars, let's not hit our wives. Let's not have one barrio fighting the other. Let's organize, vatos!

At the University of New Mexico a branch of the United Mexican-American Students (UMAS) was formed late in 1968. Like so many other organizations, this one's structure does not conform to the usual organizational form. As one young member said, "Whenever two or three Chicanos are gathered together we have a meeting." The group has so far restricted itself to protesting the Anglo students' domination of a spring campus event known as "Fiesta." The group claims that the Fiesta activities in past years have tended to emphasize the "cowboy" aspect of New Mexican culture to the exclusion of its Mexican or Spanish heritage. They wish to have included *Mariachis*, Mexican-type *Charro* events, Spanish or Mexican food at the barbecues, etc.

Although this kind of activity would seem to be merely the playful antics of college students, most observers feel that this again is only a symbol of general discontent of UMAS members and that their activities will become more serious in the future. The group declines to give names of its members, and it is at this time almost impossible to find out how many there may be. They claim a potential strength of 1,500, but this seems a little high. At meetings during the spring of 1969 on the campus of the University of New Mexico they sometimes drew up to 200, but some of these were sympathizers or curiosity seekers and not potential members.

UMAS is sufficiently well organized to publish a mimeographed bulletin entitled *Plumas de Umas* (Pens of the United Mexican-American Students), written partly in Spanish and partly in English. One of their goals is to create a Mexican-American Studies program at the University of New Mexico, preferably under the control of Chicanos. In line with this, they are beginning to agitate for the hiring of more Chicano professors. (There were thirty-nine professors, instructors, and graduate assistants of Spanish surname at the University of New Mexico in the spring of 1969, but most of these were considered "oreo cookies" by the Chicano students.)

UMAS has probable linkages with the Denver Crusade for Justice, which sponsored what it called the "Chicano Youth Liberation Conference" in

March of 1969. Delegates from New Mexico as well as from other southwestern states attended this meeting and exchanged views and techniques which will undoubtedly give a still greater homogeneity to the activities of these youth groups throughout the Southwest.

In summarizing these budding Chicano organizations, it should be noted that each one serves a somewhat different segment of the total deprived population, and although there is no overall formal organization among them there are nevertheless clear linkages through the network of individual contacts. Thus some members of UMAS may also be Brown Berets, and all look to the Alianza and its activities as somehow being symbolic of their cause as well. On the other hand, the Alianza itself seems more closely tied in with the two high school youth groups mentioned previously and may even have been instrumental in their formation. At the same time, as the individual young members of the high school groups grow up they will probably unite with the Brown Berets or UMAS, or both.

The goals of these groups are not easy to define specifically, although in general they are concerned with the lack of power of the Spanish-surname or Spanish-speaking segment of the population in this country. They feel that organized agencies in the past have not been successful in relieving the plight of the poor, and they now preach more revolutionary tactics in achieving a better way of life. Certainly there have been many instances of appalling injustice for persons of Spanish surname in New Mexico, as elsewhere. But since here most of the persons in the lowest social classes are of this ethnic group, it is sometimes tempting to suggest that they are in this position because they have been discriminated against. The author would reverse this and argue that they are discriminated against because they are in the lower class, but that being of Spanish-American origin is related to the fact that they are in the lower class. In trying to account for this, the position is sometimes advanced that they are genetically inferior and therefore doomed to perpetual poverty and low status. This is clearly a bigoted, uninformed viewpoint. On the other hand, the suggestion that these people are in this position because they have been and are being discriminated against also seems to the author to derive from an uninformed point of view.

The problem has to do with social structure and the values supporting it rather than with personal relationships, in this writer's opinion. What is meant by this is that the dominant society is structured in such a way that certain kinds of behavior are better rewarded than others. The author would thoroughly agree with the opinion that the lower-class Spanish-American's lack of ability in his second language, English, has often hindered his progress in achieving material well-being. This is most often a result of his inability to compete in schools at the lower level, and his feeling of inferiority when he recognizes that he is not being rewarded as are his Anglo schoolmates. Although there are undoubtedly some teachers who dislike or even despise their Spanish-American wards for their differences, there are also many who feel anguished by what they perceive to be a lower level of performance among these children. They are unable to advance these students according to the same set of criteria as those they use for the Anglo children, and having no other guidelines they fail the Spanish-speaking child. This position is now quite well recognized by educators in general, and it is becoming a particular issue in the Southwest. The Southwestern Cooperative Educational Laboratory, Inc. (SWCEL), a private, nonprofit educational, research and development facility, is currently conducting research and constructing programs to deal with the problem of bilingualism and teaching English as a second language in New Mexico public schools.

Given this lower level of performance in grade school, the system continues to work against the individual with this background. But at this point these individuals share more with the poverty-stricken across the nation than they do with the majority of the Hispanos in New Mexico. That is, when it comes to getting jobs, the less well educated are the ones who suffer. Without jobs, material well-being is difficult or impossible. The structure of welfare is one which prevents starvation, but welfare does nothing to improve the individual's feeling of dignity and worth. Once on welfare the individual has, in effect, "two strikes" against him socially, and it is very difficult for him to go on to anything else.

One informant, himself an Hispano with a Master's degree from the University of New Mexico, told of interviewing an eight-year-old boy—a dropout from the second grade. He asked the boy what he thought he might do when he grew up. The child replied, "Well, there's always welfare." Welfare as a way of life can clearly become a pattern which is passed on from generation to generation, and it is one of the most damning indictments against the welfare system that this should be so.

However, the alternative to poverty and low status is not necessarily complete assimilation or "anglicization," as many of the Chicanos seem to believe. There are thousands of persons of Spanish heritage in New Mexico today who live comfortably, who are able to move in any social circle they desire without fear of prejudice or discrimination, and who at the same time have preserved their sense of identity with *la raza.* Many of these speak Spanish poorly or not at all, but this is in part a function of our educational system and not necessarily because they themselves have desired to give up all that is Spanish in their background. Furthermore, many of these middle-class Hispanos retain some of the values of the traditional culture in relation to such things as family structure, religion, and everything else which forms part of the Spanish-American mystique. Social scientists have not yet investigated thoroughly and do not understand the process of acculturation, either in terms of sociocultural systems or in terms of an individual's adaptations to systems other than the one he first learns. Whatever occurs, it is not a matter of clearcut and total change in way of life and world view. One must pose further questions, such as What are the criteria by which acculturation may be evaluated? Which factors operate as independent variables and which co-vary as interdependent units?

The concept of pluralism is one with which many people are concerned today. The position that several cultures may coexist within the same society—equal in terms of material welfare, self-determination, and role in government, but each retaining its individuality and self-pride—is for some a dream and for others a very possible reality.

New Mexico, with all its faults, with all its poverty, nevertheless comes closer to the pluralistic dream of society than does any other area in the nation. It is to be hoped that current events do not further polarize the positions within the Spanish-American ethnic group to the point that some deny *la raza* altogether while others attempt to overthrow the entire system which has so far permitted and reinforced the Spanish traditions in the struggle for survival. At the same time, thousands of Hispanos have achieved positions in life which they appreciate and value—positions which they feel are dignified, free from harassment, and well remunerated. These individuals, understandably enough, resent what they see as racist militancy. Called *vendidos* themselves, many of them feel it is the militants who are "selling out" *la raza* by bringing the issue of ethnicity into what should be a war on poverty.

New Mexico needs to revamp some of its worst features. This will be difficult, because New Mexico is a part of the structure of the nation itself and as such is subject to the same pressures as are the other states. But the unique history and the pride of heritage found here among the Hispano people could be the raw materials for a true pluralism in the future—a pluralism which encompasses not just one ethnic minority but all variations on the theme of Hispanic America, as well as those non-Spanish groups which have also been involved in building the unique society of New Mexico.

SUGGESTED READINGS

George I. Sanchez, *Forgotten People* (Albuquerque 1940);
Peter Nabokov, *Tijerina and the Courthouse Raid* (Albuquerque 1969);
Michael Jenkinson, *Tijerina* (Albuquerque 1968);
Stan Steiner, *La Raza: The Mexican-Americans* (New York 1970);
Frances L. Swadesh, "The Alianza Movement: Catalyst for Social Change in New Mexico," *Proceedings of the American Ethnological Society*, 1968;
Jack E. Holmes, *Politics in New Mexico* (Albuquerque 1967).